CW00346849

LEARNING AT THE MUSEUM FRONTIERS

For the extended family

Learning at the Museum Frontiers
Identity, Race and Power

VIV GOLDING
University of Leicester, UK

ASHGATE

© Viv Golding 2009

All rights reserved. No part of this publication may be reproduced, stored in a retrieval system or transmitted in any form or by any means, electronic, mechanical, photocopying, recording or otherwise without the prior permission of the publisher.

Viv Golding has asserted her right under the Copyright, Designs and Patents Act, 1988, to be identified as the author of this work.

Published by
Ashgate Publishing Limited
Wey Court East
Union Road
Farnham
Surrey, GU9 7PT
England

Ashgate Publishing Company
110 Cherry Street
Suite 3-1
Burlington
VT 05401-3818
USA

www.ashgate.com

British Library Cataloguing in Publication Data
Golding, Viv.
  Learning at the museum frontiers : identity, race and
  power.
  1. Museums--Educational aspects. 2. Museums--Social
  aspects.
  I. Title
  069'.01-dc22

Library of Congress Cataloging-in-Publication Data
Golding, Vivien.
  Learning at the museum frontiers : identity, race and power / by Viv Golding.
      p. cm.
  ISBN 978-0-7546-4691-4
  1. Museums--Educational aspects. 2. Museums--Social aspects. 3. Museums--Philosophy.
I. Title.
  AM7.G555 2009
  069'.15--dc22

2009008176

ISBN 978-0-7546-4691-4
e-ISBN 978-0-7546-8964-5

Reprinted 2011, 2012 (twice)

Printed and bound in Great Britain by the
MPG Books Group, UK

Contents

List of Figures and Plates

Figures

Plates

Preface

Eilean Hooper-Greenhill

Learning at the Museum Frontiers: Identity, Race and Power is challenging and thought provoking, seeking to bring issues of discrimination in general and racist and sexist prejudice in particular, under a critical lens of analysis. The focus of investigation is the anthropology museum – the collections, curators and audiences – which are considered from the perspective of a professional museum educator of some twenty years standing who situates herself as a member of several excluded communities. From this perspective, Golding asks important questions about the social and inclusive responsibilities of museums which have in the past acted to marginalise and exclude. Complex philosophical ideas and theories are illuminated by extensive use of examples drawn from her educational practice where the collaborative construction of exhibitions and diverse programming reveals both the silences and erasures of Black voices in museum and the richness that can ensue following their inclusion.

This book is at one level a highly personal account, written with a deep commitment to the power of the museum to affect social and cultural change and with a strong belief in the value of hopeful striving to bring this change about. At the same time, the book is firmly embedded in what might be called 'the Leicester tradition' in that it unashamedly melds theory with practice and calls unequivocally on museums to review their received traditions in the light of new ideas, raised expectations and greater social responsibilities. Museums have the power to take a lead in cultural change and this book shows how this may be both thought through and brought into being. At a time when the exceptional educational value of museums is beginning to be fully appreciated, this book offers a new strand of analysis inspired by philosophy and grounded in practice.

I warmly recommend this book to students of Museum Studies around the world.

Eilean Hooper-Greenhill, Langtree
January 2009

Acknowledgements

In this book I discuss ideas that have been developed since embarking on PhD research in 1995 with Professor Eilean Hooper-Greenhill as my supervisor. It seems worth pointing out for postgraduate students today the juggling act that marked my PhD study, which was completed in 2000 while a part-time student engaged in full time museum work and alongside family responsibilities. To my present students in the PhD community at the University of Leicester, I know the completion of these projects presents no easy task, but I echo Barack Obama's successful campaign to become president of the United States in 2008, 'yes we can!'

My PhD progress was due in large part to my fellow students, notably Miriam Clavir, Nikki Clayton, Hadwig Krautler and Theano Moussouri. The interest and support of fellow museum professionals at Horniman during this period must also be acknowledged and I thank Margaret Birley, Sheila Humbert, Nikki Levell, Anthony Shelton, Danny Staples, Janet Vitmayer and Finbarr Whooley in particular. In addition, over the ten years I worked at Horniman I was fortunate to engage in many conversations with thoughtful schoolteachers and university lecturers who were similarly concerned to promote intercultural understanding and challenge discrimination in their working lives. Most notably amongst these colleagues from my Horniman days is Dr Joan Anim-Addo, who continues to give me unstinting support, alongside Dr Denis Atkinson, Dr Paul Dash, Juliet Desailley, Amoafi Kwappong, Karen Mears and Thelma Perkins, who I now count as dear friends. Subsequently I am indebted to discussions with the wonderful groups of Masters and PhD students in the Universities of Leicester and Göteborg where I have been working since 2002.

It was not until I joined the Department of Museum Studies at the University of Leicester that the process of actually writing this book, from PhD fieldwork, began. I am especially grateful to Dr Richard Sandell, Head of the Department of Museum Studies who has provided excellent editorial advice and consistent support over the years of writing. I also greatly appreciate the advice of my Leicester colleagues Dr Katharine Edgar, Dr Andy Sawyer and Dr Sheila Watson and who have made helpful comments on an early draft of the book. Professor Simon Knell, Professor, Eilean Hooper-Greenhill, Professor Sue Pearce, Jocelyn Dodd, Dr Sandra Dudley, Suzanne MacLeod and Dr Ross Parry at Leicester must be also thanked for academic guidance, as well Gus Dinn, Barbara Lloyd, Jim Roberts and the whole office team for ongoing general assistance.

Learning at the Museum Frontiers: Identity, Race and Power would not have been completed without the period of research leave granted by the University of

Leicester in 2005. At Leicester I was able to engage in periods of further fieldwork around the world including Korea, Japan, Sweden and South Africa, which has enhanced my initial thought considerably. The Department of Museum Studies at the University of Leicester sponsored my participation in the 2006 International Council for the Training of Museum Professionals (ICTOP) conference in Cape Town, which Dr Jatti Bredekamp organised. While I have selected District Six Museum for special mention in Chapter 4 with regards their creative memory work it was my pleasure to meet many excellent staff in Cape Town, who were all most generous in sharing their knowledge and expertise. At District Six Museum I specially acknowledge the warmth of Bonita Bennett, Mandy Sanger, Noor Ebrahim, Tina Smith and Chrischené Julius who invited me to discuss key concepts while cleaning the floor map.

In addition to the University of Leicester I am grateful to the British Academy for funding a period of fieldwork in October 2004 to present a paper at the International Council of Museums (ICOM) General Conference in Seoul, where I was fortunate to meet members of the International Council of Museum Ethnographers (ICME) thanks to the help of Dr Per Rekdal. At Seoul I invited to join the ICME Board as editor of the Newsletter, while Dr Daniel Winfree Papuga was president (2004-2007). I would like to extent special thanks to Daniel, to Dr Annette Fromm and to the other members of the ICME board for much stimulating and challenging discussion over this period.

I am also grateful to the Daiwa Foundation for funding a seminar series in Japan (2005), where I was most warmly welcomed at the National Museum of Japanese History, Lake Biwa Museum and the Edo-Tokyo Museum. I am very pleased to acknowledge the influence of this funding in Chapter 4, as well as the close contact that I maintain with Dr Nunotani at Lake Biwa Museum and Yukiko Hashimoto who organised a second seminar in Edo-Tokyo Museum in 2006.

As well as the people mentioned above there are a great many colleagues working in museums and universities around the world to whom I owe debt in this book. I am grateful to Dr Lejo Schenk, Director of the Tropen Museum, Amsterdam, who invited me to speak at conference there in 2002, together with Deirdré Prins-Solani from Robben Island Museum whose work continues to inspire me. In Göteborg Sweden my professional relationship and friendship with Cajsa Lagerkvist, Dr Diane Walters and Professor Peter Davies has sustained my research into what a museum is and can be to the benefit of its wider communities. Back home in Leicester the good humour and insights of Professor Patrick Boylan, Professor Audrey Osler and Dr Nazikat Waggle has been much appreciated.

I would like to acknowledge the earlier publication, substantially extended, of some material presented here. In Chapter 1, I refer to a Benin project that is considered in detail in Joan Anim-Addo and Suzanne Scafe's 2007 edited volume *I Am Black / White / Yellow*. Chapter 2, draws in part on long-term collaboration with Dr Joan Anim-Addo and the Caribbean Women Writers Alliance (CWWA) that continues as the Black Body in Europe research network, which was first outlined in Hazel Moffatt and Vicky Woollard's 1999 edited volume *Museum and*

Gallery Education A Manual of Good Practice that AltaMira Press now hold the copyright of. Chapters 5 and 6, reflect on three of the twelve *'Inspiration Africa!'* collaborative projects undertaken with Jacqui Callis and Tony Minion at the Cloth of Gold Arts Organisation. A part of the Telegraph Hill work discussed in Chapter 5 was published in 2004 in the *Journal of Museum Ethnography* 16:19-36, Hampshire, UK. Other *'Inspiration Africa!'* projects, not discussed in this book, have been considered in Simon Knell, Suzanne Macleod and Sheila Watson's 2007 edited volume *Museum Revolutions*, published by Routledge; Sheila Watson's 2007 edited volume *Museums and their Communities*, published by Routledge, and the *International Journal of Intangible Heritage*, Volume 1, as well as in the 2004 Conference papers that are available at the ICOM-ICME website <http://museumsnett.no/icme/> accessed on 12.01.2008.

I would like to thank Ashgate Publishing who have been particularly patient in awaiting the completion of this monograph, long delayed by periods of ill health in my family. Neil Jordan and Aimée Feenan in particular have been especially kind and helpful in getting this volume to press. I also acknowledge the meticulous work of Amy Barnes, who took on the role of proofreading and compiling the index for Ashgate, while completing her PhD at the University of Leicester.

My immediate family have provided an endless reserve of encouragement and support over the years: my mum Jean Law; my daughters Erika, Natalie, Anna and their dad David Forster. Thanks also to the close friends – the extended family – who have encouraged me to push on and helped me to refine my arguments, in addition to those noted above I thank Kofi Anim-Addo, Anyaa Anim-Addo, Ian Baker, Paul Hope and so many students, past, present and future, who inevitably become friends and part of that extended family!

Picture Acknowledgements

I must thank a number of individuals and institutions for permission to reproduce images.

Plates 1, 2, 3, 4, 8, 11 and 21 are reproduced with thanks to my colleagues at Horniman Museum, notably Janet Vitmayer and Finbarr Whooley.

Plates 7, 22 and 23 were taken during a Horniman workshop and the *'Inspiration Africa!'* exhibition by David Forster.

Section 1

Introduction: The Spatial Politics of the Museum Frontiers

I foreground this book with two powerful Black voices.[1] First let us look at a piece of creative writing taken from the Nobel prize-winning Toni Morrison's novel *The Bluest Eye*, which highlights a subtle but pernicious racism, arising from the lived experience of daily life. Morrison states:

> It had begun with Christmas and the gift of dolls. The big, the special, the loving gift was always a big, blue-eyed Baby Doll. … Adults, older girls, shops, magazines, newspapers, window signs – all the world agreed that a blue-eyed, yellow-haired, pink-skinned doll was what every girl child treasured. "Here," they said, "this is beautiful, and if you are on this day 'worthy' you may have it." … I could not love it. But I could examine it to see what all the world said was lovable. … It was as though *some mysterious all-knowing master had given each one a cloak of ugliness to wear*, and *they had each accepted it without question*. The master said, "You are ugly people." They looked about themselves and saw nothing to contradict the statement; saw, in fact, *support for it leaning at them from every billboard, every movie, every glance. "Yes," they had said you are right*. (Morrison 1990: 13, 14, 28) [my emphasis]

Morrison's *The Bluest Eye* speaks of the awful negative power of racism to adversely impact on the identity of the young Black child. Racism like colonialism objectifies people. It forces the Black 'other' to act not as agent but as subject – passively. Racism sees only limited aspects of the other – humanity the whole complex human being in social relationships is reduced to black skin. As Franz Fanon testifies:

> I found that I was an *object* … the glances of the other *fixed* me there … like a chemical dye. I was indignant, demanding an explication. … Nothing happened. I *burst apart*. Now the fragments have been put together again by *another self*. (Fanon 1993: 109) [my emphasis]

---

1   I employ the capital 'B' to describe Black people throughout my writing. This marks an act of political allegiance to address historic wrongdoing and denigration of 'Others' as not only inferior but less than human in times of slavery.

Reading Morrison and Fanon from the perspective of the museum,[2] ethical and existential questions arise. What is the role of the contemporary museum? How can museum professionals act to combat racism and its pernicious effects today? Who will take responsibility and 'speak truth to power' when it diminishes our fellows? (Said 1993: 63-75). These questions are focal points for all citizens living in the post-modern world and in my museum career with anthropology collections I have found Black writers offer a productive way forward, which I demonstrate in *Learning at the Museum Frontiers: Identity, Race and Power*. Overall the book argues that museums can hold up a hope for challenging racist mindsets essentially through respectful dialogical exchange that I term feminist-hermeneutics. My intention is to guide the reader through unfamiliar philosophical terrain that has proved useful to progress learning in the museum as Eilean Hooper-Greenhill and Hugh Genoways have notably shown (Hooper-Greenhill 2006; Genoways 2006). At this early point in the book it is only necessary to point out that I have developed feminist-hermeneutics from the politically mindful Black feminist thought of writers including Patricia Hill-Collins, Audre Lourde and bell hooks with the more abstract philosophical hermeneutics of Hans Georg Gadamer (Hill-Collins 1991; Lorde 1996; hooks 1992, 1994; Gadamer 1980, 1981, 1986). Basically feminist-hermeneutic practice is akin to Fanon's notion of 'authentic communication', which urges 'Why not simply attempt to touch the other, to feel the other, to reveal myself to the other?' (Fanon 1993: 231). Such communication in the museum is neither an easy task nor one we might simply fix forever like a mathematical equation, but it is worth striving towards and has an enduring value that lies in learning about the other and most importantly about the self – the self who does not remain unchanged.

In other words, what I want to do in this book is to look at the way in which the meaning of certain pernicious ideas about 'other' peoples and their cultures, which appear to be based on obvious factual evidence can change when they are questioned in *between* locations, at the frontiers of traditional disciplinary boundaries, and beyond the confines of institutional spaces. Specifically I present a view of the museum frontiers – a spatio-temporal site for acting in collaborative effort with other institutions, which provides a creative space of respectful dialogical exchange for promoting critical thought, for questioning taken-for-granted ideas in general and for challenging racist and sexist mindsets in particular. Ultimately I argue that frontier museum work can progress lifelong learning, 'intercultural understanding' and what is known in the UK as community cohesion (Golding 2006a, 2006b, 2007). In this I build on the work to further the social role of the museum and progress a more inclusive society undertaken by Richard Sandell, Jocelyn Dodd and David Fleming (Sandell 2007, 2004, 2003; Dodd and Sandell 2001; Fleming 2004). I also refer to the *White Paper on Intercultural Dialogue*, launched in 2008 by the

---

2   'Museums' is a generic term used throughout the book that follows American practice and includes art museums, which are commonly referred to as art galleries in the UK.

Council of Europe in Strasborg (<http://www.coe.int/t/dg4/intercultural/Source/White%20Paper_final_revised_EN.pdf> accessed on 28.11.2008).

Whether the museum holds some power to effect change in society is a large claim that may be questioned (Appleton 2001). Yet we certainly see museums increasingly present in the mass media, with stories often sparking intensive campaigns: urging the 'nation' to save 'our' treasures such as Raphael's 'Madonna of the Pinks' for example in the UK and generally to be more 'family friendly' – both calls meeting high degrees of success (RCMG 2007; Birkett 2006). Alongside this public attention, the academic literature on museology continues to expand at a rapid pace to serve the increasing demand for places on degree courses in museum related studies, as well as the changing needs of the profession over the last two decades since Peter Vergo called for a 'radical re-examination of the role of museums' or a 'new museology' (Vergo 1989: 3; Macdonald 2006, 1996: 8).

Learning at the Museum Frontiers: Identity, Race and Power bridges these public professional and academic worlds by joining the academic texts on museology with praxis, that is my own theoretically grounded educational work in the field and at the borderlands beyond the walls of the museum building. I draw on specific examples largely from my 10 year period as Head of Formal Education at the Horniman Museum, in South London, working primarily with the notable and nationally designated anthropology collection of material culture from sub-Saharan Africa. This personal focus highlights vital issues of relevance to museums around the world, such as the contested ownership of cultural property and the representation of indigenous knowledge, which have recently become the subject of much public debate and interest in the professional, academic and general press (Simpson 1996; Kreps 2003).

Thus while the book interrogates significant themes that I have grappled with at a local level and which are evident in the title, it considers these key ideas throughout from international perspectives and aims to show the wider relevance of an audience-focused learning lens beyond the UK. I shall now briefly elucidate the key themes of the book: power, learning, race and 'frontiers'.

Power. I contend the museum has in part a history of power. Museums have demonstrated the power of wealth and privilege – of the church, the king and the merchant since their inception, which in the Western world can be traced to fifteenth-century Florence, when the Medici family came to prominence and established their Palace (Hooper-Greenhill 1992; Bennett 1995). A new power – of the Nation and the citizen – can be traced to the establishment at the end of the eighteenth century, with the French Revolution and the formation from the princely collection of the Louvre in 1789, to 'stand for the Republic and its ideal of equality' (Duncan 1995: 35). The historical power of the museum can be seen not only to confirm conventional social hierarchies, but also to mark the overturning of older orders of control, and this would appear to lie at the heart of the widespread and continuing growth reported by UNESCO (the United Nations Educational, Scientific and Cultural Organisation), at a staggering rate of 90 percent since 1946 (UNESCO 1995: 184).

In today's age of globalisation, museums around the world retain the older powers of treasure house, place of knowledge, sanctuary and shrine, in combination with a newer role as a forum and a vital role in democracy, which it is a central concern to examine in this book. While this democratic exchange can spark bitter controversy, since the museum in the socio-cultural landscape of the twenty-first century can be perceived as an icon of western colonialism in particular contexts, this effect is often in contradistinction to curatorial intentions. For example at the Royal Ontario Museum's exhibition *Into the Heart of Africa*, where African Canadians protested against the museum as a storehouse of imperial loot, tainted by a colonial past, an anachronism, and at the Smithsonian where the *Enola Gay* was viewed as of no use or even a hindrance in developing a cohesive community (Philip 1994; Reigel 1996; Schildkrout 1991; Gieryn 1998). *Learning at the Museum Frontiers* argues the opposite. The museum, as it will show, has the potential to function as a 'frontier': a zone where learning is created, new identities are forged; new connections are made between disparate groups and their own histories (Philip 1992). In some cases, collections are shown to have a new and more positive power: to help disadvantaged groups, to raise self-esteem and even to challenge racism by progressing learning.

Learning is a major theme and thread running through the book. Currently in the UK, education in the museum is widely distinguished by a focus on the learner, with the department of museum education often renamed the department of museum learning and the education policy renamed learning policy. This practice mirrors the child-centred or learner-centred approaches to education long pioneered notably by John Dewey and Paulo Freire, which challenged views of education as a ladder with incremental steps of knowledge that must be acquired and measured by testing at various stages (Dewey 1968; Freire 1985, 1996, 1998). Learning for Dewey and Freire emphasises individual potential and takes metaphors from the garden – nourishment, growth, blossoming. This is distinct from the approach adopted by more conservatively minded educators, whose major concern lies with the authority of the professional educator and takes metaphors from the marketplace – the banking system, competition, assessment. I approve the direction towards learning in the museum today, which clearly does not denigrate the vital role of the museum educator. Contrariwise, the educator works hard building bridges that close the knowledge gap between the museum and the museum visitor; addressing the complex issues of diversity and developing theoretically grounded and creative approaches to learning with new audiences.

Furthermore, in the museum recent terminological changes most importantly reflect a whole museum approach to the visitor learning experience. The V&A (Victoria and Albert Museum) is one prime examples of the education department responsible for driving education policy and strategy throughout the whole museum since the early 1990s (<http://www.vam.ac.uk> accessed on 30.11.2008). The V&A operates with a broad definition of learning:

> Learning is a process of active engagement with experience; it is what people
> do when they want to make sense of the world. It may involve the development
> or deepening of skills, knowledge, understanding, awareness, values, ideas and
> feelings, or an increase in the capacity to reflect. Effective learning leads to change,
> development and the desire to learn more. (<http://www.inspiringlearningforall.
> gov.uk> accessed on 30.11.2008)

This view of learning, in the context of the museum, vitally places the learner
at the heart of provision. It recognises that since different people have preferred
styles of learning they can be engaged in the learning process in diverse ways with
a variety of stimuli throughout their lives – literally from the cradle to the grave
(<http://www.inspiringlearningforall.gov.uk> accessed on 30.11.2008).

Race. While it can be argued that the 'inspiring' definition does not pay
sufficient attention to the socio-political context of learning – the economic
poverty and racism in society, which prevents all our children from flourishing
and developing their full potential – with its emphasis on lifelong learning it is
especially helpful for museum educators concerned with inclusion in general and
antiracism in particular, since it prioritises a place for individuals who have not
achieved according to the usual timings through the school system. In the UK a
disproportionate number of Black children are included in this group as Baroness
Catherine Ashton, Parliamentary Undersecretary of State for Early Years and
Schools Standards notes, in the report of the 2002 conference, *Towards a Vision of
Excellence: London schools and the Black Child.*

> We cannot ignore the fact that the education service as a whole is clearly still
> not meeting the needs of many black children. There has been some recent
> improvement, but it remains the case that black pupils are more likely than white
> pupils to be excluded from school, and are half as likely to leave school with five
> A-C GCSEs as their peers from some of the groups. The position for our black
> boys is even more worrying. (Ashton 2002: 11)

It is almost 30 years since Rampton first highlighted the 'under-achievement'
of African Caribbean pupils in UK schools, which in recent government reports
is seen to persist today (Rampton 1981; Scarman 1981: 9, 1996; Gillborn and
Gipps 1996; Ashton 2002). In *Learning at the Museum Frontiers* I contend
that the museum can help to tackle this problem, by taking the responsibility to
examine our 'policies and methods' for signs of the 'institutionalised racism'
such as that which the Macpherson Report uncovered when investigating the
racist murder of the teenager Stephen Lawrence in South London (Macpherson
1999: 6.18). Macpherson follows Stokely Carmichael in defining institutional
racism as originating 'in the operation of anti-black attitudes and practice', which
he underlines as playing a role in this failure of society (Macpherson 1999:
6.22). Following Macpherson, multiethnic collaboration is key to success here.
Collaborative case study examples demonstrate the need for a multiethnic team,

'visibly committed to antiracism', to both develop and deliver the museum/school curriculum jointly (Gillborn and Gipps 1996). Specifically case study collaboration with Black school and university educators, creative writers, musicians and storytellers is seen to enable more creative approaches to education and learning as a useful part of antiracism at the museum frontiers.

Throughout the museum case studies presented, practical ideas are shown to reinforce the recommendations of reports such as Macpherson's in the UK, as well as global initiatives that also highlight the need for institutions to form alliances and tackle injustice, such as The International Convention on the Rights of the Child (CRC) 1989, where certain articles highlight basic human rights and responsibilities. For example the right 'to preserve identity, including nationality, name and family relations' (Article 8); the right to 'freedom of expression ... either orally, in writing ... in the form of art or through any other medium of the child's choice' (Article 13); and the right of 'ethnic, religious or linguistic minorities or persons of indigenous origin ... to enjoy his or her own culture, to profess and practice his or her own religion, or to use his or her own language' (Article 30) which are vital to all museum collaboration as will become clear in subsequent chapters (<http://UNICEF> accessed on 29.11.2008). These tenets are crucial to new ways of working at the museum frontiers.

The last of the major themes running through this book is the notion of the museum 'frontier'. It is vital to the book's antiracist intention. The 'frontiers' refers to an effective sharing of ideas and the development of programmes both inside and outside of the Museum. It is elucidated within 'feminist-hermeneutics' that brings together distinct viewpoints. Gadamer's philosophical hermeneutics helps us to understand how in a 'fusion of horizons' – the museum visitor's and the museum object's – 'meaning' or sense is made in a process of dialogical exchange, which is akin to deep respectful conversation. To engage in such dialogue the 'partners' in the exchange need to regard each other as equals, in terms of 'I' meeting 'Thou', which demands a recognition of individual 'prejudices' or prejudgements that inevitably arise from specific histories or 'traditions' (Gadamer 1981). It is only by acknowledging our historical prejudices and traditions in the 'I-Thou' dialogue, which can 'fuse our horizons' in understanding that future possibilities may be expanded. Additionally Gadamer's privileging language use in ways that echo Wittgenstein is important for progressing understanding and learning in the museum, similarly employing the concept of 'play' and 'language games' or understanding as a 'linguistic event, a game with words' (Gadamer 1981: 446-7; Wittgenstein 1974). He also crucially highlights the lifelong and life-wide nature of understanding when he states 'language games are where we, as learners – and when do we cease to be that? – rise to the understanding of the world'. Perhaps most critically he stakes a 'claim to special humane significance' for creatively entering the play of word games, which he highlights as 'a discipline of questioning and research, a discipline that guarantees truth' (Gadamer 1981: 447).

While Gadamer stoutly re-values the truth-telling of the arts and importantly defends subjectivity, noting the 'reflective appropriation' of tradition, rather than the dogmatic 'scientific' objective 'opposition and separation' from histories, he assumes an unproblematic access to such appropriation (Gadamer 1977: 28). However these apolitical notions work well with postcolonial and Black feminist theory, which offers new ways of seeing the relationships between dominant and marginalised or disadvantaged groups (Hill-Collins 1991; Lorde 1996; hooks 1992, 1994; Gadamer 1980, 1981, 1986). Most importantly the concept of the museum frontiers marks a major revaluing of Black knowledge, not simply by 'adding on' previously marginalised or excluded discourses in the temporary exhibition space – to leave the classic canon basically preserved – but rather to locate Black perspectives right at the heart of theory building. While the notion of the museum frontiers resonates in Mary Louise Pratt and James Clifford's idea of the museum as a 'contact zone' that permits connection between individuals and communities through facilitating connections – between peoples and cultures – across time and across space; it is a new theoretical positioning within feminist-hermeneutics, I argue, which in turn may more fundamentally transform the museum at the level of theory-based practice (Pratt 1992; Clifford 1999: 435-457). This distinction will be more fully explained in the case study examples. Here I offer Figure 1 to clarify these notions with reference to the collaborative research with the Caribbean Women Writer's Alliance (CWWA) and during 'Inspiration Africa!' that underpins Section 1 and Section 3.

Perhaps the enduring appeal of this frontier notion lies in part in the value of theory-based practice for individuals working within educational institutions, including the museum, at all levels of management. At the University of Leicester, Department of Museum Studies we do not attempt to impart a 'rule book' of essential theory for students to follow slavishly when they leave us to pursue their careers around the world, but rather attempt to nurture deeper critical thought as a vital underpinning to future 'situated' practice (Haraway 1991b). Thus, while in this book insights from the Foucauldian discourse, into the relation between space and power, might be shown to reinforce feminist-hermeneutic practice in London, England, insights from Marx, Confucius or the Prophet Mohamed 'peace be upon Him' may well prove pertinent at other locations. The website *The Spirit of Islam: Experiencing Islam through Calligraphy* at the Museum of Anthropology (MoA) in Vancouver, Canada provides a wonderful example of best practice – an online curriculum that consists of six lessons each providing practical, easy to use tools for educators to build their knowledge and understanding of Islam while introducing students to a rich variety of related images, ideas, audio and text. Most impressively many tools are designed specifically to address issues of stereotyping (<www.moa.ubc.ca/spiritofislam/resources/educationoverview.html> accessed on 06.09.2008). This MOA achievement has built on long collaborative relationships with First Nations people, which proved fruitful for representation in the museum and countered the 'cannibalistic' tendency to trap the 'other' behind 'our' glass case displays and frame their knowledge according to western criteria (Ames 1995: 3-4).

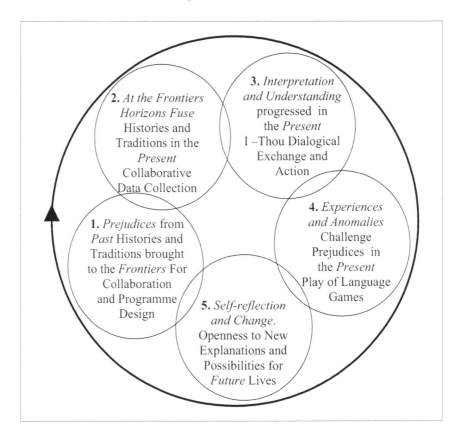

**Figure I.1 Feminist-hermeneutic research circle of
interpretation and understanding**

What needs emphasising here is that theoretically grounded practice can further
our understanding of how the museum has functioned hierarchically in the past and
point to ways in which traditional power structures can be subverted in the present,
which can benefit all our futures. In other words, the museum that traditionally
marginalised or excluded certain groups such as Black women need not – through
adhering to frontier practice – continue to do so. Most importantly, the strong
theoretical grounding of the new ways of working and the emphasis on research
can allay fears in the profession that standards will slip and vital scholarship lost,
Learning at the Museum Frontiers demonstrates the contrary, a commitment to
truth and an enhancement of knowledge.

In looking at these four major themes, I have been outlining some rather
complex notions in the abstract, but at each chapter of *Learning at the Museum
Frontiers* I offer specific museum examples to illustrate my argument. Since a

number of chapters draw on the Horniman Museum, London UK, perhaps it will be helpful at this early point to introduce this key field site.

A Brief History of Education at the Horniman Museum

Frederick John Horniman (1835-1906) founded his collections in the second half of the nineteenth century – 'the boom time in the establishment of museums' (Vergo 1989: 8). Frederick entered the family tea firm at 14 years old. He married Rebekah Emslie at the age of 23 and moved to the site of the present-day museum, Surrey House, 100 London Road, SE23, from where he also took on the duties of a Liberal MP for Falmouth and Penryn (1895-1904). His collections were displayed and shared with visitors to Surrey House or the 'Surrey House Museum' as it was affectionately known in the media. In 1889 the Horniman family, which included a daughter Annie and a son Emslie, moved their home to another house in the gardens, Surrey Mount. On Christmas Eve 1890 the objects were officially opened to the general public in the 'Horniman Free Museum' at the London Road house. The Museum was initially opened from 2.00-9.00pm on Wednesdays and Saturdays with Mr Watkins employed as the Naturalist and Mr Quick employed as Curator. Richard Quick was originally trained as an artist and his efforts to impose a rational order onto Frederick's collections largely consisted of constructing huge scrapbooks, where he pasted bills, letters and his own sketches of recent acquisitions. He speaks of aesthetics: 'rearranging' and 'relining' certain display cases 'with a light green paper, which is found to make a good background' (Annual Report 1896: 9).

Fred was not an academic university-educated scholar but a passionate collector of 'curios' as they were called at the time and purchased vast numbers from friends in the missionary and colonial services (Duncan 1972: 3-6). According to Nicky Levell, Frederick had amassed approximately 7,920 objects by 1901 (Levell 1997). The breadth and diversity of objects he desired and his 'method' of collection is explained in a letter Mrs Keddie wrote to Richard Quick in 1896, from Gaya Bengal. She states. 'Mr Horniman has asked me to send a lot of curiosities. ... He said all sorts of things' (Quick 1896: 45). Perhaps his business eye attracted him to the diversity of objects, which we see him warmly lampooned with in media cartoons (see Plate 1).

Plate 1 **Tea traits: Hornimania. Media cartoon of Fred Horniman dressed
in Chinese costume near one of the tea chests, from which the
family fortune derived, and surrounded by a wealth of 'Oriental'
and other 'curios', including the butterfly originally discovered in
his collection and named after him**

Source: © Horniman Museum, cuttings file, 1888-1891.

The richness of these collections ranging from a Spanish torture chair (a fake), mummy hands, human skeletons and gods, Elizabethan, African and Japanese Rooms as well as the special displays of live creatures including a pair of live bears and an East African monkey called Nellie – certainly proved tremendously popular with the public. Plate 2 shows Frederick and Rebeka Horniman (second and forth from left) with two friends and the curators Quick and Watkins (third and sixth from left) in the 'African and Japanese Room' or Ethnographical Saloon of the Surrey House Museum in 1892. Quick's first Annual Report of 1891 notes the museum made 'Arrangements for the reception of Schools, Societies and Clubs, in large and small numbers'. From 1891-1892, a 'total attendance of 1,070' individuals from 41 institutions, took advantage of the 'Free' admittance, and 'catalogue guide' which was 'supplied gratis' (Annual Report 1892: 8). Horniman's generous and enthusiastic nature is evident in the regular invitations he extended to children from the local board schools and orphanages, to attend organised events and activities such as races in his spacious grounds. For example on 6 July 1893 'about 100 children [from 4 local orphanages] ... were shown over the museum, and afterwards passed onto the lawn at the back, where lemonade and buns were discussed, and greatly appreciated' (Annual Report 1893: 7). Plate 3 shows Richard's Quick's children posing with parts of the collection as they might with toys at the zoo and may hint at the tactile multisensory approaches adopted by Horniman and Quick at this time – a theme I return to in Section 3.

**Plate 2 Ethnographical saloon of the Surrey House Museum c. 1982 showing
Frederick Horniman with wife Rebeka, friends and colleagues**
Source: © Horniman Museum.

**Plate 3 Curator Richard Quick's children, Richard and Louise,
        posing with parts of the collection c. 1901**
Source: © Horniman Museum.

In 1897, the Diamond Jubilee Year of Queen Victoria, 90,383 people visited the Horniman Free Museum and 120,210 visited the gardens. Frederick was inspired to commission a purpose-built museum in 1898. Two years later Harrison Townsend's art-nouveau design in Doulting stone, with Anning-Bell's decorative mosaic panel adorning the entrance, was completed at a cost of about £40,000. On 1 May 1901, in an act of great benevolence the Museum was officially given as a gift to 'the people of London for ever, as a free museum, for their recreation, instruction and enjoyment', according to the inscription on the entrance plaque which expresses an emphasis on the twin educational and recreational functions of his museum. Plate 4 shows the new museum. Horniman states as his aim for the collections, to: 'interest and inform others who may not have had the opportunity to visit other places', illustrating a democratic concern for the educational potential of the objects and a liberal view that education may lead people to a better life (Annual Report 1901: 4).

**Plate 4 Entrance to the Horniman Museum c. 1901, showing the original
building with the clock tower**
Source: © Horniman Museum.

The London County Council were responsible for administering Horniman's bequest and immediately enlisted Dr Alfred Cort Haddon, an esteemed anthropologist from Cambridge University as Advisory Curator (1902-1915), and Dr Herbert Spencer Harrison as Resident Curator (1904-1937). Haddon was concerned to make 'the museum an educational centre of great value, as well as a place of recreation' and began to organise the ethnographic artifacts according to the new 'scientific' principles of anthropology (Duncan 1972: 14; L.C.C. Report 1903). This science applied Darwin's biological theory of organic evolution to account for the different social structures around the world. The technical achievements of societies were regarded as manifest in the products of their material culture and this provided evidence of their position on the social evolutionary scale: from the most advanced and civilised or European societies, to the most 'primitive' and least technically accomplished or non-European societies. Plate 5 shows the comparative displays in the South Hall, 1904.

Plate 5 Comparative displays of material culture c. 1901
Source: © Horniman Museum.

Haddon and Harrison who were originally trained as biologists rapidly transformed the displays in accordance with the evolutionary thought which General Pitt Rivers was developing at this time, whereby 'the privileged evidence was to be that based on the comparison of artefacts' (Chapman 1984: 22). A popular series of Saturday Lectures and Handbooks on the collections reinforced the museum's new educational message of rational classification from an evolutionary perspective.

At this time the Curator's educational programmes for adult visitors perfectly complemented the museum display. Alongside this adult service an L.C.C. appointed supply teacher organised school visits to the museum and arranged for the 'instruction' of school pupils, until January 1949 when a full-time teacher was seconded from the permanent teaching service of the L.C.C.

In the 1950s the museum teacher worked with the schoolchildren and their class-teachers in a small room off the North Hall. The room was quite inadequate; lacking proper storage and display space for the children's work but the service grew in response to demand and 18,619 pupils attended the museum as part of a school visit in 1968. These school visitor figures led to the construction of a two storey Education Centre and the appointment of a second full-time teacher in 1969. The Education Centre provided excellent facilities for: art and craft work including a pottery kiln, object handling and storage, lavatories, a lunchroom and a cloakroom. A reputation for innovative educational activities with museum objects grew but the work of the museum teacher was isolated from the development of the museum displays; a situation which was exacerbated by the different salaries and conditions of employment for curators and teachers.

Throughout the 1970s and 1980s the Education Department grew under the parallel leadership of Mary Mellors for the formal (school and colleges) sector and Dr Elizabeth Goodhew for the informal (community) sector. While there was no tradition for Mellors and Goodhew to work exclusively on exhibitions they were increasingly seen as vital audience advocates in the 1990s by the Directors Richard Boston, Mike Houlihan and Janet Vitmayer who ensured a place for educational staff on upcoming exhibition teams. Alongside this role the education department worked closely from the Horniman collections and ensured the new programmes they initiated were relevant to local audience needs through direct and long-term two-way collaboration with representatives, serving on school councils for example. They held a dedicated budget for their work and set aside a proportion to maintain and expand the handling collections, through the active field research of curatorial teams from the ethnography, musical instruments and natural history departments. Thus ethnographic displays changed over these years with some wonderful temporary exhibitions curated by Keith Nicklin, Ken Teague and Natalie Tobert (Yoruba 1991; Patterns of Life 1991; Sacred Lands Devoted Lives 1994) from the ethnographic department, although an overriding presentation of 'cultural otherness' remained in the museum as a whole until the late 1990s.

In 1994 severe subsidence was discovered in the South Hall and a major programme of renovation was undertaken as a matter of urgency with Heritage Lottery Funding (HLF). Horniman was most fortunate to secure Anthony Shelton as the Head of Anthropology to progress the intellectual concept behind the development of two new exhibitions in both the South Hall and the old Lecture Theatre. Shelton's original conception was for a contrast between the two galleries *An A-Z of Collectors* and *African Worlds*, which were designed to engage in a visual dialogue with each other. I regard this work as a notable 'exhibition experiment' and return to a detailed appraisal of the *African Worlds* exhibition at Section 2 (Macdonald and Basu 2006). Before proceeding, it will be helpful to outline the whole structure and the key themes readers will encounter in *Learning at the Museum Frontiers*.

Structure and Themes

Learning at the Museum Frontiers is organised into three broad sections and six chapters, with this introduction and a conclusion. The opening Section 1 deals with the spatial politics of race, knowledge and truth in the museum. This section establishes the philosophical, political and social framework of the book. Section 1 provides an overview of museum histories and the problematic relation of truth and knowledge in the imperial, colonial and postcolonial museum context with reference to both the tangible and the intangible heritage of global communities. The material culture that underpins the dialogue here includes contemporary creative responses to objects taken as war loot from Nigeria in 1897, the Benin bronzes and maternity sculpture collected by anthropological fieldwork in the early 1900s, which is housed in the *African Worlds* exhibition at Horniman in the UK. Objects such as these are seen to raise new voices and visibilities at the museum frontiers; exemplifying collaborative practice and polyvocality (Shelton 2000).

First, Chapter 1, *Race: Repositioning and Revaluing Cultural Heritage*, investigates the stubborn persistence of the discredited notion of 'race', and the relationship of racialised ideas with enlightenment perspectives on truth and knowledge that linger in the museum context. Chapter 1 also considers post-colonial challenges to the racist fixing of meaning by 'us' in Western museum displays of 'them' the ethnographic other, against the historico-political background of thinking on 'race'. This chapter addresses controversy arising from racist viewpoints constructed by the European 'self' on the Black and Oriental 'other', in both traditional and more recent exhibitions. It explores the changing boundaries of 'Blackness' and 'ethnicities' with reference to Jews, Gypsies and Poles and critiques both multicultural and antiracist responses to this 'othering' (Back and Solomos 2000; Young 2001; Gilroy 1994a, 1994b; Morrison 1990, 1994). The contested histories of contemporary world art and culture are explored in the light of the 'art/artifact' and 'primitivism' debates through strategies underpinning seminal exhibition including *African Worlds* (Vogel 1988; Philip 1992; Shelton 2000; Arinze 2000).

Then, in Chapter 2, *Space: The Museum and the New Spatial Politics of the Frontiers*, my long-term collaborative research with the Caribbean Women Writer's Alliance (CWWA) is outlined with reference to some notes on methodology and the development of third or 'liminal' museum spaces of 'enunciation' within diaspora and hybridity theory (Bhabha 1994; Hall 1994, 1996; Said 1985, 1993). This chapter explores the specific contribution of Black women's writing to engage wider museum audiences including those in danger of disaffection, by working creatively to counter the dominant discourses of deficiency. Hill-Collins and Morrison are notable among key figures here in revaluing African ethical perspectives. For example they point us to the possibility of employing new metaphors that might progress learning at the borderlands of cultures and spaces (Hill-Collins 1991; Morrison 1988, 1993; hooks 1992, 1994; Lorde 1996). Marlene Norbese Philip's attention to sensual ways of knowing and finding expression in the Caribbean voice is also important in marking the potential for new theoretical relationships; specifically how the 'I and I' dialogue within Rastafarianism pertinently echoes Gadamer's concept of 'I and Thou' in conversation (Philip 1993; Gadamer 1981). Finally addressing issues surrounding enslavement and the abolition of the slave trade are seen to be vital for collaborative practice in the UK and in American Plantation Museums (Anim-Addo 1998; Eichstedt and Small 2002).

Overall in this opening section, attention is drawn to developing a respectful dialogical space for the 'citizen' according to the tenets of feminist-hermeneutics, which is shown to empower the socially excluded to take action in the world outside of the museum. Essentially this new location of dialogue provides an opportunity to counter the pernicious influence of the media, which too often shows the starving 'primitive' African. Respectful dialogical exchange permits the taken for granted notions about oneself and other people to be questioned, limiting self-concepts to be debated, and new hopes and dreams for a brighter future to be explored. Taken together chapters one and two suggest the need for emancipatory research and liberatory praxis, and address specific themes that contribute to the extension of this discussion in Section 2.

The two chapters in the second section of the book, *Including New Voices and Forms of Practice*, demonstrate how the passive view of the Black person, as objectively framed in traditional exhibitions, can be further transformed in ways that go far beyond the subtle subversions of knowledge, which can be achieved fleetingly through: workshops and temporary intellectual collaboration as in the UK and USA Plantation examples. The discussion is extended here to Europe and Africa, with specific reference to more intensive work undertaken by museums in Sweden and South Africa, where the struggle for stronger permanent transformation through structural changes to the management systems, with indigenous and diverse community groups taking greater control of the museum space is evident.

In Chapter 3, *Power: Inserting New Visibilities in the Museum Margins*, I consider instances of museum exhibitions which challenge our idea of what a museum is and what it might be, when there is a determination to flatten the hierarchical lines of power in the management structure from the notion of 'poetics and politics' (Karp and Lavine 1991). This chapter explores detailed artist interventions into exhibition work and intensive theoretical collaboration over museum displays that displace absolute curatorial authority. The discussion focuses on the remarkable *Museum of World Culture* (MWC), in Göteborg, Sweden that highlights issues of contemporary global concern through exhibition and artist installation, for example the *HIV-AIDS* exhibition and Fred Wilson's installation *Dwelling of the Demons*. Additionally I give an overview of the *Voices from a*

Global Africa gallery, which features historical voices of oppression and resistance as well as contemporary voices from local people with roots in the Horn of Africa and Paul Gilroy's attention to *Bob Marley*. I argue that the imaginative effort at MWC permits a vast increase in intellectual and physical access to cultures and a great widening of participation in the museum.

Chapter 4, *Control: Shifting Relationships in the Whole Museum*, focuses on South Africa to consider the historical period from the end of the twentieth century, which saw more dramatic shifts in the power structures of the museum. Indigenous groups claimed the right to their land and to democratic government. They also asserted the just claim to fully represent themselves within their own community museums where newly empowered management teams pointed to the possibility of raising controversial issues of ownership and contested histories in apartheid within a new framing of knowledge throughout the whole museum. Difficult material and troubled histories, previously hidden in traditional displays or basement stores could now be highlighted in a non-tokenistic way by those artists, writers, and academics in permanent positions inside the museum institution. The chapter is illustrated with examples of the museum offering a site of truth, reconciliation and therapeutic healing in post-Apartheid South Africa. Topics considered in Chapter 4 include management and community initiatives at *District 6 Museum* (D6M) Museum in Cape Town, South Africa, specifically creative recollection with Black Elders and imaginative intergenerational work.

Overall the two chapters in Section 2 directly confront the charge of 'tokenism' to show how the imaginative effort and political commitment of museums in the twenty-first century might positively impact on the museum poetics, to progress intercultural relationships amongst international, national and local communities today. Most importantly the museums highlighted here demonstrate the possibility of working with individual and collective memories of the most terrible histories in ways that do not continue to gnaw away destructively, deep in the psyche, but impact positively and empower communities to move forward together (Morrison 1994b).

Having laid new theoretical foundations rooted in antiracism and outlined some instances of museums' power-sharing internationally, the final Section 3 of the book, *Critical Collaborative Museum Pedagogy*, focuses on inclusive museum education and learning, and in particular on innovative opportunities for the construction of new identities with diverse young audiences. Overall, Section 3 investigates new forms of practice to raise schoolchildren's voices through a new theory-based practice seen in a project of two years duration entitled *Inspiration Africa!* This section emphasises the role of the museum in addressing the low self-esteem, which impacts on poor motivation and weak academic performance amongst socially excluded communities, especially Black learners. The two final chapters offer a number of success stories, which demonstrate the value of creatively re-reading traditional objects, not only to spark imagination and curiosity, but also to highlight the need for negotiating rights and responsibilities within a global citizenship agenda that might enhance social cohesion and intercultural understanding in contradistinction to stereotype and fear (Osler 2007).

Chapter 5, *Identity: Motivation and Self-esteem*, explores the roots of Black underachievement as well diverse ranges of holistic mind and body museum approaches, to raise self-esteem, motivation and 'flow learning' (Csikszentmihalyi 1995; Falk and Dierking 2000; Hein 1999). The objects, which are central to the discussion here, revolve around material culture displayed at Horniman including the Haitian shrine and the Igbo ijeli mask. These objects are utilised innovatively in writing, dramatic telling and performing of new identities and new stories, in collaboration with writers, storytellers and musicians. With a focus on voice and language activities the chapter demonstrates how new ways of creative interpretive working can facilitate the construction of more positive, diaspora hybrid identities, so vital for audiences who experience social exclusion.

In the final Chapter 6, *Towards a New Museum Pedagogy: Learning, Teaching and Impact*, the learning of new museum audiences, in terms of teaching impact, is subject to evaluation. Firstly drawing on French feminism, learning is regarded as importantly an active 'power to' see, hear, move, and speak in the Foucauldian sense, which reinforces a constructivist museum position and a radical new museum pedagogy. Next, the differing terminology in the UK and the USA to describe disabled children is closely considered. Then the chapter examines the use of an Ashanti stool as the focus for imaginative work on the theme of 'respect' with a special audience of younger learners, who have Special Educational Needs (SEN), specifically Educational and Behavioural Difficulties (EBD). Overall, Chapter 6 critically considers the idea of progressing embodied knowledge or more sensual and cross-cultural routes to knowledge. This is seen to be achieved with reference to a most disadvantaged audience by employing the 'both and' sensory approaches of feminist-hermeneutics at the museum frontiers, to promote active learning in contradistinction to the 'either-or' of binary reasoning.

Taken together these two chapters outlining '*Inspiration Africa!*' at the frontiers of the Horniman Museum develops a respectful dialogical space, where socially excluded individuals and groups, too often Black youth, might become citizens and empowered to take action in the world outside of the museum. Essentially this new location of dialogue is seen to provide an opportunity to counter the influence of the media that perpetuates negative ideas of Black people, such as weak-mindedness and criminality.

Then the concluding chapter draws the common threads of the six chapters, covering the learning of diverse audiences at three continents, together. Overall I argue it is the museums promoting an open yet respectful dialogical space, one that shares characteristics of my own feminist-hermeneutic praxis, which progresses notions of democracy and global citizenship. The strengthening and expanding of the relationship between museums and communities through questioning traditional cultural authorities and reasserting new power structures and identities is shown to be a principal theme of the book and one of the most urgent concerns for contemporary museums. Through museums, the citizen may honestly examine taken for granted notions about other people and oneself, subject limiting self-concepts to rigorous debate, and imaginative interpretation; then new hopes and dreams for a brighter future may be explored.

The conclusion further demonstrates and justifies the value of creative collaboration at the museum frontiers for diverse audiences. Taken as a whole the book illustrates a new praxis that highlights both the differences and the similarities between and within seemingly diverse or unified groups of people; thereby agreeing with Gupta and Fergusson's point that the distance between rich people in different continents is often closer than that between 'different' classes in 'same' city (Gupta and Ferguson 2002). Overall the book not only addresses the ways in which factors of class, gender, race, disability and sexuality intersect within fields of power, but also points to helpful ways of empowering disadvantaged peoples by re-analysing certain sorts of negative experiences that have been felt in the mind and the body and result in dis-ease (Trinh 1989).

Chapter 1
Race: Repositioning and Revaluing Cultural Heritage

Introduction: Racism and 'Post' Thought in the Museum Today

Issues of 'race', racism and social justice remain pertinent for the twenty-first century museum: national UK television and the Danish print media face charges of racism over the publication of some notorious, not very well drawn cartoons, satirising the Prophet Mohamed – peace be upon him; 'race riots' are seen in Paris France, legal cases of race-hate murder are being dealt with across Europe; while in the USA the notorious lynching rope is once again seen in the streets and Universities, specifically targeted to threaten Black citizens. Set against such discord, this book lights a different pathway, a new collaborative museum practice, which is interdisciplinary, heterogeneous and multiple. It is essentially dialogical across races and nations. It is aligned with the wealth of work in contemporary museums that aims to undermine the historical pattern of museums speaking about and speaking for 'others', usually Black others.

As a mixed race disabled academic I have strong feelings on these issues. While the overwhelming election victory of Barack Obama as President of the USA in 2008 makes me optimistic for the future, I consider it urgent for museums to address the historical background of slavery because the pernicious legacy of racism lingers. Toni Morrison illuminates this history. She comments.

> From a woman's point of view, in terms of confronting the problems of where the world is now, *black women had to deal with "post-modern" problems in the nineteenth century and earlier*. ... Certain kinds of dissolution, the loss of and the need to reconstruct certain kinds of stability. Certain kinds of madness, deliberately going mad in order, as one of the characters says in the book, "in order not to lose your mind" ... *Slavery broke the world in half, it broke it in every way. It broke Europe*. It made them into something crazy. You can't do that for hundreds of years and it not take a toll. They had to *dehumanise, not just the slaves but themselves*. They have had to reconstruct everything in order to make that system appear true. It made everything in World War II possible. It made World War 1 necessary. Racism is the word that we use to encompass all this. The idea of scientific racism suggests some serious pathology. (Morrison 1994a: 178) [my emphasis]

I open this chapter with the words of Toni Morrison in conversation with Paul Gilroy, since I take a post-modern feminist position throughout this book, but follow Morrison's regard for the limited and Eurocentric notions of the concept. To define the key terms, modernism, in sociological thought, may be distinguished by 'reflexiveness' and 'an aesthetic self-consciousness' involving a break with the paradigm of 'realism' in 'representation', while modernity is identified with paradigm shift from a God created universe to a belief in man's [sic] rationality and the triumph of scientific truth that characterised the Age of Enlightenment in the eighteenth century, which I consider below (Jary and Jary 2000: 392). At this point let us simply note that post-modernism like feminism is 'contested terrain', which it is difficult to define precisely and briefly (Usher and Bryant 1994). Carole Boyce Davies helpfully critiques the 'post' in postmodernism and post-colonialism for being premature, totalising, recentering the status quo male position against the resistant discourses of women (Boyce Davis 1994: 81). She detects pessimism and belatedness in 'post' theorising, against a radical energy and creative optimism directed to the future by new subjects and 'uprising' texts that we shall see in subsequent chapters.

Toni Morrison's discussion of postmodernism is illuminating for showing transatlantic slavery or in my preferred term the Atlantic holocaust to reveal the bankruptcy of modernism, as characterised by a faith in rationality and the progress of science, as the Atlantic holocaust necessarily heralds a new period of postmodernism for the enslaved peoples. Specifically Morrison refigures and relocates the notions of the postmodern historically with reference to the Atlantic holocaust and within Black feminist politics. This particular lens illuminates the postmodern disillusionment with grand narratives and expands our understanding of these ideas for the museum context.

For example her language is wonderfully economical in its destructive analytical force on *slavery*. She employs just three words to note: *It broke Europe*; six words to observe *Slavery broke the world in half* and six more to detect slavery fragmenting the world to pieces *it broke it in every way*. It is useful to recall the power of such textual economy when developing museum text and facilitating audiences to construct their own textual responses. Furthermore Morrison notes the problem of racist 'knowledge' emerging when a 'scientific' world-view based on observation and realism treated Black subjects as inanimate objects, and excluded the investigating self from its objectification; for the contemporary museum, this urges self-reflexivity and striving for more equal subject positions. Morrison's stress on the potential of employing 'fragmentation' and a series of subversive strategies informed by Black feminist thought as techniques of resistance when a grand logic of emancipation may prove impossible, also provides a refreshing perspective for inserting small scale project work into wider museum planning (Lyotard 1984).

Thus Morrison's text points to exciting possibilities for museum learning, where new audiences may be empowered to look through new lens of their own make. In brief there is no orthodoxy and I argue that postmodernism can present a useful framework for progressing museum learning, since it marks a questioning of universalising tendencies and a collapse of the essentialist, 'grand narrative' of the centre in favour of multiple diverse mini-narratives at numerous new mini-centres. Yet it is important to note here that I incorporate certain radical and liberatory features of the modernist discourse into a postmodern-feminist stance in the museum. Therefore my view does not abandon us to an, 'anything goes' dispensation (Crimp 1985: 44). On the contrary I consider it a 'political necessity' to open up the museum to a range of fruitful positionings, blurring the traditional boundaries between the 'personal and political' realms, dissolving the opposition between 'theory and practice', to open the 'closed system' of the museum to the 'discourse of others', to a 'heterogeneity of texts' and multiple re-writings (Foster 1985: viii-ix).

Overall this chapter cites ways of thinking and working which demand a restructuring of museum 'knowledge' and the whole notion of what counts as knowledge in the museum context. It cites a more engaged positioning for museum researchers and workers, which most importantly emphasise a new sensitivity to difference and similarity. This is an optimistic view. It follows the Gadamerian discourse on knowledge, which seeks out multiple meanings and a praxis based on the Black feminist thought that facilitates a number of ways for 'situated' subjects to produce their own 'little narratives' of self-legitimation and constant reinvention (Gadamer 1981; Lyotard 1984: 60; Haraway 1991b).

Next the chapter explores the general terrain of 'race' and 'racism' in society, as well as the interaction of these issues on the museum of the past, the present and the future. First the emergence of the term 'race' is sketched historically from the eighteenth century, the age of Enlightenment, imperialism and colonialism, when 'lower' Black 'races' were treated in abhorrent and inhuman ways to profit 'superior' white 'races' under the growth of European capitalism to the changing discourse on 'race', 'racisms', 'ethnicity' and 'difference' that came about under the 'New Conservative' and 'New Labour' governments in the UK during the last decades of the twentieth century and the first decade of the twenty-first. Having covered the historico-social background, albeit briefly, I return to a more detailed consideration of the binary distinction that lies so stubbornly at the root of western thought in the context of the modernist museum. Specifically I look at the postmodern and postcolonial challenges to the binary notions of 'self' and 'other', 'art' and 'artefact', which have negatively impacted upon representation to result in controversy in the museum, but which need not, as I demonstrate with key examples of African art exhibitions, continue to do so. In the main, reference is made to the UK situation within which most of my professional work takes place, although points of contact are made with other regions of our globalised world – USA and Canada – to address the pernicious effects that taken-for-granted ideas of race and racism continue to play in the museum and in the wider social world today.

Defining 'Race': Biology versus Language and Socio-political Change

In 1943 the American anthropologist Ruth Benedict gave us the 'briefest possible definition', stating 'race is a classification based on hereditary traits' (Benedict 2000: 113). Benedict notes the confusion of hereditary traits, 'outward visible signs such as the colour of skin, colour and texture of hair' with learned, socially acquired behaviours such as language. The term *Aryan*, which refers to an Indo-European language group not the German race, is one example of a mistaken focus on biology that leads to racism or 'the dogma that one ethnic group is condemned by nature to congenital superiority and another group is destined to congenital inferiority (ibid. 114).

Benedict further observes how language in the 'culture bearing animal' may be a cause for 'domination over all creation' precisely since it is not given at birth in 'germ cells', like the communicating behaviour we observe in wasps and ants (Benedict 2000: 115). She contends the importance of cultural change and transformation and points to non-biological transmission permitting greater adaptability and change in cultural groups so that the aggressive Scandinavians of the ninth century become the peaceful citizens of the twentieth, while the Japanese who were prized for traits of aesthetic appreciation and ceremoniousness and enjoyed a peace unrivalled in the west for 11 centuries of their recorded history, began to increase military aggression and become one of the most warlike nations of the world from 1853. It is provincialism according to Benedict that writes history as a celebration of one particular group although this obscures the dynamism of human culture, which results from the contribution by many diverse peoples over time, not whole 'races' but 'certain fragments of an ethnic group which were for certain historio-political reasons favourably situated at the moment' (Benedict 2000: 118).

One 'favourable moment' for the development of the modern museum is the age of the Enlightenment in post-industrial Europe. Despite differences of emphasis in Europe, the Enlightenment can be understood as signalling a decisive break from traditional to modern thought, and social organisation, notably the French Revolution.

The contemporary museum arises out of these new rational ways of thinking and organising social space such as the pedagogic aims of universal education. It is also intimately connected with the ideologies of imperialism, racism and social Darwinism, which I consider next.

Imperialism, Colonialism, Humanism and the Enlightenment

It is argued that racial ideologies and practices interact with other sets of ideas and values in specific historical circumstances and further that these notions persist over time (Said 1993). For the contemporary museum to combat racism within the western world and the racialised social relations in the wider world today, some understanding of the rise of western imperialism and colonialism from the eighteenth century is required.

First to define the key terms: imperialism can be defined as an overarching ideology, which serves to legitimate colonialism – the economic and military control of one nation over another by settlement (McLeod 2000: 7-8). Colonialism is therefore regarded as one specific historical experience of imperialist ideology. This means that while in the current 'postcolonial age' – a moot point as we noted earlier – resistance of previously colonised peoples that secured independence from settlers, the wider imperialist mindsets can be seen to persist from the earlier times.

Against imperialism, what is important to highlight here is that taking a long perspective, phenotypical and cultural differences were not simply produced from the mid eighteenth century onwards, nor even from the sixteenth century period of European expansion and exploration in the world. In earlier periods and looking back to ancient societies in Egypt, Greece and Rome, while differences on the basis of skin colour and 'curly hair' were noted, it was not with any significant social consequences attached. It was in the eighteenth and nineteenth centuries that notions of race as sets of discreet categories of physical appearances were developed, and it was upon these physical attributes that diverse theories justified oppressive social practices.

Nevertheless while the notion of race has taken various forms in different national contexts over time, it is the mid eighteenth century, at the high point of the Enlightenment, when ideas about race and racism became articulated. At this time popular, scientific and political discourses began to divide humanity into distinct groups with shared physical characteristics and the dissemination of such notions was progressed through the rise of print media. Additionally, different origins were attributed to the groupings and different socio-cultural significance attached to the racialised boundaries (Bulmer and Solomos 1999: 7). To take just one example, Edward Long's 1774 *History of Jamaica*, a British colony, portrayed enslaved Africans as lazy, lying, profligate, promiscuous, cowards, savages debased, ugly and therefore demonstrably inferior to their white masters who were fulfilling a role of natural superiority. On the other hand, Black 'Sambo' characteristics are contradictory in Long. He uses opposing terms to describe the Black 'other' who is childish but sly, slavish and cunning, a lap dog and a wild animal (Solomos and Back 1996: 40-41).

These contradictory perspectives highlight the inherent difficulties in dualist positioning, which emerge in the humanist ideology of the Enlightenment period. In short, humanism as a philosophy set up Essential and Universal ideals of 'Man' based on a view of 'Human Nature', which is seen as at a remove from history, geography and socio-political circumstances. Humanist man of the Enlightenment age was seen as the measure of all things, in opposition to earlier claims that God created and ordered the universe. Enlightenment man could draw on scientific method to justify claims to Universal Truth and Knowledge as certain and objective. Alongside his human nature, man was gradually thought to have certain inalienable human rights and responsibilities as citizens in the democracy of the nation state. Yet as certain postcolonial theorists note, the early notions of the humanist 'man' are exclusive. Man is European. European man was more and more aggressively engaged in global expansion, increasing trading networks and gaining power over 'other' indigenous people and their lands throughout the eighteenth century. At this time the 'scramble for Africa' divided the continent into colonies under imperial rule. Said highlights this European expansion and appropriation of 'other' lands as, fundamentally, acts of geographical violence (Said 1993: 1-15). Fanon also points to the violent negativity of a British colony, where 'Man' 'the settler ... plunders ... violate and starves' the colonised dehumanised 'other' (Fanon 1990: 40). He states:

> That same Europe where they were never done talking of Man, and where they never stopped proclaiming that they were only anxious for the welfare of Man: today we know with what sufferings humanity has paid for every one of their triumphs of the mind. (Fanon 1990: 251)

Fanon further highlights how 'Western bourgeois racial prejudice' towards 'the nigger and the Arab is a racism of contempt; it is a racism which minimises what it hates', while at the same time the bourgeois ideology invites 'the sub-men to become human', taking 'as their prototype Western humanity as incarnated in the Western bourgeoisie' (Fanon 1990: 131). Fanon's words recall John Stuart Mill, who wrote in 1859 of 'The sacred duties which civilised nations owe to the independence and nationality of each other', which is distinct from the 'barbarous people' who have 'no rights as a *nation*, except a right to such treatment as may, at the earliest possible period, fit them for becoming one' (Mill 1984: 118).

Benin City, Nigeria: 1668 to Today

In offering a concise overview there is a danger of over simplifying the issues, continuing to make sweeping statements and global assertions along the lines of the older essentialism and universals, when what is required in critique is the need to observe the complexity, the significance of particular instances (Young 2001). A brief outline of educational work with material culture from Benin, Nigeria may address Young's concern.

In the context of museum learning today we can stress the changing accounts of Europeans on African 'others' from the sixteenth century, since favourable images of Black people exist in historical narratives and can be productively employed in the museum. For example, the first impressions of Benin City in Nigeria by the Dutchman Olfert Dapper in 1668 highlight the grandeur and sophistication of the Oba's (the ruler's) kingdom, which he compared more than favourably with the city of Amsterdam at the time (Golding Teachers' Pack 1996: 3). Accounts such as Dapper's demonstrate a sophisticated society and early cultural production in Africa to counter views of 'primitive' lack that was the 'white man's burden' under colonialism. Similarly the Royal Courts and craft guilds of medieval Europe mirror aspects seen in the City of Benin at the same historical period.

We can note in passing that intellectually Thomas Paine's *Rights of Man* (1791-1792) was equally applicable to woman and the enslaved, yet as the 'other' of man and as the colonised 'other' of the European both were excluded. Annie Coombes points to Benin as a typical case illustrating the contradictory attitudes and mindsets in the eighteenth and nineteenth centuries that underpin museum collecting and exhibitionary practices and displays of artifacts of the period and she observes how historical accounts of the period 'tell us more about the speaking subject than they do about the African' (Coombes 1994: 22). To illustrate her remarks with reference to Horniman we might cite R.H. Bacon, an intelligence officer to the 'punitive expedition' and Richard Quick, curator of the Horniman Museum in 1897. Bacon writes in contradictory terms about the Edo, who are 'liars' and mentally 'slow', yet also 'courageous' in battle. The point about the Edo 'courage' transparently adds greater prestige to the British military victory in Benin. Quick's public writing on Benin in 1897 highlights the evidence of 'civilisation', at a time when Benin objects are dismissed in the media as 'hideous bronze heads' or a 'hideous Benin god', and his later writing in 1899 shows a greater appreciation of Benin culture. His words cherish the 'fine deep carvings' made by extremely 'skilful craftsmen' which proves for him 'that artists of no mean talent were formally attached to the King's court' (Quick 1899: 248, 251, 254).

At Horniman, teaching Benin across the curriculum for 5 to 11 year old pupils and as part of the art curriculum for 11 to 16 year old pupils together with teacher collaborators, Quick's highlighting of Benin material culture as Art was emphasised. This revaluing of material culture from Africa was vital to raising pupil's self-esteem and achievement as I have demonstrated elsewhere although the notion of Benin as 'art' was contentious at the 1999 MEG (Museum Ethnographers Group) conference hosted at Horniman (Golding 2000, 2007). I shall outline the art/artifact debate as it remains contested today and since all my collaborative practice challenged this binary opposition, not only during Benin projects but also during the Horniman case studies discussed throughout this book.

The Art/artifact Debate and Learning Programmes at Horniman

One important factor during collaborative Benin project work, when funding permitted, was engaging contemporary Black artists, storytellers, writers and musicians to work alongside the class teacher and myself with the pupils. Employing contemporary artists at the museum frontiers provides positive live role models for the students and thwarts any fixing of Benin arts in an 'extinct' past (Picton 1992). Additionally making new pieces of art and engaging imaginatively with the personal meanings of the historical objects in the museum for each viewer in the present day does not prevent giving careful attention to the original context and contextual meaning of the museum objects, Benin plaques in this example, and thoroughly interrogating the social world(s) in Africa and London during the time of their original making, their life and use as well as their movement, too often forced or resulting from 'spoils of war', into the museum collection and the contemporary use there [1897] (Howell 1993: 215).

For example, the fact that the Benin plaques are made according to royal patronage, to commemorate historic events, and for overriding religious purposes does not irrevocably sever them from the world of western art at this time. On the contrary, systems of religious and royal patronage are found throughout the 15th century art world. Historically workshops of artists and apprenticeship systems existed in the west, that bear some similarities to the historic guilds of brass-casters in Benin City. The Romantic notion of an individual artist working in glorious isolation from any patronage is comparatively recent, and moreover a largely imaginary conception. Artists in the west and in Africa remain dominated by the demands of the Global art market.

John Picton also stoutly defends the notion of African art, but he deplores the way this global market privileges the arts of 'tribal' or 'auto-didact' artists over 'academic' artists today (Picton 1998: 281). At Horniman, students sometimes had the opportunity to work with a contemporary academic artist from Nigeria. Chike Azuonye is one collaborator who highlights Picton's proposition that, 'The academic artists are concerned to hold on to and explore their place within the traditions of practice inherited from the past; it is they who use these traditions as among the resources with which to explore current concerns' (ibid. 284-5). Collaboration with Azuonye was vital to the success of projects, which would otherwise have been fixed onto distant historical aspects. Additionally Azuonye shared the experiences of travelling across cultural horizons with the multicultural multiracial student groups who came to recognise specific African art-skills, within a framework of African knowledge and history, which had previously been obscured or hidden from them.

Programming with contemporary artists such as Azyonye vitally adds the live voice, the living human mind and body, to the interpretation of material culture in exhibitions on display. Perhaps most importantly during Benin work with Azuonye the participants all became active participants, re-forming and redefining a relationship to the derogatory notion of a primitivised, colonised 'other', through an empathetic engagement with historical *and* contemporary Benin arts (Hiller 1993: 285). We saw how collaboration during Benin projects might challenge the notion of any childlike or 'primitive other' and help to combat the idea of the museum as a site of white supremacism, since as Marlene Nourbese Philip notes:

> For Africans the museum has always been a significant site of their racial oppression. Within its walls reasons could be found for their being placed at the foot of the hierarchical ladder of human evolution designed by the European. Proof could also be found there of the "bizarre" nature and "primitive" anatomy of the African. ... The museum has been pivotal in the expansion of the west's

knowledge base about the world, seminal in the founding of its disciplines and indispensable in Europe's attempt to measure, categorise and hierarchize the world with the white male at the top. (Philip 1992: 104)

Philip is another Horinman collaborator who cites here the shameful and tragic case of Saartje Baartman, the Khoi-San South African woman who was known in early nineteenth century London as the 'Hottentot Venus' for her large backside, and made a live 'display' (Bennett 1996: 202-203; Gilman 1994). Saartje suffered an early death at the age of 24, when her genitalia was preserved, similarly exhibited and then stored in the Musee de l'homme, close by the preserved brain of the 'advanced European' craniologist Paul Broca. Saartje's remains were finally returned to the Khoi-San people in 2002 following considerable diplomatic pressure from the new democratic government led by Nelson Mandela.

It is worth highlighting the 2007 exhibition, *Between Worlds Voyagers to Britain 1700-1850*, at the National Portrait Gallery in London, which highlighted the complexity of Saartje Baartman's historical position. This exhibition celebrated Saartje's agency and highlighted her refusal to break her 'contract', which in a certain sense implied she choose to be displayed, although I would question the notion of choice in such circumstances of economic necessity. Whatever our opinion on the matter of choice here, the Saartje case exposes 'Primitivism' as a western notion about art in the nineteenth century. A time when Europe defined itself against the 'primitive' as an essentially superior point, while in the twentieth century Modernism saw in the notion of 'primitivism' aspects of a 'noble savage' a more natural self 'lost' by 'us' in our 'rapid evolution at the centre' (Hiller 1993: 285, 87).

Benin project work at the Horniman Museum addressed issues such as those raised by the Saartje Baartman case in an attempt to 'widen our aesthetic horizons to include African sculptures', without rendering 'invisible the facts of historical and cultural difference', and 'the brutal history of European colonialism' (Bryson 1992: 96, 100).

Evaluation of the Benin programmes revealed an overwhelmingly favourable response towards the idea of *African Art* as opposed to *African Craft* (Golding 2007a). The term art was felt to more fully celebrate and honour African human achievement. In terms of pedagogy, teacher collaborators further argue that if China has art and craft, India has art and craft but Africa lacks highly valued art and has only the lesser-valued craft then this communicates a negative message about Africa and African-heritage children, which the multicultural/antiracist curriculum aimed to counter.

Art is one of the highest accolades in terms of western thought. I understand the western term art as derived from the Greek word '*techne*', which translates as 'human skill' in making an object (COD 1976: 52). Therefore, although there may be no term denoting art in any African language, it seems preposterous to deny Africa has any skilfully made objects of art (Vogel 1988). African material culture is often superbly crafted and the makers obviously employ a sophisticated aesthetic

sense in their construction, since a serious attention to the formal relationship
between visual forms is displayed. My experience shows museum visitors can
better appreciate this aesthetic through engaging in creative activity.

My approach to Benin learning programmes in this respect is situated in my
own professional art training, which the contemporary artist Rasheed Araeen
shares. Araeen wants to praise the 'extraordinary formal qualities' of African
sculpture, without being accused of 'reducing them' to these aspects (Araeen 1993:
165). Araeen does not deny the ritual function of the African works, but sets this
function alongside sponsorship within market economies. Clearly art museums
abound with Western works of art, which have been produced for ritual purposes
and are similarly ripped from their original context in the church, by placing them
in the new location of the art museum.

These issues may be further clarified with reference to western exhibitionary
practice. I select three major exhibitions: from the USA, Canada and the UK to
interrogate the main points.

The Art/artifact Debate and a Seminal Exhibition in the USA

I consider Susan Vogel's text on the seminal 1988 *Art/artifact* exhibition at the
Centre for African Art in New York, where she became executive director in 1984,
casts light on these points that remain pertinent today. Vogel's paper refocuses the
lens of attention in museums towards a more reflexive stance about exhibitionary
practices, which challenges the taken for granted assumption of a 'neutral' museum
position. It does this not by presenting an exhibition 'about African art or Africa'
nor more broadly one entirely about 'art', but rather about 'the ways Western
outsiders have regarded African art and material culture over the past century ...
(both literally and metaphorically) ...' (Vogel 1988: 11; 1991: 195). Vogel notes
the importance of the extent to which much of 'our vision of Africa and African
art has been conditioned by our own culture', or how the image of African art we
have made a place for in our world 'has been shaped by us as much as by Africans'
(ibid.).

This 'shaping' is demonstrated in the *Art/artifact* exhibition by showing the
power of the museum's exhibitionary practices to affect visitor perceptions through
the construction of different environments, such as the art space or the traditional
ethnographic space for the objects in their collections. Ivan Karp emphasises this
point with reference to *Art/artifact*, where viewers are 'forced to question' what
they see and how this is fundamentally affected by the framing of objects within
the museum settings that include the: cabinet of curiosities, natural history, art
museum and gallery (Karp 1991). Vogel herself reinforces Karp stating the aim of
Art/artifact was to 'empower the visitor to look critically at works of African art
and at the same time to heighten awareness of the degree to which what we see in
African art is a reflection of ourselves' with the 'museum as the 'subject' (Vogel
1991: 193). *Art/artifact* is presented over five exhibition spaces or rooms, each

organised according to specific display styles. In one clean 'white cube' room a 'Zande' fishing net wrapped up for transport is displayed to privilege its formal qualities with minimal labelling; in a second room of Mijikenda posts displayed aesthetically as sculptural objects a video showed the installation of a Mijikenda memorial post with a label pointing to the privileged original audience experience; in a third 'curiosity' type room reconstructed from 1905 man-made and zoological objects are mixed; a fourth room laid out in a natural history museum style includes a diorama of the Mijikenda installation, and in the fifth room objects sit behind plexi glass privileging their art status.

Just as the *Art/artifact* exhibition displays are clearly not neutral but communicate values so, Vogel contends, does the whole institution. Not overtly but in the programming and audiences it addresses, the size and emphasis of respective staff departments, in object acquisition, selection and location of objects for display or storage, as well as in lighting and labelling (Vogel 1991: 200). Elaine Heumann Gurian reinforces this point with reference to Stephen Weil. Weil states that the museum is not 'a clear and transparent medium through which only objects transmit messages' and urges museums not to attempt to 'purge' itself of values but to make their values 'manifest' and to bring them to the consciousness of visitors (Heumann Gurian 1991: 189). To raise consciousness or levels of learning in the visitor, Gurian argues for exhibition makers to embrace 'theatricality' and 'playfulness', and not to shy away from including the 'sensual and emotive' alongside the 'intellectual' to prompt critical thinking in the viewer (Heumann Gurian 1991: 182-3).

Art/artifact was vital in museum studies and practice for drawing attention to the historical western gaze and its systems of classification. James Clifford clarifies this when he speaks of non-western objects categorised by museums into two major groups 'as (scientific) cultural artifacts or as (aesthetic) works of art' (Clifford 1994: 262). This classification determined an absolute distinction between what Stuart Hall terms 'the west and the rest' – 'ourselves' and 'others' – that was made visible with reference to the display of material culture in different museum displays over time. Clifford importantly points out the movement between the 'boundaries of art and science, the aesthetic and the anthropological' that encompass western categories of 'the beautiful, the cultural and the authentic' and further notes the importance of increasing transparency in representing self and otherness. In other words he calls for greater historical self-consciousness; or the historical, economic and political processes underpinning the production of exhibitions of other cultures, to be made a feature of museum display (Clifford 1994: 266). In the last decades of the twentieth century *Art/artifact* was a landmark exhibition that went some way to achieving this end, importantly commenting on the historical differentiation between self and other, 'superior' and 'inferior' races (Hallam and Street 2000: 5).

Self and Other/s, Margin and Centre/s

Said's work on Orientalism – a term describing a whole field of studies and accruing to it a wide range of meanings and associations – casts light on this 'self-other' notion. For example notions of the depraved other in comparison to the European rational, virtuous, mature, normal self emerged out of the racial clichés of Oriental despotism and Oriental sensuality, within the academic field of Orientalism. Museums, as a field of research similarly draw upon a huge body of written texts including eyewitness accounts from missionaries, colonial administrators; traders and travellers; anthropological writing; newspapers; novels; poems and films, which underpin collecting and exhibitionary practices (Said 2003: 40, 203). While some of these texts may acknowledge the greatness of the other – as a construct created by the self – the majority of texts mark the other as essentially a sign of difference and weakness. This served as a force to maintain Western superiority against the inferior other, or as Pearce states, it 'keeps the right and proper in place' (Pearce 2003: 350).

The important point for our discussion of the art/artifact distinction in African material culture here is the way prestige objects of western and certain Asian cultures (including India, China and Japan) were designated fine art status and housed in the art museum while the ethnographic museum housed the other objects, including the craft or ritual objects of Africa. For educational purposes, if Africa has no prestigious objects of art the underlying messages seem to be that the African is a sub-human other, devalued by this limiting classification.

Clearly educators must be aware of regarding the formal properties – the power of strong line, tone, form, and so on – of African art in isolation from the rich cultural context past and present. The purely formal interpretation would reduce the African work to a mere 'footnote' in the development of art in the west and to neglect vital questions of content, such as iconography as well as intentionality (Karp 1991: 376). It would also present a simple adding-on to the centre, work from the margins, when a more fundamental reassessment of the intellectual framework that marginalises and makes 'other' seems to be required, if we are to present a thorough challenge to racism. What I am suggesting is that human understanding necessarily occurs through our own conventions, our ways of thinking and imagining that are based in part at least on ways of looking, which is a circular infinite process. This is not to argue for a universalising notion of art but rather to highlight points of contact between diverse cultures. As Ivan Karp notes, to see the other negatively presented as exotic and lacking the rationality of the west is also to present the other as in some sense the same. In other words, to see difference we must also see similarity, and then differences that at first appear great, can be seen as 'only surface manifestations underlying similarities' (Karp 1991: 375).

In today's plural society this points to a vital task for museums – to help to construct new ideas of ourselves as a nation by mediating the claims to the representation of diverse groups. Yet it is by no means easy, since we need to explore 'this multicultural and intercultural terrain consciously and deliberately, in spite of the snares that may await' (Lavine and Karp 1991: 8). Controversy is a particular snare for museums that aim to speak not only for those powerful visitors, ones with a vested interest in telling the traditional stories to those who are less powerful and who may only listen, but to widen participation on the notion of who can speak, who can listen and why, as I shall demonstrate with an example from Canada.

The Making of Controversial Exhibitions

In addition to the *Primitivism* and *Art/artifact* exhibits we have just considered, the original proposals for the interpretation of the *Enola Gay*, which eventually opened in 1994 at the Smithsonian saw World War II veterans and American-Japanese heritage peoples clash. At the Royal Academy in London UK in 1997 and later in New York *Sensation* also saw conflict between the sensibilities of the conservative Catholic community and the right to artistic freedom of expression. I shall now examine what makes an exhibition controversial and cultures clash through one seminal case from Canada, *Into the Heart of Africa* curated by Jean Canizzo at the Royal Ontario Museum (ROM) in 1990, which illustrates some key issues. In my discussion of this case I shall highlight Marlene Nourbese Philip, since she has commented so pertinently on it from the perspective of the Black 'other', with recommendations to museums striving to avoid future negative conflict. I shall also refer to Henrietta Reigel's perceptive remarks on exhibitionary practice, which are relevant to Philip's points.

In short a public outcry followed the opening of *Into the Heart of Africa* at the ROM, which infamously juxtaposed negative images of Black people with 'ironic captions' taken from missionaries and colonial administrators. The protesting public considered the use of irony as an exhibitionary device served merely to reinforce negative stereotypes that are racist, imperialist and thought to be obsolete.

Philip quotes John McNeill, acting director of the ROM at the time, who deemed the controversy surrounding the exhibition, which led to a number of museums cancelling the tour, to impinge 'on the freedoms of all museums to maintain intellectual honesty, scientific and historical integrity and academic freedom' (Philip 1992: 103). She further notes how McNeill's remark's are echoed in the print and electronic media's overwhelming portrayal of the protesters – mostly African Canadians – as 'irrational, emotional and unable to grasp the irony', which was the linchpin to a true rational and sophisticated understanding of the exhibition. Accordingly, to the media and the museum, the protesters – the Black Others – were at fault.

In contrast, at an individual curatorial and at a wider institutional ROM level, Philip charges the ROM with a failure to perceive 'how thoroughly racism permeates the very underpinnings of Western thought', despite Cannizzo's stated wish for the exhibition to 'help all Canadians understand the historical roots of racism', which she declared in writing to the *Toronto Star* newspaper (5 June 1990), following the controversy. Philip highlights how the African Canadians *outside* the museum were an integral and indispensable part of the cultural text *inside* the museum, since their knowledge of the history of colonialism is intimate and painful. Their different historical location inevitably determined the alternative reading of the artifacts 'as the painful detritus of savage exploration and the attempted genocide of their people' by the Black audience. While the ROM viewed its exhibition as an instance of self-reflexivity, holding up a mirror to its historical practice, the audience perceived the museum as the cultural arm of the same powers that had long exploited Africans historically.

Yet the hostile reception of *Into the Heart of Africa* marked a contrast with the curator Jean Canizzo's curatorial aims. Philip welcomed and understands Canizzo's aspirations: to study the museum as an artifact, to read curatorial collections as cultural texts and to discover the life histories of objects, and understand something of the complexity of cross cultural encounters. For Philip, these goals highlight the possibility of an interpretive 'framework' that might have provoked 'less adversarial' responses (Philip 1992: 104). Unfortunately as Philip wryly comments, Canizzo's notion of a cross-cultural encounter was only acceptable to the museum if it maintained the flow of power and knowledge from the museum as subject centre, out to the object African Canadian peoples at the margins. She strongly contends the Black Canadians brought different, but not inferior, ways of knowing to the museum objects, which were linked for them with the 'ongoing struggle against white supremacy.' For Philip, the ROM missed the opportunity to recognise the oppressive history of the collection and failed to support the ongoing Black struggle for equality. She regards the major failure in the making of this exhibition was not working collaboratively, '*with African Canadian involvement*' from the outset (Philip 1992: 107). It is unfortunate that the ROM did not grasp the potential to find other ways of looking and settled for a traditional display, but Philip ends her paper with some challenging suggestions for the ROM to respect and celebrate Black achievements, in the spirit of Canizzo's original aims. Firstly she wonders if the ROM might 'donate a portion of the proceeds of the gate' to assist the formation of a permanent African collection, under the aegis of the ROM but with African Canadian participation. Then she asks if the ROM might also consider compensating the African Canadian community of Ontario for the historical theft of their 'cultural and spiritual patrimony', by donating and storing certain pieces on their behalf, to be displayed by the communities on appropriate occasions (ibid.).

Henrietta Reigel reinforces some of Philip's points. She also notes the public objection marked a contrast with Canizzo's aims: to draw attention to historical collecting practices underpinning ethnography in Western museums and to celebrate 'the rich diversity of African cultural practices and artistic traditions' (Reigel 1996: 91). For Riegel, a major problem for the ROM lay in a failure to be specific and critically focused on the actual material on exhibition. Rather the ROM material appeared to be presented in a neutral and distanced tone that served to abnegate institutional responsibility. She notes how adopting a critical view of historical collecting in general, but not 'critical of the practice of collecting *these* objects', left many visitors with the impression that the Rom lacked self-reflexivity on the socio-political processes and the constructs that underpinned the display and were rooted in the history of the institution.

Overall Riegel seems to take a less radical position than Philip, one that might maintain a hierarchical position for the curatorial authority of the museum over a rather passive audience. Specifically, Riegel speaks of the exhibitor's role to mediate and translate objects in ethnographic collections – distanced geographically and temporarily from originating communities and contemporary audiences – into meaningful frameworks to promote visitor's understanding in the present day and notes this distance may be reproduced by the museum 'through rhetorical, stylistic and linguistic strategies', as indeed we saw at ROM (Reigel 1996: 88). She draws on the ROM case to ponder whether visitors will give the 'same signifying weight to images and written texts' arguing that many visitors 'read a very few of the text panels and labels', a point which visitor research calls into question (Reigel 1996: 93).

Visitors Reading Text and Image

Hirschi and Schriven in the USA demonstrated that question enhanced text panels, well located, promote reading activity in family groups (Hirschi and Schriven 1996). They note the importance of active reading by visitors to inform them on matters of difference and similarity, between Chinese and Japanese Asian peoples for example. Their work reinforces Paulette Macmanus's research in the Natural History Museum UK that family groups tend to designate a 'reader' who addresses the text conversationally, with the purpose of progressing social interaction as much as to gain knowledge of the exhibit (Macmanus 1996).

Roger Simon and Lynn Teather cast light on this matter with respect to shocking images of racially motivated torture and murder in the USA, specifically into visitor reactions to the *Without Sanctuary* exhibition of James Allen's collection of photographs and postcards. Allen's collection depicts the lynching of Black people from the mid nineteenth century to the 1960s with some cards showing the lynching as a spectacle being watched by white family groups, including children. The images can be accessed at a dedicated website where Allen introduces them with the following words.

> Without Sanctuary is a photo document of proof, an unearthing of crimes, of collective mass murder, of mass memory graves excavated from the American conscience. Part postal cards, common as dirt, souvenirs skin-thin and fresh-tatooed proud, the trade cards of those assisting at ritual racial killings and other acts of a mad citizenry. The communities' best citizens lurking just outside the frame. Destined to decay, these few survivors of an original

photo population of many thousands, turn the living into pillars of salt. (Allen
<http://www.withoutsanctuary.org/> accessed on 11.12.2008)

Simon and Teather's visitor research team are examining visitor responses at
two contrasting exhibitions: the Andy Warhol Museum where the terrible images
were largely permitted to 'speak for themselves' with little interpretive text and
the Chicago Historical Society where the stories of selected lynched individuals
were explained in detailed yet easy to read text panels. Their evaluation research
of the visitor comments books casts interesting light on the value of contextual
information. It shows the Warhol visitors would appear to be more emotionally
moved, according to their comments that were written in greater depth on this
feeling aspect, than the Chicago visitors. We await the publication of Simon
and Teather's report findings, since a number of factors could account for these
different responses including socio-economic grouping, political persuasion, types
and levels of education. At present a definitive case cannot be made for or against
interpretive text colouring visitor perception and informing their understanding.

We will return to the active visitor reading and re-writing the museum text
and display in Chapter 2, but let me offer one final example in the discussion of
African art here. I return us to the UK.

Africa: Art of a Continent, UK

A major focus of the *Africa: Art of a Continent* exhibition at the Royal Academy
London was on 'authentic' objects of art deriving from pre-colonial times,
which had a tendency to 'fix' cultures in a 'tribal' timeless past. This approach
was premised on Vogel's notion stated earlier that objects of art hold a power to
communicate 'aesthetically' across time and space. What is required is a sensitive
observer, skilled in visual literacy; one who is able to respond to the objects of art
emotionally and intuitively, irrespective of any prior knowledge of the cultural
context, which may actually impede such access to the work in her opinion (Vogel
1988: 136-7). Perhaps it may be questioned whether the emphasis on visual literacy
here is inclusive towards non-literate visitors, or whether this approach may serve
to exclude the less knowledgeable. For example, we might note that Africa does not
recognise the art/craft, high/low dichotomy that is central to western aesthetics, and
which has resulted in the neglect of objects such as ceramics, basketry, furniture
and textiles in the western art museum. Moreover this western distinction has
served to denigrate the status of the African maker in comparison with the western
one, 'recognising their manual dexterity but implying that they lack the capacity
for creative, intellectual endeavour' (Court 1999: 150).

Here we return again to the self-other binary and the argument that the high
status of the artist has too long been reserved for the western, usually male, genius,
as Philip contends (Philip 1992: 94-97). There is considerable support for Philip's
questioning of Picasso's 'discovery' of African art at the Trocadero in 1907 by

pointing to the clear links between the formal qualities of 'Les demoiselles d' Avignon' and the Nok heads on display there. Court for one echoes Philip's observation that the notion of the 'primitive' sub-Saharan central and west African arts as having more 'direct' and 'elemental' expressive qualities of fundamental 'human emotions', reinforces the link with African people and nature and the body as opposed to the mind, which I shall examine with reference to a Royal Academy (RA) exhibition in London UK (Court 1999: 152).

Africa: Art of a Continent at the RA was the major exhibition of 'Africa 95' – a season of national events held in museums across the country showcasing the extraordinary achievement of Africa and African heritage peoples past and present. The RA exhibition was curated by Tom Philips who took a geographical and temporal approach to the display of more than 800 exquisite objects, selected for their merit as art according to western criteria and in a manner reflecting the western artist-genius, which remains contentious. The range included an Egyptian sculpture of a 'female torso, probably Queen Nefertiti' carved in quartzite c. 1352-1345 BC (Russmann 1995: 84); Sudanese '*Kardaru*' stem pots made from animal dung, painted with earth pigments and air dried for a girl's trousseau (Mack 1995: 135); 'engraved ostrich eggshell flasks' made by San peoples of South Africa (Davidson 1995: 192-3); 'Nkisi nkondi' power nail figures from Kongo (Biebuyck and Herreman 1995: 246-245); 'Head of a queen mother from Benin' Nigeria (Picton 1995: 395) and 'folios from a Quran manuscript' Tunisia (Insoll et al. 1995: 561).

Objects were gathered for display under seven cultural groupings and the visitor route led geographically from Ancient Egypt and Nubia, East, South, Central, West and North Africa. Material culture from Central Africa was located in a spacious gallery in the middle of the visitor route, which as Court observed permitted reflection on the 'canonical forms' of art from Africa, including 'power figures (fetishes) and masks' (Court 1999: 161). Throughout the galleries, not just in the rooms displaying colourful textiles as conservation-minded visitors expect, the rooms were subject to very low levels of light with key objects spot-lit, which echoed late nineteenth century notions of the 'dark continent' for some critics, including myself.

A question that arises here concerns the power and control of representation, whether it may be possible to restructure the western aesthetic canon, which is rooted in the visual as well as discredited racist ideas and values, to permit more diverse pathways of connecting visitors with African art and African people, perhaps through more multisensory engagement to promote embodied knowledge that I consider in Section 3. Linked questions and criticism of *Africa: Art of a Continent* concern the privileged referencing of named western modernist artists against the nameless African makers. Kobena Mercer's comment on a five-seated stool from the Ngombe area of Zaire, which was displayed vertically to resemble Brancusi's Endless Column sculpture clarifies this objection to the museum environment where African objects are appropriated for purely aesthetic qualities, since this exhibitionary approach can erase the complex historical relationships of power (Court 1999: 163; Biebuyck and Herreman 1996: 307).

Yet it is precisely the aesthetic approach – revaluing what is counted as the beautiful – that other critics praise. Andrew Graham-Dixon celebrates the exhibition for breaking with colonialist attitudes to demonstrate 'that it will no longer quite do to consign such art to the wunderkammer [cabinet of wonders or curiosities] or marked 'Primitive' or 'tribal' (Court 1999: 163). Interestingly the exhibition catalogue provides literate visitors with broader and deeper knowledge, which notes how the original function of the Ngombe stool is unclear, but was possibly used by the warrior society as a means of symbolically linking them to a common case, or for judges to sit on and hear the pleas of the accused.

The catalogue accompanying the exhibition is visually striking and substantial at 612 pages and has contributions from Africanists with many decades of experience in the continent as well as a small number of African-heritage scholars. Some commentators do not find this imbalance problematic. As Eki Gbinigie stated 'The fact that you may not be from a particular culture does not mean that you cannot understand and appreciate something as deeply as somebody who is from that culture' (quoted in Shelton 2000: 19). Furthermore the seemingly easy option of assigning a member of a particular cultural group as spokesperson for the whole community clearly presents an impossible task; one fraught with another set of problems, not least those revolving around issues of tokenism. It is also noticeable the extent to which African heritage and other scholars comment on colonialism and the politics of display, including Cornel West and Patricia Davidson (West 1995: 9; Davidson 1995: 185).

I agree with Gbinigie's point – we are not trapped in sealed worlds where intercultural exchange and understanding would be impossible – yet as an educator, I am aware of the need to bear in mind the oppressive colonial histories and the continuing negative legacy. Additionally, it seems vital here, to recognise Kwame Anthony Appiah's emphasis on the overriding effect of global capitalism and the art market. Appiah notes the power to speak, write and represent lies to a large extent with the buyer located at the centre of the western economy. He cites the wealthy David Rockefeller, purchaser of traditional and contemporary African art, as illustration. Rockefeller is able to link 'considerations of finance, aesthetics, and décor' in appraising his art on display; while his sponsored artist, for example Lela Kouakou the economically 'poor African' maker, who 'dwells at the margins' here is merely a silent commodity or informant for the powerful purchaser (Appiah 1996: 56-57).

To sum up the criticism, *Africa: Art of a Continent* was felt to totalise Africa representing it as a fixed and homogeneous entity, which was exacerbated by the exclusively historical focus and failure to address the African and Diaspora artists of today. This was felt to result in othering that was again amplified by a lack of African curatorial voice (Court 1999: 170). While there is undoubted truth in these views it must be admitted that it was the *Africa 95* programme as a whole that was intended to serve this wider remit and which did so effectively in certain respects.

For example at the Whitechapel Art Gallery *Seven Stories about Modern Art* presented a challenge to the notion of African Art as forever fixed and traditional by offering a series of diverse views informed by the concerns of contemporary artists themselves. Taken as a whole there was some multivocality in this Africa 95 exhibition with 60 artists represented and 23,000 visitors, and my research team of Horniman teacher-collaborators made some productive study trips with their school pupils to challenge the equation of Blackness with ugliness and to revalue western categories of the beautiful in the context of African art and in relation to historico-political processes (Golding 2000).

I shall return to this self-other theme when I explore the potential of imaginative learning communities for resistance, for subverting and inverting the traditional museum narrative and the spatial politics of the museum in Chapter 2. First to conclude this chapter, let us define the boundaries of Blackness as a political category that might inspire unity in diversity.

Conclusion: Blackness, Science, Race and Physical/Socio-political Boundaries

When Sander Gilman poses the question 'are Jews white' he traces the growth of ethnological and 'scientific' literature of the mid nineteenth century highlighting the 'swarthy' or 'black yellow' skin, and the 'Hawknose' of the 'bastard' and 'ugly' Jewish race. Gilman provides us with some particularly horrid comments, from the 'liberal' Bavarian writer Johan Pezzl, who wrote of Jewish 'filth ... stench, disgust, poverty, dishonesty, pushiness' and their status as 'supposed human beings' who seemed 'closer to the Orang-Utang' in the 1780s (Gilman 2000: 231). Gilman also cites Robert Knox who lists a 'whole physiognomy of the Jew' not simply skin colour 'which is like that of the black African', effectively 'removing him from certain other races' (Gilman 2000: 230-232). Knox's 1850 *Races of Man* fixed biologically distinct racial types in a hierarchical order and attached each with corresponding moral and intellectual qualities, so that Anglo Saxons were the most developed and highest, with Celts, Gypsies, Jews, African and finally Aboriginal Australians at the lowest rungs of the evolutionary ladder (Solomos and Back 1996: 43). Methods of measurement, external, moral and intellectual, which were a key concern of nineteenth century 'scientists', return to prominence a century later in the context of Nazi rule 1933-1945. Again the 'racial' nature of the German nation state stemmed from a variety of imagined factors and shaped the articulations of anti-Semitism and racism, such as the uprootedness of the cosmopolitan Jews versus rootedness of the Volk.

This is a vast field of scholarship, which has been admirably addressed elsewhere. Perhaps what needs to be stressed here is that Anti-Semitism in Nazi Germany can be seen as part of an attempt to construct a racially pure society where the stereotype outsiders, Jews, gypsies and blacks joined 'others', the 'abnormal, insane, homosexuals and criminals (Solomos and Back 1996; Young 2001). I want to make two points here. Firstly to note for socially conscious museum studies and museum learning the wide groupings of 'others', subsumed under the derogatory label of 'Blackness' in the historical literature. This illuminates racism in the world today where gypsies are widely referred to as 'black' in Eastern European institutions including the museum.

Secondly, while 'Blackness' is a category that has been used historically to oppress the 'other', contrariwise more recently it has been employed to unite diverse groups politically in a struggle for equality and social justice during the second half of the twentieth century. For example the Southall Black Sisters Co-Operative in London UK, united Asian women with African Caribbean women in social and political action. Perhaps most notably in the 1960s the Black Power movement in the USA critically addressed overt and covert racism. Their attention to the dynamics of language and meaning pointed to the possibilities of subverting negative meanings, specifically by inverting the equation Blackness equals ugliness in the slogan 'Black is beautiful'. Similarly in the twenty-first century Gobineau's conception of humanity hierarchically 'divided' into three races white, yellow and black is inverted in the Black Body Research network that I belong to, notably our united publication *I Am Black, White, Yellow* (Anim-Addo and Scafe (eds) 2007; <http://www.goldsmiths.ac.uk/blackbodyineurope/about.php> accessed on 30.11.2007).

It is to collaborative programming with Anim-Addo and the Caribbean Women Writers Alliance (CWWA) – an earlier research network – that I turn to in the next chapter. Specifically in Chapter 2, I shall outline collaborative ways of working with notions of spatial politics to challenge racism in the museum.

Chapter 2

Space: The Museum and the New Spatial Politics of the Frontiers

Introduction

Marlene Nourbese Philip has written extensively on spatial politics. In the historical context of the museum she comments:

> As I wandered throughout this museum, I recognised many of the displays – these silences were mine as much as they had belonged to the people they had been taken from.
>
> "Return them," I demanded of the proprietors. "You must return these silences to their owners. Without their silence these people are less than whole" … It had been theft originally, I continued, now it was nothing but "intimidation!" … It was mine – ours – I challenged, to do with as we pleased – to destroy if we wanted. They told me the silences were best kept where they could be labelled, annotated, dated and catalogued …
>
> It was one of the world's wonders, they told me, this Museum of Silence – never had so much silence been gathered together under one roof, and they were proud of it. (Philip 1998: 136-7)

In this chapter I shall outline my long-term collaborative research with the Caribbean Women Writer's Alliance (CWWA) at the frontiers of the Horniman Museum in London. This alliance, which continues within the Black Body research network, aimed to break the museum 'silence' CWWA member Philip alludes to above (<http://www.goldsmiths.ac.uk/blackbodyineurope/about.php> accessed on 10.01.2009).

The collaboration I discuss here arises from what Fanon describes as 'bottom up' impetus – my own, from a position (Head of Formal Education) outside of the senior management team staff structure together with a small local community group from outside of the museum – rather than the 'top down' approaches, which characterised the exhibitions considered in Chapter 1. CWWA collaboration is shared as an example of a European museum touching on issues of ownership and cultural heritage, notably the raising of new voices and visibilities in the museum, in ways that echo the concerns of indigenous communities in North America, Canada, Australia and New Zealand, for example, that have positively impacted on contemporary practice of 'decolonisation' around the world in the last decades of the twentieth century. As Fanon states:

> Decolonisation is always a violent phenomenon. ... Its usual importance is that it constitutes, from the very first day, the minimum demands of the colonized. To tell the truth, the proof of success lies in a whole social structure being changed from the bottom up. The extraordinary importance of this change is that it is willed, called for, demanded. The need for this change exists in its crude state, impetuous and compelling, in the consciousness and in the lives of the men and women who are colonized. But the possibility of this change is equally experienced in the form of a terrifying future in the consciousness of another 'species' of men and women: the colonisers. (Fanon 1990: 29)

I will draw on examples of CWWA collaboration to elucidate how museum knowledge and professionalism, if respectfully and sensitively balanced with migrant voices and narratives, can facilitate a new political space of enunciation, which involves the museum in dealing with contentious issues, such as colonialism and its negative legacy, yet positively (Hall 1994). To paraphrase Fanon, I shall outline a 'decolonisation' of the traditional museum space, which is neither a 'violent phenomenon' nor points to a 'terrifying future' for the museum or the community group but rather, to brighter and broader 'horizons' for both (Gadamer 1980). The opening poetic extract taken from a CWWA workshop organised by the Canadian woman of African Caribbean heritage, Marlene Nourbese Philip exemplifies this view and highlights the vital role of creativity in building new feminist-hermeneutic theory.

In short I contend that while voices such as Philip's are certainly challenging for the traditional cultural authority of the museum, in my experience the benefits of working within a 'collaborative paradigm' proves helpful to the museum promoting intercultural exchange and 'community cohesion', which far outweigh any disadvantages (Philips 2003; Home Office 2001). The chapter aims to show that collaboration brings clarity of thought, especially in terms of ethical considerations about power-knowledge relationships at the museum frontiers for all parties at the local level, with repercussions that extend to the global.

The chapter is subdivided into sections. First I offer some background information on CWWA. Then I expand theoretically upon the borderlands or 'frontier' methodology, informed by feminist-hermeneutics that was developed together with CWWA. Next, two collaborative programmes: *Re-writing the Museum* and *Emancipation Day* will serve to highlight the ways in which our praxis resonates in the third or 'liminal' museum spaces of 'enunciation' within diaspora and hybridity theory, as well as the social constructivism that is more established in the context of museum learning (Bhabha 1994; Hall 1994, 1996; Said 1985, 1993; Silverman 1995; Hein 1998; Falk and Dierking 2000). A most important point of this programming lies in privileging new 'standpoint' texts and 'situated' knowledges from Black theorists, who may also be poets, to transform the museum space from temple of high cultural worship into a democratic forum space of freedom (Hill-Collins 1991; Harraway 1991).

My argument draws attention to the complexity of the issues considered in the UK context including the importance of museums: working with insider and outsider readings or interpretations, prompting diverse multi-sensory ways of knowing and seeing, and facilitating empathetic understandings in audiences. This UK research flags up the interconnection between the individual and the collective, as well as the dynamic nature of the boundaries of social group and this is reinforced from a global perspective with collaborative examples from American Plantation Museums in the USA (Eichstedt and Small 2002; Gable 1999).

Overall this chapter highlights the importance of museums addressing difficult issues such as historical enslavement, dealing positively with the contemporary legacy of racism and breaking out of limiting stereotypical moulds both the 'dingy' (Trevelyan 1991) museum and the Black woman as 'sexual siren' (Anim-Addo 1998: 102) entrapping the white man in her 'goatish embraces' (Long 1774: 260). At the end of the chapter, I reflect on the nature of collaborative research considered and draw some concluding remarks on the strengths and weaknesses of this effort.

Let me begin by providing some brief notes on the CWWA community group – their particular histories and experiences that directed collaborative museum work. Then I shall outline the theoretical perspective, which directed our actual practice at the museum frontiers.

CWWA: Background Information and Collaborative Theory-building

Dr Joan Anim-Addo, who was born in Grenada, is Director of the Centre for Caribbean Studies (CCS), founder of CWWA, and a Senior Lecturer at Goldsmiths College University of London. Anim-Addo's extensive writing includes poetry, history, literary criticism and drama (Anim-Addo 1998, 1999, 2007, 2008).

At the time of Horniman collaboration in the mid 1990s there were more than 160 international members of CWWA with ages ranging from teenagers to elders. I was a founder member and a large proportion of our local members were teachers or lecturers who subsequently attended, and/or collaborated with me on organising museum In-service Training of Teachers (INSET), as well as on the organisation of educational museum-school projects and museum visits for their pupils.

However, we should note here at the outset the multiple subject position of CWWA members, which impacted upon collaborative practice. In addition to their professional lives, CWWA members may be: sisters, mothers, grandmothers, daughters, friends etc., with extended family members including those on holiday from other countries visiting the museum at weekends. Additionally, perhaps most importantly, class allegiances were vitally seen to overlap with gender and ethnic loyalties for the group and indeed for myself – a disabled woman with dyslexia (but not severe), of mixed race (but who usually 'passes' for white and whose

English speaking ability is often praised by strangers), born into and living for the first 18 years of my life in economic poverty. It is also pertinent to note that the features listed as defining CWWA members need not fix individuals essentially in subject positions. From a feminist-hermeneutic perspective, deprived backgrounds do not necessarily limit what Gadamer terms our 'horizons' as my own undeniably middle-class position today exemplifies.

Let us listen to Gadamer on 'tradition' and the 'nation state', which are topics that have been exercising the British government's articulation of 'Britishness' following the bombings on the London transport system on 7 July 2005, by our own 'home grown' terrorists from the north of the country (Brown 2006). Gadamer states:

> My thesis is ... that the thing which hermeneutics teaches us is to see through the dogmatism of asserting an opposition and separation between the ongoing, natural "tradition" and the reflective appropriation of it. ... the historian ... is so little separated from the ongoing traditions (for example, those of his nation) that he is really *himself engaged in* ... he belongs to the nation. (Gadamer [trans Linge] 1977: 28)

It is important to state here that these words are not advocating a relativist notion of truth. Gadamer vitally challenges the persistent dualism of Enlightenment thought as well as contemporary relativism and a lazy 'anything goes' postmodernism. He interestingly saves us from relativism with the 'concept of play', which refers to the serious language games humans the world over engage in. He notes:

> The way in which the weight of the things we encounter in understanding disposes itself is itself a linguistic event, a game with words playing around and about what is meant. ... when we understand a text ... we are drawn into an event of truth. (Gadamer 1981: 446)

My research partner Joan Anim-Addo and members of CWWA have been inspired by Gadamer's concept of the 'reflective appropriation' of history and the 'play' of language, which is a 'discipline of questioning and research ... that guarantees truth' (Gadamer 1981: 447). On behalf of the museum I established an open and trustful research dialogue with CWWA members from the earliest days of meeting, which centred on sharing of personal histories and complex subject positionings in dialogue or conversation, the 'living speech' of language (Gadamer 1981: 331, 432). The oral – the live voice – is vital to the success of the philosophical hermeneutic dialogue, which respectfully engages one human with another or with a work of art. This is an infinitely enriching process leading to renewed knowledge and understanding on particular topics. The process in dealing with complex human themes is never finally completed like a trivial chitchat exchange at the shops, but rather adjourned for us to pick up reflexively again and again, like deeper human conversations.

Now let us ground and clarify these ideas, which can appear rather abstract and difficult, with reference to the politics of representation at Horniman. I turn to one example of spatial politics considered with CWWA at Horniman, which proved fruitful for praxis.

The Frontier or Borderline Museum Space and 'The Races of Man' Displays

While human societies are rarely static but rather marked by generations of movement and mixing that mark CWWA membership, we may still observe a fixing of the natural landscape and social organisation in traditional ethnographic 'reconstructions' or interpretive panels located in natural history museums around the world today, as Monique Scott has recently demonstrated (Scott 2007). In the North Hall housing the Horniman Natural History Collection, tucked away at one edge of the gallery in a narrow space made corridor-like by the original mahogany cases c. 1901, there are a series of displays including dogs' heads showing diverse canine types, and a collection of skeletons with physical characteristics showing the 'development' from ape to human types over the ages. Near the skeletons there is a panel entitled 'The Races of Man' [sic] which is reproduced at Plate 6 This panel shows a map of the world overlaid with a thick black cross and portrait photographs representative of physical 'types', arising from specific regions. Some types smile, some do not. No types are allowed a voice. They exemplify the silent objects of western study. The 'Races' panel gives the impression of the world without movement and mixture. It is a fantasy neutral grid. One that rigidly divides the world space and peoples as fixed into four distinct quartiles where pure origins remain, forever, just as the nearby cases of natural history specimen fix the animal kingdom and demonstrate hierarchies of power and control.

The Horniman 'Races' panel and the skeletons that reinforced the ideas underpinning the display that linger from the curatorship of Watkins and Haddon in the early twentieth century are of interest for other museums with similarly antiquated exhibitions and lack of funds. Exhibits like these can inspire creative new voices, as evident in the extract from Marlene Nourbese Philip's 'Museum of Silence' that foregrounds this chapter and which arose out of a creative workshop intervention into the North Hall Gallery space. Her imaginative text gives voice to the silent 'types' on display that exemplify the silent objects of traditional western museum study and authorship. Similarly, Philip's poetic text raises the visibilities of the originating communities whose material culture was part of a 'concise display' of anthropology, taking up one third of the floor space at the end of the Natural History Gallery, at the time of collaboration. It was decided that this temporary display arrangement – mixing Natural History and Material Culture – was necessary while the Anthropology Gallery was being refurbished or the entire collection would have been put in store, although the Museum struggled long and hard with the underlying mixed messages that this exhibitionary practice was reminiscent of. Namely, certain non-western peoples are 'primitive', closer to nature and the lower animal kingdom, which is evident in the physical closeness of the display cases. This point echoes our discussion of the art/artifact debate in Chapter 1.

Plate 6 The 'Races of Man' display at the Horniman Museum, 2008
Source: Author.

Nevertheless working with Philip and CWWA in this, by no means ideal space, the value of the edge and the border came to the surface. The notion of 'borderlands' was considered literally in the tight viewing space between the display cases as well as the 'Races' panel, as a 'narrow strip along steep edges' (Anzaldua 1987: 3). Physically space was extremely narrow in this part of the museum as the children's bodies crowded around their drawing boards at Plate 7 shows. Moreover this compact visitor space was mirrored in the space of the display cases, packed tightly with wonderful material culture in traditional ethnographic fashion, but with little contextual information. The barest labels such as 'Afo Maternity figure, wood, Nigeria c. 1900' stated the largely obvious and failed to account for CWWA lives as intellectual border crossers (Giroux and McLaren 1994).

**Plate 7 Drawing in the narrow space between cases in the
       North Hall Gallery, 1999**
Source: David Forster.

On the other hand, the border here became a bridge, a space of movement, reinvention and re-articulation. As Fanon notes, helpfully for CWWA praxis, museum frontier collaboration demands 'introducing invention into existence … going beyond the historical, instrumental hypothesis' to initiate a 'cycle of freedom', through negotiation of physical and metaphorical boundaries. Fanon elucidates this freedom at the borderlands as new subjects rejecting 'thingness' to assertively reinvent the self, through enunciation and re-articulation of selfhood against the 'primitive' stereotype that lingers in the twenty-first century. Fanon further illuminates the individual struggle for selfhood as a 'battle for the creation of a human world – that is, of a world of reciprocal recognitions' – for the museum and the community group (Fanon 1993: 218). Here Fanon articulates a human project of negotiation in which the restrictive stereotypical boundaries – the physical and metaphorical borders – can be traversed in a *leap* of invention and travelling through a world, 'endlessly creating' the self (ibid. 229).

This optimistic stance is not to ignore the danger of the borderlands. The frontiers may provoke a fear of contact with the 'other' – out there in the untamed territories – for both Black and white people. I shall turn to address this issue next.

Fear and Travelling Theory

Black thought has illuminated ideas of racism in the white and the Black imagination, where whiteness is equated with normality and goodness, while Blackness is associated with abnormality and evil. Fanon hearing the words 'Mama, see the Negro! I'm frightened' uttered by a small boy on the Paris train *feels* the weight of racist history inside his body (Fanon 1993: 112). He is led to reject his skin, his history and wears the white mask of normality to survive the othering of the gaze that fixes him in a distant location, both geographically and socio-historically, the land of the 'tom-toms' and 'cannibalism' as he comments.

Stuart Hall points out that simply reversing the equation and replacing the old bad Black object with the new good Black subject will not suffice to remove the fear of difference and bell hooks considers these issues from a Black woman's perspective. She notes the 'deep emotional investment in the myth of 'sameness' that white people hold and further contends that on the contrary 'whiteness' is 'often 'connected with the mysterious, the strange, and the terrible' in the Black imagination' (hooks 1992: 166-7). She connects this fear of whiteness with the need to be 'safe' in white supremacist society, an important point we shall return to, and as 'a response to the traumatic pain and anguish that remains as a consequence of white racist domination' (hooks 1992: 169).

This focus on the lived experience of Black people in general and women in particular has important lessons to teach us in terms of museum theory. It points to the need for becoming sensitive to barriers for participation that prevent inclusive learning in the museum. For example hooks counters Clifford's notion of travelling theory, which conjures up 'rites of passage, immigration, forced migration, relocation, enslavement and homelessness' in the Black imagination (Clifford 1997; hooks 1992). In the USA she further states:

> Travel is not a word that can be easily evoked to talk about the Middle Passage,
> the Trail of Tears, the landing of Chinese immigrants, the forced relocation
> of Japanese-Americans, or the plight of the homeless. Theorising diverse

journeying is crucial to our understanding of any *politics of location*. ... To travel, I must always move through fear, confront terror. (hooks 1992: 173-174) [my emphasis]

In the location of the museum, there is a responsibility to assist visitors in this movement through fear, which involves the tasks of examination and deconstruction. This is a task in language, of naming to 'both name racism's impact and help break its hold', which may 'decolonise our minds and our imaginations' (hooks 1992: 178). For museum practice this is also a spatial task, which interrogates the frontier between similarity and difference that Charles Taylor has examined. CWWA widely concur with his recent criticisms of supposedly neutral 'difference-blind' principles, which are 'in fact a reflection of one hegemonic culture' (Taylor 1994: 43).

Taylor further argues that dominant cultures actually suppress differences in the notion of 'blindness' and force minority groups to take an 'alien' form. He calls for an active 'politics' which recognises and respects *both* the differences *and* the similarities amongst *all* members. Ultimately Taylor recommends Gadamer's concept of the 'fusion of horizons' as a way of learning to live in a broader framework and making 'real judgments of worth'. He notes how we may be 'transformed by the study of the other, so that we are not simply judging by our original familiar standards' and he distinguishes this approach from condescending and ethnocentric 'favourable judgment made premature' that 'praise the other for being like us (Taylor 1994: 70-71). Taylor's complex and detailed essay highlights Gadamer's point that the individual is perpetually *transformed* through dialogical experiences of 'play' with the 'other', and in the subsequent chapters this point is emphasised. A view is taken which is averse to any 'fixing' images of the 'other' in opposition to 'ourselves' that 'ethnographic encounters' in traditional museums present, and which the research teams' collaborative work contests.

The important notion to stress at this point is that the museum frontier marks a boundary that is also a site of transformation. As Homi Bhabha observes a boundary is not the point at which something stops but 'from which something begins its presencing' a space of 'creative intervention' (Bhabha 1994: 5, 9). It is at the museum frontiers that fixed imperialist and colonialist notions of purity seen in the 'Races' panel can give way and the museum space becomes a place for diverse CWWA voices to speak from. Even here – at a site that appears full of incommensurable contradictions – the notion of the museum frontiers can offer a third space within which people inside and outside of the museum can speak of survival, resistance, become 'politically active and change' our limited views of each other, in coming to explore and challenge the traditional politics of display (Bhabha 1995: 67).

There are clear similarities between our use of the term frontiers with James Clifford and Mary Louise Pratt's notion of museum 'contact zones', which it may be helpful to consider here as it also highlights spatial politics. The contact zone accounts for histories of colonial 'encounter' and ongoing relations 'involving conditions of coercion, radical inequality and intractable conflict ... radically asymmetrical relations of power' and Clifford employs it to view the museum space as an ongoing site of exclusion and struggle but also of political negotiation (Pratt in Clifford 1999: 438). My own and CWWA preference is for the term frontiers. Although both concepts privilege and foreground marginal in-between spaces to disrupt the notion of the museum as established centre, we consider frontiers more accurately describes the necessity of the 'other's' agency, as well as more fully accounting for the danger, risk and fear of otherness involved for all parties in stepping outside of traditional comfort zones. It is to the notion of agency that I turn to next with reference to one example of collaborative CWWA project work.

Agency: Black Women Re-writing the Museum

Anim-Addo originally conceived the Alliance to embrace mainly, but not exclusively, Black women, to facilitate a movement into agency – self-representation and new forms of writing – by peoples whose voices were regarded as misrepresented, marginalised or silenced by hierarchies of power in the established academies, including the museum. As Toni Morrison points out *Playing in the Dark* 'is not about a particular author's attitude toward race' but a project that marks 'an effort to avert the critical gaze from the racial object to the racial subject; from the described and imagined to the describers and imaginers; from the serving to the served' (Morrison 1992: 90). These words echo in the history of the ethnography museum, and Anim-Addo organised a series of 're-writing the museum' workshops to raise Caribbean women's voices, which after a two-year period were satisfactorily marked by the publication, *Another Doorway Visible in the Museum* (Anim-Addo 1999).

Anim-Addo concisely describes the purpose of the re-writing the museum project, 'to insert a hitherto largely absent presence, that of the Black woman's, into the museum context' (Anim-Addo 1998a: 93). Anim-Addo also highlights the multiple resistances and refusals to be mute objects of the western and male gaze in the re-writing. In collaborative museum practice the women vitally asserted themselves as subjects determined to break the historical silencing of their voices.

As Donna Haraway observes a 'special significance' is attached to writing 'for all colonised groups', since it 'has been crucial to the Western myth of distinction between oral and written cultures, primitive and civilised mentalities' (Haraway 1991: 175). Harraway further notes from a feminist perspective the importance of writing as a vital means of disrupting the notion of the traditional centre by, 'attacking the phallogocentrism of the West, with its worship of the monotheistic, phallic, authoritative, and singular work, the unique and perfect name' (Haraway 1991: 175).

Another Doorway Visible in the Museum points to the UK today as vitally pluralistic, composed of Diaspora cultures, which bring many centres of pluri-vocality into the heart of western philosophy, to enrich thought and theoretically-grounded museum praxis. Successful collaboration with CWWA was seen to enhance the museum by resisting the demand or desire for 'perfect communication' in favour of 'a powerful infidel heteroglossia', which is more akin to 'a feminist speaking in tongues' (Haraway 1991: 181). Anim-Addo explains how this might be achieved by stressing she is not advocating 'an either/or interpretive situation' – the Black women's or the usually white male ethnographer's – but rather posing the exciting possibility of a museum audience accessing 'alternative or even competing interpretations' (Anim-Addo 1999: 96). She also emphasises the necessity of ironic reading of the museum as cultural text when confronted with a collection in which the Black woman recognises aspects of herself despite the exotic 'othering' of the traditional ethnographic framing and stereotyping.

Anim-Addo notes 'One space where the Black woman is unquestionably configured, is as a maternity figure', so fecund she suckles one adult child at her breast while nurturing two others at her back. The powerful maternity figures of women, notably one simply labelled 'Afo maternity figure, wood' at the time of the re-writing workshops and reproduced at Plate 8 served as an inspiration for much creative re-writing. Further research in the Horniman Library informed our CWWA group that men traditionally used the figure as part of a prayer 'for fertility in their wives' and subsequent investigations suggest the figure is from the Eloi and not the Afo peoples (Picton 1995: 368). I had previously regarded this figure simply as a strong powerful woman with a rather innocuous label cited earlier, but the object triggered more complex responses in Anim-Addo and the terms 'fertility' and 'maternity' on the label held a tragic history of meaning for many CWWA visitors to the museum. This particular history was inextricably linked to their Diaspora experience of enslavement during the transatlantic trade, when the bodies of enslaved Black women were primarily used as human vessels for the production of more slaves. The relevance of these interpretations may be illuminated through Anim-Addo's poetic voice in 'Was that Sethe or her sister?' (overleaf).

In this poem Anim-Addo joins the history of an African museum object with her own tragic community history in transatlantic enslavement and her admiration for the creative writing of Toni Morrison in her Nobel prize-winning novel *Beloved* (Morrison 1988). She takes pride in the human capacity for survival and her play with language here is part of the ongoing 'Black woman's resistance', to erasure or misrepresentation in the context of the museum (Anim-Addo 1998a: 100). The writing of this poem followed an object handling session that included musical instruments and voice work, aspects of which echo here in the 'bu-dum bu-dum bu-dum' of the imagined heartbeat and the heart-rending cry of 'No-ooo!' Perhaps it is notable that the group meetings in the Education Centre of the museum and at the Caribbean Centre included sharing food, the absence of which features in the text 'Was that Sethe'.

Plate 8 Eloi maternity figure in *African Worlds* at the Horniman Museum
Note: Photographed by H. Schnebeli.
Source: © Heini Schnebeli.

Was that Sethe or her Sister?

Maternity figure of woman
on Ashanti stool
suckling child
- wooden, still -
milk-breathed
and at one.

Maternity figure of a woman
another situation we know full well
no child to suckle. Child done gone.
Sold. Mother wooden - still -
too drained, too whiplashed.
A stone; no stool.

A stone is not a stool.
In this hard place no comfort; no rest
where body thieves
separate sister, husband, infant.
Even the wisdom of elders absent.

How to cook without a stool?
How to grind peppers for the pot
with earth spirit not knowing libation
and palm oil an acrid memory?
In this corner, the heart of man
is only stone

echo-ing a faint, faint
bu-dum, bu-dum, bu-dum.
So, infant body wooden now
stiff still. No to mothering
in this stone place.
No. No. No-oooh!
Howling into stone
On stone/through stone
Maternity figure of a woman
Wooden. Still.

Figure 2.1 Was that Sethe or her sister?
Note: After Toni Morrison's *Beloved*.
Source: Anim-Addo 1998b: 39–40.

Anim-Addo contends it is a strong sense of absence that impels the Black woman to 're-memory' and 're-write' a richer picture of herself into the museum, which she has achieved in this homage to *Beloved*. She also notes how each re-writing of a more three-dimensional woman character brings a 'shock' of recognition 'that before the invention there was a gaping absence, a concerted silence' (Anim-Addo 1998a: 98). The space of this creative intervention, with all the weight of racist representation that such a juxtapositioning of natural history and material culture implies, is also notable here.

It may be objected that the CWWA re-writing devalues museum 'scholarship' and museum truth (Appleton 2007: 122). Let us address this question next.

Truth, Objectivity, 'Situated Knowledges' and 'Standpoint Texts'

Poetic interpretations of museum objects are clearly subjective and do not claim any scientific objectivity. Nevertheless, I argue that CWWA writing has a claim to knowledge and truth. Perhaps the value of the poem is as a work of art and its truth lies closer to the psychoanalytical space whereby difficult histories struggle to speech? In the context of the traditional museum space, what Ricouer terms the 'saying true' of psychoanalysis might account for the creative resistance to relations of power (Ricouer 1982). The psychoanalytical notion of this movement of troubled histories into speech also returns the discussion to the politics of representation in the museum, within which CWWA were determined to speak truth to power (Said 1993: 63-75).

Again Donna Haraway is helpful to museum praxis here. Haraway provides a re-definition of 'objectivity' for feminist epistemology in her idea of 'situated knowledges', which insist 'on irreducible difference and a radical multiplicity of local knowledges'. In addition her thesis most crucially repossesses 'ethics and politics' (Haraway 1991: 187). At the museum frontiers her demand is to make the community involved in presentation and perception responsible, accountable or 'answerable for what we learn how to see' (Haraway 1991: 190). Here Haraway highlights Hill-Collins's point outlined in the introduction on the political value of working at spatial and intellectual borderlands, drawing on new voices – creative and theoretical – to expand the notion of what counts as knowledge in the museum context and progress ideas of how diverse theoretical perspectives might underpin museum learning for new audiences (Hill-Collins 1991). My research partner Anim-Addo makes a strong argument for breaking the frontiers between theory and creativity that Hill-Collins recommends. She notes 'our poets are also theorists', which is a necessary if unusual methodological stance since more established theoretical views have tended to ignore or misrepresent Black positionings (Anim-Addo 2007a: 25). Perhaps this point on creative agency and truth can be justified with reference to the literature and its affect on collaborative museum practice.

**Beloved as a Key 'Standpoint Text' for CWWA
'Call and Response' Collaboration**

Anim-Addo's poem 'Was that Sethe' took inspiration from observation of a specific museum object, an Eloi sculpture, and Morrison's novel *Beloved*. Morrison dedicates this novel to the estimated 'Sixty Million and more', enslaved African heritage people who died during the Atlantic Holocaust. The novel is an attempt to access the interior lives of the enslaved, their emotions and thoughts, which are unrecorded. In the plot of *Beloved* Morrison imaginatively reconstructs the appalling history of enslavement in the USA, through the collaborative resistance of people and events surrounding one enslaved woman, Sethe. Morrison based her novel on historical evidence of a woman who murdered her baby rather than see her enslaved.

A vital point I have learnt from reading *Beloved* as a museum educator, is that all the subjugated Black and poor white characters – including Sethe, her Mother Baby Suggs, and the white girl Amy Denver who aids the birth of Sethe's baby *Beloved* – come to their *own voice* and genuine dialogical exchange in the novel. For me the collaboration Morrison outlines in her book contrasts with exhibitors giving voice to 'others'; and also to the slave testimonies recorded by white abolitionists, where with the best intentions a 'master narrative' was constructed, which 'spoke *for* Africans and their descendants, or *of* them' (Morrison 1992: 50).

Furthermore Morrison's novel does not advocate separatism, which is vital for developing collaborative museum pedagogy. *Beloved* importantly highlights the possibility of movement and collaboration across gender and racial lines and the new class allegiances that may be achieved. For example this is seen the relationship that develops between the Black character Sethe and the white character Amy Denver. It is also seen in the dialogue modelled on the African 'call and response' musical tradition, which at one point in the novel moves both the individual and the collective in the special forest Clearing space. Morrison notes how a deep telling and listening there merges the personal and the political in a distinctive space of freedom where Baby Suggs 'called and the hearing heard' (Morrison 1988: 209, 177; Golding 2005). It is in this space that Baby Suggs expounds the sensuality of her vision predicated on love. She states:

> And O my people they do not love your hands. Those they only use, tie, chop off and leave empty. Love your hands! Raise them up and kiss them. Touch others with them. (Morrison 1988: 88)

The call and response here is not merely concerned with voice but with the whole human being, mind and body. CWWA storytellers worked with Horniman on call and response that involved audiences in active learning. In African and Caribbean storytelling the tale-tellers' pose an initial question, by calling out 'Crick', which means 'do you want to hear a story?' To hear the story the audience must then respond by voicing, suitably loudly, the word 'CRACK', which means 'YES'.

CWWA musicians also engaged audiences in call and response musical forms that highlight the sophistication of African rhythms, which helps to re-value African knowledge(s).

I shall return to the themes of storytelling and music making in Section 3. Here the vital pedagogical points for the museum context that arise include firstly drawing present-day connections between community histories and historical collections, and secondly exploring more sensory ways of knowing the world (Howes 2005). In other words the personal *and* political aspects of pedagogy developed with CWWA overlap and demand an unlearning of the slave mentality – object-hood, which is seen when Baby Suggs experiences the first moments of freedom and recognition of her subject-hood; she re-imagines and feels the bodily roots of this freedom when she simply states, 'These my hands' (Morrison 1988: 141). A point Freire echoes when he questions whether people who enter the discourse as objects can later become subjects (Freire 1972: 101).

In addition for Morrison, when the enslaved come to voice and agency as well as social and historical connection in the Clearing, this unsettles established social orders and points to the possibility of transforming hierarchical positionings in the future. Finally at the end of the novel Morrison describes another call and response – a call for help from Sethe's daughter, Denver, and a responsive action in the socio-political world, a world of nurturing for Black women. Morrison speaks of a gathering of the community of women raising their voices in a 'cape of sound' outside Sethe and her daughter Dever's house at 124 Bluestone Road, which liberates the individuals inside from the ghost of their tragic history in enslavement (Morrison 1988: 261).

Reading *Beloved* as part of early collaborative programming with members of CWWA, the power of creative collective activity to liberate, psychologically, the individual in the group, proved inspirational to subsequent museum praxis. While the novel addressing the horrors of enslavement in the USA had no direct connection with Horniman's public exhibitions, in addition to call and response it related directly to the history of museum collecting, where wealth built upon enslavement financed collections such as the Tate Galleries in the UK that were founded on the profits made from the family's sugar empire, which proved an intriguing theme for CWWA dialogue. The willingness of the museum to open its space for consideration of these largely hidden histories was appreciated by and resonated with the particular CWWA audience, who came to perceive the enormous possibilities of collaboration for the benefit of their community, just as the museum recognised the benefits of collaboration for widening audiences and developing more inclusive creative practice.

It should be clear now that the notion of museum frontier space I have been expounding refers to more than physical structures; it alludes to spatial practices – experiences created through interaction between people in a spatial location where they feel safe to explore creatively individual and collective histories. It is a 'third space' where people can begin to feel at ease and engage with others in horizontal relationships even if the participants do not share all aspects of histories in common nor attachments to specific geographies and languages, as is the case with the vastness of the Caribbean. Most importantly frontier space requires the museum to facilitate relations of trust and solidarity (Lownsbrough and Beunderman 2007: 28). Horniman built this relationship over time with CWWA by slowly dismantling the barriers of 'otherness' and recognising concerns that humans share collaboratively. This is distinct from the hierarchical provision of programmes by the museum as if they were simple 'goods' that might be delivered without due regard to specific circumstances and the dynamic relation of the individual within the collective over time and space. Rather, re-writing their absence into the museum led CWWA to collaborate on diverse programming. One particularly important programme was Emancipation Day and I shall outline this next.

Emancipation Day and the Museum 'Homeplace'

In contrast to Philip's words of indictment on the 'silencing' role of museums above Anim-Addo commends Horniman. She notes how on 1 August 1997 'a multiplicity of voices' were heard 'side by side' when 'sixteen artists commemorating sixteen decades since the passage of the British Emancipation Bill shared their work in the Conservatory of the Horniman Museum' for the first time (Anim-Addo 1999: 9). Anim-Addo further observes how this event enabled a community of 'two hundred or so' people, to come 'together out of a shared need to remember an important moment in African-Caribbean history' (ibid.). Emancipation Day became an annual collaborative event on the Horniman Calendar although the format took different turns each year. Notably in the Conservatory of Horniman in the summer of 1999 Anim-Addo directed an extract of her Opera *Imoinda* with an original musical score from the musician Juwon Ogungbe and with Horniman artifacts from the handling collection of African objects (Anim-Addo 2008). Anim-Addo explains how *Imoinda* re-writes Aphra Behn's *Oroonoko* for several reasons, principally because Imoinda is given no autonomous voice by Behn and because the subject of slavery is a part of her history, which she has reclaimed in the writing of the opera.

Imoinda points to the endless reality of enslavement for woman, whose body laboured under appalling conditions during daylight hours and was the regular object of the master's sexual pleasure at night. Anim-Addo observes the emotional complexity of this relation – miscegenation – for the enslaved woman Imoinda feels love for her baby whose father is white. This focus of *Imoinda*, like the poem 'Was that Sethe' cited earlier, on woman's reproductive function, raises the question of essentialising the Black woman as emotion against the white male as reason. Anim-Addo replies there is no divide between her 'scholarly' concern with motherhood and her personal concern that arises out of her own motherhood, both are 'grounded within a specific reality', which she connects with re-memory. Looking back to the African reality within the Diaspora she comments on a historico-philosophical space where there was a strong sense of community. She observes how even today a woman can be seen carring her child closely 'wrapped to her body for years ... kind of swaddling with their children' (Anim-Addo in Guarracino 2007: 217-218). This is a warm situation that she contrasts to the conditions under enslavement, where this vital human connection was severed.

Anim-Addo's *Imoinda* articulates the history of enslavement and the long resistance struggles around the world, which is marked by 'people negotiating their sense of freedom as a whole group' within the context of Pan Africanism (Anim-Addo in Guarracino 2007: 214). *Imoinda* also articulates the positive idea of women working together, since at the end of Imoinda, it is a network of women that survive and come to voice in the Chorus in ways that echo the ending of *Beloved* noted earlier. In this creative Diaspora movement at the end of Imoinda, empire 'sings back' and the museum experience is transformative as we come to 'change our point of view, or point of hearing', which echoes in Constance Classen's sensory cultural theories that I consider in Section 3 (ibid. 219; Classen 1993).

The transformative museum experience was dependent at least in part on the quality of the spatial environment at the Conservatory, which aided the process of successful social interaction. The glass structure made the layout and routes into the gardens clearly legible, its lack of an overarching dominant message made it relevant to a range of community events such as parties and weddings – celebratory events that became magical in the evening with the effect of lighting. It was a 'space of potential' where people could come together to exchange ideas and information on issues of common concerns for one-off creative events 'in-between' the museum itself and the CWWA community venue (Lownsbrough and Beunderman 2007: 18-19).

Anim-Addo illuminated the special nature of this transformative space. She states. 'No-one could have predicted that the Conservatory could so easily have been transformed into a Caribbean *homeplace*, evoked through song, story, poetry, prose, *lest we forget*' (Anim-Addo 1999: 10). This feeling of being at *home* was crucial to the success of Emancipation Day, where African Caribbean individuals were reminded of their connections to 'groups, the nation, the human family', and most importantly for CWWA, finding a way of healing a painful history (Silverman 1995: 163). Homespace is a vital notion to collaborative practice that I shall consider next.

Collaborative Reconstruction of Knowledge

For all participants, Emancipation Day performances reaffirmed lost, 'discredited knowledge' to use Toni Morrison's words (Morrison 1984). Morrison elucidates the concept of African Caribbean knowledge from the 'standpoint' of CWWA (Hill-Collins 1991). She speaks of 'the way Black people looked at the world', which she imaginatively reconstructs in her novels as a, 'blend' and an, acceptance of the supernatural and a profound rootedness in the real world at the same time with neither taking precedence over the other. ... And some of those things were discredited only because Black people were discredited therefore what they *knew* was discredited. (Morrison 1984: 342)

In the imagined world of books such as Morrison's *Beloved*, and in the construction of the museum as homeplace, there is a special overlapping of time and space. This can jolt museum visitors out of taken-for-granted notions and behaviours, towards more empathetic and active listening and thinking, in the process of feminist-hermeneutic dialogue. On Emancipation Day, active listening enabled the conscious remembering and articulation of the 'unspeakable thoughts unspoken', which are the ghosts of the Middle Passage that loudly haunt the spaces of the ethnographic museums, demanding to be 're-memoried' in ways which are 'painful' but 'not destructive' (Morrison 1988: 199).

In addition to this global point, CWWA argue that their partnership work is fulfilling an important national recommendation laid out in the UK Macpherson Report, which followed the racist murder of Stephen Lawrence in the local area close to the museum in south London. Macpherson state:

The importance of and the need for genuine multi-agency *partnership* and co-operation to combat racism, and to bring together all sections of the community with this aim. ... there must be a 'multi-stakeholder' approach involving all parts of the community. (Macpherson 1999: 45.18, 45.20) [my emphasis]

Collaboration with CWWA certainly seemed to promote a feeling that the museum is sensitive, 'not just to the experience of the majority but to minority experience also' (Macpherson 1999: 6.32). However, reading the Macpherson Report leads me to question the UK museum as an institution, and specifically to examine our 'policies and methods' for signs of 'institutional racism' (Macpherson 6.18). Macpherson follows Stokely Carmichael in defining institutional racism, which 'originates in the operation of anti-black attitudes and practice' (Macpherson 1999: 6.22). In terms of the framing of 'knowledge' in the museum CWWA contend that to an extent 'a sense of superior group position' prevailed during our collaboration, since the traditional displays were constructed by a specialist 'white' middle-class profession (ibid.). Nevertheless, the museum hierarchy did encourage the education department to collaborate with CWWA, and thereby increased the construction of new 'knowledge' at the museum frontiers, if initially only at a 'tokensitic' level of temporary project work.

My role as museum educator in this collaboration involved firstly doing what Gayatri Spivak terms my 'homework', which importantly included re-reading texts such as *Beloved* and listening to music that is important to the group (Spivak 1988). Re-reading such texts and museum objects as texts together, gradually enabled us all 'to construct and construe the contradictory texts that constitute [our] lives' (McCabe in Spivak 1988: xix). However, it may be argued that this

CWWA collaboration occurs 'at the margins' of the main museum discourse, which left the centre of museum exhibition unchanged. Certainly CWWA programming involved women joining together to subtly subvert the master narrative and yet the influence of this intense, theoretically grounded collaborative practice was far reaching and eventually radically transformed not only the wider Horniman Museum space but also affected praxis in Europe as I shall explain in Section 2. CWWA group leaders maintaining a close relationship to the Anthropology Department who were truly concerned to reform the outdated and indeed racist display made this possible, in part at least; for example regularly engaging Shelton and Levell in dialogue, sharing publications and mealtimes, which ensured warm and stimulating relations throughout the building of the new exhibitions in the South Hall Gallery and the old Lecture Theatre.

Before outlining the new exhibitions at Horniman and elsewhere, which draws upon issues of power and control, let us briefly explore the themes of challenging racism and the politics of space through programming outside of the UK. Next I shall review programming at Plantation Museums in the USA.

Telling 'Other' Stories

Colonial Williamsburg is the largest outdoor museum in the USA and a middle-sized corporation and resort (with two golf courses and three hotels). A for-profits business side manages a 250 million dollar endowment and the museum or education side manages events in a 175-acre complex of 100 gardens and 500 restored or reconstructed buildings replicating Williamsburg, the capital of Virginia in the colonial era on the eve of the American Revolution. Fifty houses are open to the public and attract one million visitors, spending 120 million dollars a year in the 1990s (Gable 1996: 179-182).

In his seminal paper 'Maintaining boundaries, or "mainstreaming" black history in a white museum', Eric Gable outlines his ethnographic research at the Colonial Williamsburg museum spaces. Here approximately 500 mostly white frontline staff, called interpreters, wore period costume and worked in the houses. Plus, at the time of Gable's research, 12 black interpreters from the Department of African-American Interpretation and Presentation (AAIP), who led walking tours in the grounds and in two kitchens, using role-play interpretation techniques. Gable's paper examines live interpretations with roots in the late 1980s 'new social history' movement, which was interested in exposing class relations and conflict, and had a desire to use history to effect positive political change in the present. At Colonial Williamsburg the new social historians became interested in telling new stories of slave-master relations and Gable's research shows enduring notions of racial 'identity' causing difficulties in telling stories about race relations. His focus is on pedagogic practice among 'frontline' or guiding staff that 'tell' the Museum's stories, and on the question of miscegenation (Gable 1996: 177).

Gable argues that the history of laws against miscegenation, codified in eighteenth century, coupled with their systematic violation, is at the root of the invention of racial categories. To tell stories of miscegenous kinship denied at the Williamsburg spaces would mean that a largely white audience and a largely white frontline staff would have to rethink the category of race itself in ways ostensibly more threatening to their identities than their Black peers. Gable's research uncovers white guiders' resistance to the new stories of miscegenation, which is revealed in their preferred 'just-the-facts' approach that distinguishes white frontline staff from the Black guides, who they believed played 'fast and loose with the facts' (Gable 1996: 179). In contradistinction the new historians criticised white history as too clean and sanitised, primarily concerned with 'silk pants patriots rather than the 50 percent of the population who were enslaved. The new historians were concerned to make the site more inclusive and tell more critical stories of 'the other half', to 'mainstream' these other stories and make them part of every 'morally correct' eighteenth century story told by the guides at the main sites, which would result in less pedagogic space for the celebratory narratives (ibid. 181).

The Foundation was committed to notions of melting-pot equality in the 1980s and hoped Williamsburg could participate in black enfranchisement and assimilation. Perhaps cynically in financial terms they felt new audiences might be attracted to this new storytelling and provide new sources of income.

Miscegenation at Wythe House: Instances from Field Research

Gable notes miscegenous unions have become a kind of archetype in museums; an older white master takes a black mistress and aids the child of the union educationally and financially. Society's mistreatment of the mistress and disenfranchisement of the child then become symbols for the fundamental inequalities of slavery itself rather than the white master (Gable 1996: 182). At George Wythe's House new historians told an alternative story of the great white intellectual and liberal thinker's relationship with his cook Lydia Broadnax and her son, Michael Brown, whom he educated and left property to in his will, which was repudiated by the white interpreters who evaded this sensitive issue in their talks, arguing that there was a lack of hard evidence for the alternative story (ibid. 183).

The notion of sufficient evidence is questionable. One house used posters requesting information on runaway slaves but the interpreters still argued there wasn't enough material to discuss issues of slavery. The same white interpreters used certain documents as evidence of Wythe's liberalism – Lydia the cook chose to stay with him as a paid employee after gaining her freedom, therefore Wythe is surely a kind boss – while disregarding other documents as circumstantial such as the runaway posters as evidence for poor treatment of slaves.

On the subject of runaway slaves one white guide told Gable, 'I say I don't do that and I don't do ghosts either. … I tell visitors if they are interested in that they need to ask elsewhere' (Gable 1996: 186). This guide thus portrays herself as a disinterested defender of the truth and links stories of miscegenation with ghost tales to further discredit them. Similarly towards the end of a two-day training, a white guide asked about miscegenation and the trainer responded with 'interesting' material about the much clearer situation in the distant Caribbean with white overseers who were probably responsible for miscegenation. These double standards are seen in contrasting theatrical performances: 'Christmas' and 'Affairs of the heart'.

'Christmas' documents a time when the black cooks were said to have important roles. While the speeches of the enslaved in this narrative hint at a fear of dismissal, and a view of Christmas as a time when they did more work for cheap presents, the masters were portrayed as generous spirited in their speeches. For example one master comments: 'it will be a great long time before we can find a way to abolish the system, meanwhile we must treat them as humanely as we can' (Gable 1996: 192). 'Affairs of the heart' documents the story of a miscegenous union. A white master's marriage announcement allows his black mistress to express her fear that his new white wife will ill-treat their son. Finally the master leaves the room, undecided about how to deal with the situation. This performance was flagged as a 'composite' tale whereas white interpreters flagged the 'Christmas' performance as a 'true' tale of hard facts. Gable notes the epistemological sloppiness of this distinction since although Christmas included biography it was also a theatrical mixing of stories (Gable 1996: 194-5).

Gable concludes that groups in the centre (white here) appear to resist the notion of 'mainstreaming' black stories, with a 'just the facts' policy, although he contends they seem more naive than wilfully resistant. What a pity then that the new historians were unable to instruct or guide the guides, which left the Black employees as scapegoats in a fact/fiction debate and white Americans with an idea of the fundamental impermeability of racial boundaries that other research has identified at a level of tacit knowledge.

American Plantation Museums:
Live Interpretation and Symbolic Annihilation

Jennifer Eichstedt and Stephen Small's recent research also highlights the power struggles involved in live interpretation narratives at American Plantation Museums (Eichstedt and Small 2002). They gathered data by attending the public tours on offer at the museum sites, where the majority were white-centric, normalising and valorising white ways of organising the world, specifically the system underpinning enslavement. This is observed in the frequency of mentioning, for example mahogany furniture in aesthetic neutral terms, without any reference to the routes and the human suffering that the pieces are inextricably entangled within. They regard this aesthetic tactic as one instance of 'symbolic annihilation', which they saw employed as a primary strategy at 65 sites, with 3,250 mentions (Eichstedt and Small 2002: 109).

Their concept of 'symbolic annihilation', which is defined as 'a powerful rhetorical and representational strategy for obscuring the institution of slavery' and can be seen when certain groups are 'absent, trivialised, or condemned for taking non-steroetypical gender roles', proves useful for analysing the preferred narratives presented by live interpreters at the museums (Eichstedt and Small 2002: 106). Eichstedt and Small record symbolic annihilation in 'cases where slavery and the enslaved are either completely absent or where mention of them is negligible, formalistic, or perfunctory', for example when enslavement is mentioned on three or fewer occasions. They found nearly 56 percent of all sites employing the strategy of symbolic annihilation, with twenty-five percent of all sites in three states failing to mention enslavement at all and thirty percent of sites mentioning it less than three times (ibid. 108).

Eichstedt and Small further note the way certain sites employ strategies of 'trivalisation and deflection', which is defined as making absent or fleeting mention of the enslaved with little or no detail or context, while focusing discussion on a tiny elite population of the plantocracy. Instances of these strategies involve the interpreters using language to make universalising ahistorical statements when referring to the wealthy white experience, using the euphemisms 'servants' and 'servitude' rather than 'slave' as well as the use of the passive voice and neutral pronouns to discuss the achievements and labour of enslaved African American people.

However there were instances of 'other' African American stories being told. I shall briefly review some of these next.

Eichstedt and Small's 'Other' Stories

Professor Eichstedt took part in the 'Other Half' Tour at Colonial Williamsberg with 22 other white and seven Black visitors. The group met their African American costumed guide at the Lumber House, at the far end of Parson's Green from the Governor's House. She told a complex story strongly informed by a race and class analysis, explaining that slavery was 'based on a class system plus racism plus prejudice' for example (Eichstedt and Small 2002: 180-181). Her interpretation consistently drew historical connections between poor white and poor black people who she declared were closer than rich and poor whites people, although three poor whites were thought to be worth one Negro. She emphasised that the poor included 80 percent of white people, who typically lived in a 12 x 15 foot, dirt floor shack.

This interpreter's narrative ranged across diverse sources of material evidence and the clever use of learning styles and multiple intelligences to make key points

(Cassels 1996; Gardner 1996).[1] For instance, when speaking of the diaries written by slave ship's captains she used kinesthetic active learning to demonstrate how slaves were packed 'either lose or tight' on slave ships. Visitors were asked to stand side by side then face neighbour's back and pack themselves 'loosely or tightly' as if their bodies were inanimate goods. This exercise highlighted her point that 25 to 30 percent of 'tight packed' Africans died during the crossing, while those who survived were made to 'dance' two weeks before reaching their destination to strengthen them (Eichstedt and Small 2002: 181). The horror of enslavement was tempered with positive stories such as that of Alfonso Johnson, one of the original 20 Africans brought to Jamestown in 1619 who gained his freedom to own 250 acres and five indentured servants. In addition to kinaesthetic learning she engaged the visitor's interpersonal and intrapersonal intelligences during and after the tour, since several visitors stayed behind to ask more questions.

We would argue that this interpreter has dialogical skills that echo in the openness of feminist-hermeneutics. 'Yes blacks owned slaves too' she answered when questioned by a white visitor. Then she related the story of John Punch the African American descendant of enslaved people who ran away with two white indentured friends. After they were captured the Court ordered them all to be whipped thirty times, then the white friends were to serve a prison sentence for two years, while John was to serve the rest of his 'natural life' (Eichstedt and Small 2002: 180).

The complex issues involved in the best live interpretation tours demand not only an excellent script but flexible actors who can move out of the first person character and into a third person contemporary role with ease and often humour to further learning[2]. For example at *Carter's Grove* an interpreter asked members of the audience what the spectacles on a woman's head were, whether the children went to school and how happy the little Negro children were now that they were allowed to read and write, while she told her moving tale 'The Soul of a Sharecroper' (Eichstedt and Small 2002: 183). Out of character she explained how the programme developed. She wanted to look at freedom, what it might mean in

---

1 Howard Gardner observes eight intelligences: logical-mathematical, spatial, naturalistic intelligences, bodily kinaesthetic, musical, linguistic, intrapersonal and interpersonal intelligences, which individuals hold in different combinations (Gardner 2000). His pluralistic view of mind importantly revalues the standard western concept of intelligence as equated with mathematical-linguistics to the exclusion of other ways of knowing and experiencing the world through more sensory means. The concept redresses ideas of value attached to the limited western view that has disadvantaged Black and working-class children in intelligence testing systems. However, it is culture bound as we shall see in Section 3 since it excludes taste and smell for example as ways of knowing (Howes 2005: 6).

2 First person interpreters keep to the language and manners of the period at all times, while third person interpreters step in and out of past and contemporary roles to clarify difficult points for visitors.

1862, and how fear can infect all people, black and white (Eichstedt and Small 2002: 186).

Half-truths or More Inclusive Stories?

A major problem identified with the 'Other' tours is that audiences were largely self-selecting, attended by Black visitors and numbers were low at 10-20 percent (Eichstedt and Small 2002: 199). While regular 'white' tours may distort or obliterate the horror of slavery, in 1998 one tour 'Enslaving Virginia' at Colonial Williamberg broke the segregation of knowledge by interspersing a Black perspective mini drama, which involved 'enslaved' people plotting to run away, running, and being chased by slave hunters in the regular tour. Visitors gasped in shock and tears welled in their eyes as they were asked to act on behalf of the runaways. This drama seemed to raise awareness of slavery in the general population and brought more African American families into the site and one wonders why it only ran for one season (Eichstedt and Small 2002: 201).

Small and Eichstedt recognise some African Americans want to avoid exposing their children or themselves to difficult issues such as slavery, just as many white people do. Yet they note the costs for Black people and white people today when racialised hostility of different kinds is perpetuated, being told half truths distorts and rewrites history with a narrow focus (Eichstedt and Small 2002: 256). In mainstream stories upholding the dominant social narrative of race, where whiteness is constructed as moral, generous, democratic and hardworking, lies are built that separates the imagined white self from Black others. White-centric perspectives not only tend to erase links between history and contemporary inequality but are transparently self-contradictory narratives. For example images of 'docile happy servants' seem to be contradicted by stories of goods needing to be locked away since the servants have a tendency to steal. Furthermore, we note there is an added danger that these stories of Black theft connect Black people with the contemporary stereotype of crime, as predominantly perpetrated by Black people.

Conclusion

The best sites in the USA seem to avoid stereotype and show the individual human dignity of Black agents in the face of oppression by linking Black histories to the larger social, economic and political world, and to the racialised ideologies of the historic time that also persist today. This leads Eichstedt and Small to argue that it may be worth trying to engage more docents at sites to explore the possibility of telling more inclusive stories, which was a motivation behind of the CWWA examples I raised earlier in this chapter.

CWWA colleagues also echo Eichstedt and Small's argument that moral human beings would not want to work in spaces of social injustice, to perpetuate dominance and oppression, to reinforce silence and stereotypes. Furthermore our UK work has shown, like Eichstedt and Small's in the USA, that the museum unthinkingly legitimising racialised social forgetting can be transformed by pedagogical attempts to create a socially just society. This requires recognising the past injury afflicted, engaging in full and open discussion of this history and relating it to contemporary inequalities. Then release from the oppressive weight of the past might be experienced and healing permitted to occur. To paraphrase Eichstedt and Small, in these cases museum collaborators and site interpreters can become teachers for a just future (Eichstedt and Small 2002: 270).

Let us conclude on this optimistic note. In the next section I shall examine the power and control issues that have arisen here with reference to case study examples in South Africa, Sweden and the UK that also resonate with feminist-hermeneutic praxis that has been outlined in this first section.

Section 2
Including New Voices and Forms of Practice

Including new voices in the museum can be achieved in terms of programming as we have seen in Section 1. However, programming may not incorporate new forms of practice and more fully address issues such as racism, within the museum as a whole. Staffing structures are key here.

Staffing the Museum

Racism in the museum needs to be addressed in terms of staffing structure as well as representation. In the UK as the Black academic Stephen Small noted at the end of the twentieth century Black people will no longer satisfied if museums open their doors 'only slightly', they want to be fundamentally involved in the decision making processes, not only regarding access to but also control of representation and resources, and furthermore they are not willing to permit 'non-blacks' to 'dictate what when and where' this may be allowed (Small 1997: 62). Small reinforces the view of my Horniman CWWA collaborators, in highlighting the possibilities of using the museum as a 'contact zone', or social space where the boundary lines of separation between the 'self' and the 'other' are 'not fixed but always shifting', while emphasising the need for museums to address historical hierarchies of power, which remain in the museum staffing structure (Clifford 1999; Loomba 2002: 71).

UK Readers may be asking themselves if it is significant that the loudest voices to address racism in the UK museum are those of Black people and whether – to invert the infamous phrase – racism here is the 'Black man's burden'? The answer to this question must be no or at least, not entirely. For example, the Museums Association has been working closely across racial and institutional lines, notably since 1999 with Richard Sandell at the University of Leicester on 'Diversify' (<http://www.museumsassociation.org/diversify> accessed on 19.10.2007; Sandell 2002). Diversify is a positive action training programme to fund BME (Black and Minority Ethnic) people or people of visible ethnicity minorities to undertake Masters level courses at UK Universities and placements in the museum workforce. In 2008 it is heartening that this project has seen some success, with more than 60 graduates now employed in the museum world, although the proportion does not yet equal that in the UK population. For example, as Helen Denniston notes in our capital city, while '27% of Londoners are black or minority ethnic' (BME), the London museum workforce comprises 'less than 4%' of individuals from BME communities (Denniston 2003: 21).

At this point I should like to return to Horniman. In Section 1, I outlined collaboration that it may be argued occurred at the margins of the main museum discourse, inserting Black narratives into interpretive programming at Horniman with CWWA, which left the centre of museum presentation, the stories told in main programming and exhibition, unchanged. A similar point may be made for the new live interpretation events at the Plantation Museums in the USA.

Certainly CWWA programming involved women joining together to subtly subvert the master narrative and yet the influence of this intense, theoretically grounded collaborative practice was far reaching. Most importantly the CWWA group leaders maintained a close relationship to the Anthropology Department who were truly concerned to transform the outdated and indeed racist display. CWWA members, Golding, Shelton and Levell regularly engaged in dialogue, shared publications and mealtimes, which ensured warm and stimulating relations throughout the building of the new exhibitions in the South Hall Gallery and the old Lecture Theatre.

At Horniman the redisplay of the South Hall and the Lecture Theatre galleries were envisaged as working together, almost in conversation with each other. This was seen as reinforcing Pearce's point that the history of collecting and displays shows we are always 'collecting ourselves', and it was hoped that if we ensure this factor is made a transparent and visible aspect of an exhibition, as visitors we may come to 'learn as much about ourselves as about them', the other cultures displayed (Pearce 2003: 159-177; Ames 1995: 45; Shelton 1992). The old Lecture Theatre space now houses the visually stunning, 'three dimensional Mondrian' designed *Centenary Gallery: A Hundred Years of Collecting*, which opened in 2001 and works as the sister gallery to *African Worlds*, which opened two years earlier in the South Hall. The development of this gallery is intriguing. A major underlying aim was to take account of account of the debates I outlined in Section 1, which as Ruth Phillips notes is shared with three other notable western museums, who engaged in the radical redisplay of African material culture in the last five years of the twentieth century. In addition to Horniman's *African Worlds* Phillips discusses a 1995 reinstallation at the Michael C. Rockefeller Wing of the Metropolitan Museum of Arts, the 1999 *Africa Voices* at the Smithsonian Institution's US Museum of Natural History, and the Sainsbury Galleries of African Art located in the basement of the British Museum's Great Court in 2000 (Phillips 2007). Since *African Worlds* has been influential on the Swedish projects considered in Chapter 3, as well as the focus of '*Inspiration Africa!*' project work that I return to in Section 3, a brief outline here will prove helpful.

Consultation: *African Worlds*

Anthony Shelton, Head of Anthropology at the Horniman, declares his role to be 'curator as author' or 'producer/director' of the, 'ideas driven but object-centred' exhibition *African Worlds* (Shelton 2000: 5). The focus on the second largest collection of 17,000 African objects in a dedicated permanent gallery space of 380m², the South Hall, was unique in the UK at the time of opening in 1999 and the high quality of the material culture – part of the Horniman's designated national collection of ethnography – remains of international significance. Additionally at a local level it was widely felt in the museum during the inception of the project that this focus would resonate particularly well with the local African Caribbean communities and schoolteachers, who had built up strong collaborative relationships with the museum and were eager for a permanent site – not only to showcase the historical achievements of African heritage peoples, but also to affirm their continuing creative virtuosity in a 'live artists' area of the gallery that would provide inspiration for youth; a subject I return to in Section 3.

African Worlds presented us as staff at all levels of Horniman with the opportunity for considerable self-reflexivity on the direct museum culpability in the 'long and tortuous history' of 'capitalistic colonialism' and oppression, which was to be uncovered, acknowledged and in a certain sense mark an apology, initially through exhibitionary practice and in a sustainable sense through an ongoing education department commitment to collaborative effort (Shelton 2000: 8). This extremely ambitious and wide remit determined the direction and sponsorship of field research and active collecting in areas of Africa that were under represented in the existing collection, notably for the project discussed in Section 3 of this book: a Haitian Voudou shrine, as well as a radical re-evaluation of how all the objects might best be displayed and by whom. These questions and the persistent drive for sensitivity and innovation in exhibitionary practices notably led to Horniman commissioning an outstanding Ijele, the largest mask carried by one person in the whole of Africa, from the Igbo area of Nigeria, which is shown at Plate 9. In addition to the impressive pieces made in African communities who were keeping their cultures alive, the rolling live artists project held in the balcony area which encircles the South Hall effectively illustrated the hybrid nature of global identities with the programme of artists trained in the contemporary art schools, which combated any notion of African culture as fixed or stagnant. Osi Audu was the first artist to exhibit in this space and Horniman was able to purchase one of his pieces *I have a Landscape In My Head*.

**Plate 9 The Igbo ijeli seen from the balcony in *African Worlds* at the
            Horniman Museum with Benin displays in the distance, 2007**
Source: Author.

In the early planning stages of *African Worlds* Shelton stated a major concern for
polyvocality – to raise many diverse new voices in the exhibition and towards this
end three advisory panels were formed: an international Anthropology Advisory

Panel (AAP), a local Community Consultative Forum (CCF) and a Voices group. The AAP included two esteemed Nigerian curators Joseph Eboreime Director of the National Museum of Benin, Nigeria and Emanual Erinze from Nigeria's National Commission for Museums and Monuments, the Caribbean artist Kathryn Chan, and two other UK curators with deep knowledge of Africa, Keith Nicklin and John Mack. The AAP worked most closely with the designer Michael Cameron to develop the intellectual content and make the final decision on issues of representation – negotiating creative answers to the what, why, by whom, for whom and how questions. Additionally as educator and as trade union (GBM) workplace representative I suggest that regular formal meetings of the whole staff group to communicate the complex messages of *African Worlds* throughout the museum staffing structure was key to the success of the project.

The AAP met in London twice a year. I was fortunate to have Dr Eboreime stay in my family home with its constant stream of visitors. This arrangement naturally meant the local CWWA and CCP members who were working on Benin benefited from Eboreime's ever generous sharing of expertise over and above his contractual work. For example, readers can imagine how the children, from economically disadvantaged backgrounds, were quite overwhelmed when the Director of the National Museum of Benin Nigeria and I made a visit to their school in Brixton!

Design and Text

The AAP and CCP decided at the outset to bridge the, pernicious and mistaken in our view 'aesthetic' – contextually light versus the 'ethnographic' – contextually dense divide; by firstly developing series of themed narratives *and also* presenting the material culture of Africa with an abundance of contextually enriching video footage, both archival with contemporary voice over and footage from recent fieldwork as well as 'layered' text panels. Text panels were designed at four levels of density from large 16-point single sentence pithy quotations that were taken from interviews at the main object text panels, which were designed to provide a 'kind of poetic hinge' or connection point with the object, to the provision of highly detailed booklets offering further information and made available in slots to the sides of the object cases. Layered text was designed to cater for different levels of audience interest and ability as well as supporting the object as 'hero' in aesthetically pleasing manners (Cameron quoted in Shelton 2000: 12). One important feature of the original design for the object text panels to visually break up the block of solid text, encourage reading and help to connect visitors geographically, was a map of the world locating the object. Unfortunately the map was lost in the final panels due to space, the overriding demands of readability and maintaining reasonable point size.

Rejecting the chronological and geographical approach common in traditional ethnographic museums, it was hoped that eight key themes: Patronage; different natures; men/women; ancestors and morality; royalty and power; text, image, history; cycles of life; parody and humour, might counter the persistent view of the African as the 'exotic primitive other', as well as the media emphasis on the 'problems' of Africa today. *African Worlds* themes vitally draw out similarities and differences between and within cultural groups. Most importantly, displaying within these themes objects were not to be made subservient to and illustrative of abstract concepts in the manner of traditional displays that 'demonstrated' higher and lower races; rather the themes were employed to enhance and celebrate the beauty of the objects on display, and the originating communities of makers and users, in accordance with criteria from contemporary art museums that endow high value and prestige through the selection as 'art' that we discussed earlier.

Alongside the AAP the education department formed a local Community Consultative Forum (CCF) who included school children, teachers, Black families, storytellers, musicians and artists. The CCP were able to offer a wider range of perspectives as well as providing valuable advice on mock-up panels to ensure the design concepts might be successfully imparted to audiences. Most importantly they made a vital input into the displays through participation in the Voices project led by Patti Peach. Peach worked hard to gather some extremely rich oral material from almost thirty interviewees, drawn extensively from the local African Caribbean population. Peach's method was refreshingly simple – she simply asked the interviewees to offer their immediate responses to the material selected for display by the AAP.

The final text panels used original authored texts from 36 individuals: 12 from local people, 12 from people in African, the Caribbean and Brazil and 12 from professional writers. Plate 10 shows the text panel at the Midnight Robber carnival mask display. The immediacy of the impressions given at interview imparts a lively feel to the textual displays they were incorporated into and the portrait photograph of the speaker further humanises the text. It is these features that encourage reading of exhibition text and provoke empathetic understanding; I expand upon audiences and readers in Section 2 but Ayan Ayan-dosou, one of the drummers who had long worked with school groups at Horniman, illustrates this point here. He noted at interview:

> When I look back at all these masks in the museum, I feel sorry they are not being used … To me a masquerader is like a musician. A musician cannot play on his own. (Ayan Ayan-dosu 2001)

Ayan highlights the importance of the local social group in his text. Members of the AAP, in addition to conducting some original academic research into the objects such as uncovering names and histories of the previously anonymous chiefs who figure on the Horniman Collection of Benin plaques by consulting elders working today in the Oba's Court, also made more personal and global political observations. In their introductory text panel they highlight the problematic of ownership, forcefully opining on the British army sacking of Benin in 1897 and appealing 'to the conscience of the world for a peaceful resolution of this shame of history', but not leaving the reader to dwell negatively on restitution, they further note how the 'Horniman Museum is working with Benin and with the Nigerian Commission ... developing joint projects to promote a better understanding of Benin's history' (Eboreime 2001).

Plate 10 An example of a layered text panel showing the Midnight Robber carnival mask with a family of visitors reading in the background at the Horniman Museum, 2007

Source: Author.

One crucial 'joint project' that permitted a more equitable flowing of knowledge between the Northern and Southern hemispheres was the installation of a computer with internet access for visitors to use at the National Museum of Benin. I understand from Dr Hassan Arero, the present Head of Anthropology at Horniman, that the museum is continuing a lively exchange programme of skill sharing with Museums in Nigeria. For example the Head of Conservation Louise Bacon has shared her considerable knowledge of conserving the enormously diverse materials that comprise Horniman's anthropology collections, making consultation and training field trips to Nigeria.

Emanuel Arinze locates *African Worlds* as a 'success story' offering a 'glimpse of Africa' in the new context of the 'post-colonial' world (Arinze 2000: 1, 3). He attributes the success of Horniman collaboration to seven factors: involvement of collaborators from the very beginning; personal and institutional commitment from the host museum; a trusting atmosphere; flexibility and acceptance of different styles; open communication throughout the museum; shared interests and a common vision; willingness to share influence and control of the decision making process (ibid.). Arinze wryly notes the importance of active 'listening' for genuine and effective collaboration – 'for the collective good of all, for as the Igbo say: *Ada-akwu ofu ebe enene mmanwu'*, which in English translates as 'you do not stand in one place and watch the mask dancing' (Arinze 2000: 4).

Plate 11 The uplighting of the *Nkisi* Power sculpture
Source: © Heini Schnebeli.

Plate 12 One entrance to *African Worlds* at the Horniman Museum, showing the central walkway, 2007
Source: Author.

Shelton highlights the demands on design for the development of 'a new visual language' that would vitally reinforce the political messages. He praises Cameron for his ability to work allegorically: 'to manipulate objects to evoke different emotions and feelings' and to treat objects as 'embodied texts' (Shelton 2000: 12). For example, through focused down-lighting at the almost closed eyes of the Pende *mbuye* masks to enhance the melancholy feeling of 'spirits at the point of earthly death', and as we see at Plate 11 through judicial up-lighting of the *Nkisi* power nail sculptures from Kongo to increase the sense of their commanding presence (ibid.). Plate 12 shows one entrance to the exhibition with the central walkway. This rises up in the central section and down to displays of Ancient Egypt or Khemet at one end, and a concrete lion sculpture at the other end. The walkway is very strongly down-lit with lighting hanging from a ceiling gantry to evoke the hotness of an African sun shining on an African road. The hot feeling is reinforced through colour, with the red-sanded walls evoking adobe architecture. Small children of course delight in whizzing up and down this central road, yet they are also caught as shown at Plate 13 in what Greenblatt notes as 'awe and wonder', for example at the vast scale of the Dogon masks on open display here as no section of glass could be made big enough to contain them at almost 20 feet tall; and enthralled by the video showing the strongest men dancing so gracefully with the 40 kilo weight, moving so swiftly and even sweeping the ground with the very tips like the antelope, in the fragment of masquerade shown (Greenblatt 1991).

Plate 13 Small visitors caught in awe and wonder with the Dogon masks in
**   *African Worlds* at the Horniman Museum, 2007**
Source: Author.

Throughout, Cameron's design employs cube and rectilinear elements and also makes extensive use of non-parallel angles, which serve to disrupt our sense of balance and jars with the softness and exquisite plaster details that marks the original arts and crafts style of architecture of the South Hall. There is also a resounding 'modernism' in terms of the prime materials used for the postcolonial *African Worlds* exhibition space for so many objects collected in colonial times: steel framed display cases fitted into the walls holding precious Benin plaques, soaring cases of plate glass housing masks from Zaire. This is all expressly intended 'to convey a sense of alienation in the gallery', to mirror the displacement of the objects 'far removed from conditions of usage and original signification' and to highlight the partial perspectives of postmodernism; the fragmented nature of the objects 'masks without costume; figures without shrines; shrines without sacrifices' (Shelton 2000: 13).

The fragments of African material culture exhibited in *African Worlds* echo in the absences and deliberate gaps left in the display, which were intended to offer opportunities for new voices and viewpoints to be inserted alongside those in the main text panels. The text panel introducing visitors to the exhibition acknowledges the subjectivity of the selection panel and states the exhibition 'does not present one but the many different Africas in the minds and imaginations of the people who have contributed to this gallery' and further emphasises that 'we' the exhibition makers, 'can never give more than the most fleeting impression of these objects before they came to Europe.' Overall the exhibition recognises that representing cultural identities is never a neutral or a holistic process, and this one privileges contemporary African Caribbean authorship within a strong post-colonial narrative thread, which emphasises the dynamic nature of culture.

Perhaps *African Worlds* exemplifies what Ruth Philips terms a 'collaborative paradigm' in the development of a public exhibition space, which aims to develop a 'space of coexistence for multiple perspectives', acknowledging both the voices of community members whose heritage is on display and Western interpretive devices for understanding object 'identities, functions, and meanings', thereby deconstructing 'the singular, distanced, and depersonalised authority of the modernist museum' (Philips 2003: 164-165). The collaborative paradigm also highlights the need for 'visitors to consider their own historical position in relation to colonial anthropology and the displacement of objects it achieved', which is what earlier CWWA collaboration managed albeit with specific targeted programming (ibid.). Certainly the intense collaboration and sincere effort over the making of the *African Worlds* exhibition demonstrates that an attitude of self-reflexivity can expose the politics of knowledge construction, past and present, to bode well for the future. Most importantly in addition to an exhibition, *African Worlds* with its deliberate gaps for new textual material to be added for diverse audiences and with its large open spaces, works particularly well as an intercultural forum space of dialogical exchange – a democratic space, where members of different cultures can 'sit well with each other' and learn to exist with the tension between diverse points of view (Shelton 2000: 19; Ames 1995: 24).

Finally it is worth highlighting here that evaluation shows teachers welcome the wide range of viewpoints in the exhibition. Most importantly for key stage 2 history teaching is the new displays of Ancient Egypt, Khemet, which is firmly located at the heart of African culture and takes up a prominent position over a whole wall of display at the entrance. This renews the historical trade routes across the Sahara that united the continent and disrupts the notion of Ancient Egypt as somehow attached to Europe and Ancient Greece, which Martin Bernal's linguistic research has uncovered (Bernal 1987). The Khemet display in *African Worlds* counters Bernal's account of Ancient Egypt as the birthplace and cradle of western civilisation in the minds and imaginations of the west, which historically demanded a distancing from the 'primitives' of sub-Saharan. This distance, albeit unintentionally, is still evident in the spatial separation of Ancient Egypt from the African Gallery in the British Museum.

In short *African Worlds* remains a special exhibition, with which I am proud to be associated. Next I shall turn to explore an extension of these ideas – of exemplary collaborative practice underpinning the powerful displays – at other field sites outside of the UK.

Conclusion: Looking Beyond the UK

Much museum attention has recently been drawn to the examination of issues surrounding the representation of image and identities, the aspects we hold in common as human beings with specific rights and responsibilities as well as the distinguishing factors such as religion, language and sexual orientation that are safeguarded the UDHR (Universal Declaration of Human Rights 1948). I noted the importance of Human Rights in my introduction now in Section 2, I shall argue that new exhibitions and programming can address these concerns through shifting traditional power relations and structures of control in the museum.

Over two chapters I shall now draw attention to the collaborative exhibition of museum objects, the gathering and representation of human life histories, and to the creative retelling of contested histories firstly in Sweden and then in South Africa. Overall the chapters aim to demonstrate that museums sharing traditional cultural authority, power and control, can aid community cohesion via explorations of human unity in diversity, which profitably challenges stereotype and division to an even greater degree than the *African Worlds* example I have outlined here.

Chapter 3
Power: Inserting New Visibilities in the Museum Margins

Introduction

The Swedish citizen Abdullah Said traces his heritage to the Horn of Africa. He powerfully makes diverse aspects of Horn identity visible in one piece of museum text, noting:

> I left my country albeit young, unwillingly and unprepared. I left everything behind me, near and dear, brothers and sisters. I left my school, I left childhood friends and I left all memories. I left the football made of old socks, the one we used to shoot towards the goal made of stones. The porridge before sunrise during Ramadan, the juice after sunset and the weekend candy – all this I left together with the traditional games of my country. I left the lust and playfulness of youth. I left mountains, valleys, hills and fields. I miss the sun and the moon and the sea. I also miss the brown desert, the one I look like, the one that looks like me. (Said, A. 2002: 49) [Abdellah from Rebirth – my land and life]

Said inserts feelings of loss and longing for home elsewhere in this text. He highlights the way in which the personal overlaps with the socio-cultural past that Stuart Hall has illuminated in terms of migration. Hall states.

> We need to situate the debates about identity within all those historically specific developments and practices which have disturbed the relatively settled character of many populations and cultures, above all in relation to the processes of globalization and the processes of forced and free migration which have become a global phenomenon of the so-called postcolonial world. Actually identities are about using the resources and history, language and culture, in the process of becoming rather than being. (Hall 1996: 4)

In Chapter 3 I offer a detailed case study from Sweden Europe, where Said's text was constructed. This case study provides a critique from a position outside of the exhibition planning process. It aims to examine instances where the hierarchical lines of power remain in the museum management structure, but project-work, is shown to displace the absolute curatorial authority in museum exhibitions, to a far greater extent than the examples considered in Section 1 and in *African Worlds* discussed earlier. My focus throughout the chapter is on the National Museum of World Culture (MWC), in Göteborg Sweden, where I have been privileged to contribute, since 2002, to the international MA course in Museum Studies at Museion that is hosted there.

The galleries at MWC I shall consider, demonstrate the possibility of imagination and collaborative effort permitting different interpretations to be housed in the museum, and for people to come to recognise and value each other beyond superficial factors, such as skin tone. Most importantly for this book there is a shifting of activity at MWC to foreground the Black subject and MWC does not shy away from thinking through the complexity of issues such as colonialism and the legacy of racism and stereotype, which are made visible through different media and in the object rich displays that aim to increase intellectual and physical access to diverse cultures and widen participation in the museum.

I shall outline particular creative interventions with world-renowned: artists, cultural theorists and migrant communities. In the main I shall concentrate on the opening exhibitions including: *Horizons: Voices from a Global Africa* where a multitude of voices, historical and contemporary were invited to be heard by the exhibition team leaders alongside the museum's own voice; *No Name Fever* on the global HIV Aids epidemic and the artist installation *Site Unseen: Dwelling of the Demons* completed by Fred Wilson. In these exhibitions issues of emotion and reason in the politics and poetics of display come to the fore, which includes notions of diaspora identities, the body and metaphor that progresses understanding across borders in a fusion of horizons (Karp and Wilson 1999; Golding 2005; Gadamer 1981).

Within this remit it is the *Horizons* exhibition that permit a detailed consideration of these key themes and link with my Horniman discussion. *African Worlds*, with its collaborative exhibition ethos and the notion of plurivocality that underpins the 'glimpses' of Africa and the diaspora provided a 'point of reference' for *Horizons*, developing these key themes and extending them specifically into the areas of antiracism (Horizonter Brief 2001: 5, 8). For example we can hear Franz Fanon, Sojourner Truth, Paul Gilroy and Bob Marley's voices alongside many others and together these voices break down the binary divides and essentialism of Enlightenment thought that I have discussed, to feature 'fusion, diaspora and hybridity' (ibid. 6). These voices offer a radical representation of historical enslavement and resistance, urban and rural Africa, traditional and contemporary perspectives, notably the 'stories of routes and roots' voiced by Swedish communities who have migrated from the Horn of Africa, which movingly speak of the impact of migration on the individual's life today that is heard in Abdullah Said's identity poem above (ibid. 19).

First I shall begin with an overview of MWC from inception, its aims and objectives as a National site before moving onto consider the new architectural spaces. Then from a gendered perspective I consider the *No Name Fever* displays and explore the controversy that exploded in the press at the time of widespread 'Islamaphobia' in Europe. Next I address the *Voices* exhibition and engage in a critical discussion of identity politics, exploring political issues around class, race and gender that intertwine there in a poetics of display (Karp and Lavine 1991). Finally, I look at the artist intervention by Fred Wilson before drawing some concluding remarks.

Developing the Museum of World Culture

It was a Swedish government idea in 1996, to connect the old Göteborg Ethnographical Museum with three Stockholm museums (the Museum of Ethnography, the Museum of Mediterranean and Near Eastern Antiquities and the Museum of Far Eastern Antiquities), and establish a consortium of museums as The National Museums of World Culture (MWC). The left wing Swedish government of the time is to be congratulated for recognising the potential of the museum – specifically international and non-European collections – for progressing intercultural understanding between diverse communities in Sweden, which comprises 20 percent of the population. A government report of 1998 expresses this clearly:

> The National Museums of World Culture shall create something new in the world of museums ... They will mirror similarities and differences in ways of thinking, lifestyles and living conditions, as well as cultural change in Sweden and in the world. The visitor shall be given an opportunity to reflect over her own cultural identity and over other people's identities. (Official Government Report, SOU 1998: 125, 28; Lagerkvist 2007: 1)

The government required the consortium to develop new audiences that might more fully reflect the diverse local population and advised originality in terms of museum communication and collaboration with key stakeholders from outside of the museum world to achieve these ends. Thus government initiatives heralded the birth on 29 December 2004 of a new museum building in Göteborg, at a cost of 38 million euros from the architects Cécile Brisac and Edgar Gonzalez. The founding Director Dr Jette Sandahl led the MWC project and adopted a collaborative teamwork approach from the outset, to facilitate some innovative methods of consultation and representation, which remain exceptional in the contemporary museum world.

Dr Jette Sandahl highlights the key concepts that underpin the mission for the MWC. She states:

> In dialogue with the surrounding world and through emotional and intellectual experiences the museum wants to be a meeting place that encourages people to feel at home across borders, to trust and take responsibility for a shared future in a world in constant change. (Sandahl <http://www.intercom.museum/ conferences/2002/sandahl.html> accessed on 01.02.2009)

MWC comprises a versatile series of spaces in steel, concrete and vast areas of glass, nestling at the foot of the Liseberg. The architects have employed light – natural and artificial – to full advantage, including a light box extending across the entire length of the top fifth floor, which changes colour from misty green, to white and vibrant pink at dusk. A glass wall also runs along almost the complete length of the building at ground level, providing natural light to visitors inside the *Horizons: Voices of a Global Africa* Gallery, where the objects are protected from the direct glare of the sun by large banners with colourful photographic images advertising the museum.

Once inside, the building opens into a expansive central atrium with a vast staircase leading off to the café on the first floor, and the five exhibition galleries on three other floors. Do ho Suh (1962-), A south Korean artist's, screening zones the café area and encloses the seminar rooms without losing the openness of the space. Suh's screens represent cultural difference within the global village, particularly the emphasis on the individual in the USA where he lives, which contrasts with the celebration of the collective in traditional Korean society. His screens work with the repetition of elements, to comment on the negotiations necessary between collective states of anonymity and individual identity. The screens take two forms. His open fretwork screening consists of hundreds of plastic human figures, both men and women – wearing trousers and tops – whose individuality only appears on close inspection. Each figure in bright but not garish colours has spread legs, raised and spread arms, which are pegged together so that they may stand on and support each other to form a six feet high screen or mesh wall that seems to emphasise the possibility of humanity working together as part of 'one world'; a 'rainbow nation' effect as Plate 14 shows. A photographic image of this screen is printed onto the plate glass walls of the seminar rooms, which effectively allows extra light into the discussion spaces while obscuring the visitors passing by.

Coloured benches and the broad steps of the main staircase provide welcome rest and conversation points for visitors in the atrium, which attracts audiences of all ages in small groups or in larger audiences, for the regular public performances that are held on the small stage area facing the stairs. MWC has operated a strong programme of music, dance and theatre, seminars, lectures and public debates on a theme related to the exhibitions or a current event since its inception. Input from a high percentage of non-Europeans (60 percent of the artists and lecturers and 50 percent of the international guests), whose cultures are represented in the museum, enriches MWC programmes. Two comments, from visitors at a Teddy Afro (Ethiopian pop) concert audience survey, are taken as typical evidence of appropriate programming:

> It is very rare to be able to see this kind of thing in the public sphere, not only in private associations. This feels as if it is a public space. Wonderful that these things get a place here.

For me it is of great importance. My daughter listens to his music. She has got to know Ethiopia through Teddy Afro's music. (Lagerkvist 2007)

These comments are reinforced by audience surveys showing programming can be effective in reaching a youthful and 'diverse' target audience whose average age 'is unusually young for a museum, with 60% of visitors being under the age of 30' (<http://www.varldskulturmuseet.se/> accessed on 20.12.2008). All programming is developed in consultation with target audiences, and with opening hours until 9pm Wednesday to Friday, the museum is able to host events such as world music performances including 'club nights' with a DJ in response to the needs of diverse local community groups. MWC also programme 'Community Nights', which provide opportunities for diverse groups and organisations to 'use the museum as an arena for their own events', although MWC takes responsibility for preventing racist or anti-democratic opinions infiltrating the museum space by stipulating all groups must respect the law and the Universal Declaration of Human Rights (UDHR) (Lagerkvist 2007).

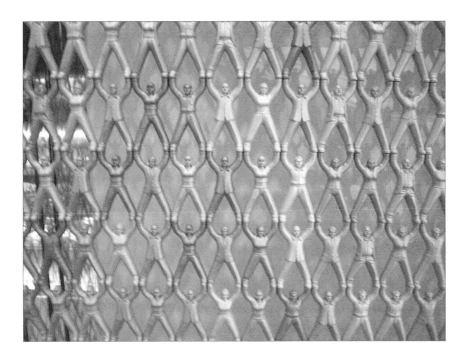

Plate 14 Doh ho Suh's sculptural screen at the Museum of World Culture, Göteborg, Sweden, 2006
Source: Author.

Thus we see in programming, as with exhibition making, MWC has taken to heart Richard Sandell's call for museums to 'radically rethink their purposes and goals and to renegotiate their relationship to, and role within, society' in order to achieve a more equal representation (Sandell 2003: 45). It is an intense process of 'dialogue' and 'negotiation' that marks the movement of MWC away from the traditional role of the museum (Lagerkvist 2006: 57). Instead of highlighting the hierarchies of power in society, the greatness of those who rule, usually male, his wealth and his deeds, we see MWC fulfilling the aim of promoting a plural society, with close to one million visitors since opening attending hundreds of activities, 600 school programmes and 250 conference events annually (Dubin 1999: 3).

MWC constructs more than five new exhibitions each year for visitors to attend. Next I shall consider three exhibitions in the light of an underlying ethos, which I recognise as political and poetical.

The Politics and Poetics of Design

Jette Sandahl illuminates the way the MWC mission translates into exhibition policy. The MWC exhibition mission declares:

> Through its exhibitions the museum will create dialogue with audiences that are diverse relative to age, class, gender, education, ethnicity. The museum will develop an experimental and questioning style for its exhibitions, so that many different voices can be heard and also ambiguous and conflict filled subjects can be articulated. Exhibitions will explore the unique understanding, poetry and power embedded in museums objects. (Sandahl <http://www.intercom.museum/conferences/2002/sandahl.html> accessed on 01.02.2009)

Here Sandahl emphasises the importance of 'politics and poetics' in museums. Nearly two decades after Ivan Karp and Steven Lavine first highlighted these ideas I agree with Jette Sandahl, Henrietta Lidchi and Julian Spalding in regarding the concept as important and relevant today (Karp and Lavine 1991; Lidchi 2003: 151-222; Spalding 2002). The two notions inextricably work together, with the poetics of display providing visitors with points of emotional contact with others. I shall explain this point with reference to one of the earliest western sources, before outlining how the overriding liberal political perspective at MWC is progressed through poetics.

In the *Poetics*, Aristotle considers the nature and value of art or what we term today aesthetics. Aristotle attempts to explain the way in which 'great art' or tragedy in his text enriches the understanding of audiences not only in terms of the play but also in terms of the human place in the wider world. To summarise, at the risk of oversimplification, he attributes the power of the art on the spectator to the circular relationship between the 'parts' and the 'whole' in artistic production. This relationship in tragedy might provoke 'empathy' or 'pity and fear' as well as a 'catharsis of such affections', but only in a viewer possessed of the codes to read the work (Aristotle, Telford translation 1961).

From Aristotle's time to the present day the poet is able to condense meaning, to express some vital emotional elements of experiences that make us human, into the poem. It is this emotional impact between the exhibition maker and the visitor through a 'kind of systematic order' that museologists employ in their discussions of poetics (Bann 2004: 67). Julian Spalding clarifies this when he writes of a primary challenge for museums today, which lies in creating 'displays that express emotional, not just factual, content' (Spalding 2002: 69). At MWC museum poetics involves facilitating human experiences with objects in spaces that are deeply moving – even earth shattering – in ways that more straightforward presentations of information in a standard distanced 'scientific' or didactic fashion do not so readily achieve. Spalding speaks about reaching the 'hearts and the minds' of visitors and he prioritises their 'seeing, feeling and comprehending', through the display of original objects. He stresses the importance of the awe and wonder these experiences can evoke in an age of globalisation where the world of the original object is close, at least for those with the finances to travel. Spalding, who comes from a working class background as I do, contends this heritage sensitises him to the 'advantages that education, class, wealth, race and where we live bring' (Spalding 2002: 10).

Spalding offers many examples of museum exhibitions progressing poetics and I highlight Jette Sandahl's work on the 'At Night' (1993) exhibition, at the Women's Museum in Aarhus, here. This exhibition explored emotions such as 'fear' of being attacked, and the way in which ordinary objects such as a bunch of keys, when imaginatively displayed with reference to their use as a defensive weapon clutched in a fist, acquire great symbolic power. Additionally we may note how such displays can overturn taken for granted notions in presenting possibilities for woman as actor-subject and not the eternally passive-object or victim of crime. Gaby Porter also observes how this exhibition explores feelings and associations shared amongst many women 'fear; desire and pleasure; dreaming; nursing the very young and very old; working ... in factories and theatres' (Porter 1996: 121).

Porter's writing on the representation of women in museums, although commenting on the situation in the late 1990s, remains largely true today. She highlights the relational role of women in museum displays as the 'other' of man – 'relatively passive, shallow, undeveloped, muted and closed' in contrast to men who are seen as 'relatively active, deep, highly developed and articulated, fully pronounced and open' (Porter 1996: 110). Women, she argues, are consistently the passive background against which man acts and she also notes a relegation of the feminine to the realms of the 'irrational' (Porter 1996: 110-111). We might further argue that as woman's passivity in museums reflects her place in the wider world, where she is silenced and marginalised if not altogether excluded, the socially responsible museum holds a moral and political duty to counter this inequality and silence.

It is to the political notion of breaking such silencing that I turn next. First I consider silencing and emotion with reference to the poetics of an opening exhibition at MWC *No Name Fever* – Aids in the age of globalisation, which began travelling in 2006.

Poetics and Politics in Exhibition Design and Intent at MWC

The MWC exhibition *No Name Fever – AIDS in the Age of Globalization* provides an in-depth study, challenging the silence, the myths and the wider socio-economic issues surrounding the HIV/AIDS pandemic. It aims to raise awareness of HIV/AIDS, which forty million people across the globe are living with today. The exhibition is interesting in imparting a broad and emotional understanding of the disease to visitors.

Jette Sandahl notes that since the MWC mission was 'to be an institution with relevance to our contemporary age', this necessitated tackling 'themes that are defined by contemporary problems. She notes HIV/AIDS as 'a microcosm of our eras unsolved economic and power-related relationships, encompassing all the mechanisms, antagonisms and conflicts of globalisation', and the determination of her team to 'take a stance' on the issue, which is at once political and poetical in museum terms (<http://www.actupny.org/reports/WorldCultureMuseum.html> accessed on 02.01.2009). The exhibition title is derived from the refusal of the Chinese authorities to acknowledge the disease when people first began presenting symptoms, contracted from contaminated blood sold by poor farmers to illegal collectors. Lu Guang's photographic work uncovered this blood donor scandal in Henan province and features amongst a large display of posters from 'Act Up', a New York-based protest group.

The Danish company KHR Arkitekter, whose earlier design of mobile HIV clinics won an international competition in New York, structured *No Name Fever* around seven emotive themes based upon two decades of typical reactions to the pandemic: Denial, Fear, Rage, Lust, Despair, Sorrow and Hope. In these themes KHR take an apposite and uplifting approach to an emotionally charged subject. As Sandahl observed from the museum perspective 'in the midst of all the tragedy, it has been a life-giving process to work with this theme' since 'ranged against the sadness, the anger and the powerlessness is all the empathy and the determination generated among people living in close proximity to the disease – expressing solidarity without borders'. HIV/AIDS is a disease that respects no geographical, social or economic boundaries; it carries extreme reactions in its wake and sufferers across the globe are subject to enormous prejudice, indifference and taboos, from the poorest rural regions of China in the East to the richest states of the USA in the west.

**Plate 15 HIV condom costume at the Museum of World Culture,
          Göteborg, Sweden, 2004**

Source: Author.

The KHR design emphasises the indiscriminate disease, affecting gay, straight, haemophiliac, young, old, women, men, poor and rich. Design considers each of the seven emotions separately within a tall white polygon shape that refers to the haemoglobin cells the virus attacks. The location of projectors within each polygonal space, so that we cast our shadows as visitors, is affective and prompts our reflection on the objects and the information. Key objects include wonderful artwork made by established artists and ordinary citizens from around the world. For example in the 'Horizons of Hope' section visitors can see part of 'Dressing Up For Aids', two beautiful dresses in hot reds, pinks and oranges, and a black suit, which is a project by the Brazilian artist Adriana Bertini who uses hundreds of brightly coloured condoms to make elegant clothing that can be seen at Plate 15. On the wall behind the clothing one short factual text in white lettering states: 'Youth at Risk. 58% of all adolescent AIDS cases in the United States are young women', which is a typical example of the way the exhibition offers a deep intellectual experience by circling emotional messages and factual information around the visual material culture. This intermingling of emotion, object and information provides visitors with a comprehensive overview of the topic and access to resources. Perhaps this mixture, coupled with a free choice of multiple routes rather than a single fixed route and a linear historical sequencing of the material also facilitates openness in the visitor to consider the subject anew and from diverse perspectives.

Personal stories abound and tell the heartache caused by rejection. One email from India speaks of a family even refusing contact with their son's dead body. Moving testimonies such as this, point beyond the medical problem to the social economic and ethical issues of HIV/AIDS, the misunderstanding and the stigma. Individual memorial quilts made by friends and family-members of deceased AIDS sufferers from Sweden and the Philippines also have heart-rending messages: 'No one should die alone', 'Hurts inside, Discrimination outside, Peace in death', 'Take care of my kids and Mom' which incorporates a favourite check shirt of the dead Nick. Another set of personal objects that tell poignant stories are the display of cheap cosmetics and jewellery belonging to Bangladesh sex workers.

Perhaps what is vital to this exhibition is the way emotions and politics cohere in the museum media, the use of light, projection and colour in spaces that relate emotionally to the human body *and* intellectually to the mind. For example some of the contemporary art and craft refers to traditional techniques like the 'family' of beaded dolls, which include two life-sized figures from South Africa as Plate 16 shows. The brief wall text at this polygon display speaks powerfully of the disproportionate impact of the disease on women who suffer the 'greatest HIV risk factors', especially the world's poorest women. Since women are chief caregivers the world over this is consequently a tragedy for children. Throughout the exhibition there is a vibrant mix of factual information, films, examples of political activism and campaign materials from around the world, music, a wide range of fine art and craftwork, sculptures, photographs and personal testimony that I have outlined.

Finally it is worth highlighting the use of light and shadow once more. Outside of the polygons four large projection screens run along one wall and chronicle information on the impact of the disease over the whole world since the 1980s, with the red AIDS ribbon serving as bullet points. Two of these four screens show images of people with the AIDS virus, which relieves the eye from solid text. The shocking facts of deaths worldwide are counted at a clock in the top corner of this section, which reached 20m in 1997, 24m in 2004. One more person dies every tenth second and there are 14,000 new sufferers diagnosed every day.[1]

1   This exhibition reached 230,000 people during the two years it was open in Göteborg and proved attractive to a high proportion of the target audience of teenagers and young adults. The exhibition is underpinned with substantial research by an interdisciplinary team of academics, activists and policy makers. It was a collaborative project led by MWC and Museion at Göteborg University and part of the knowledge gathered to support the displays is available in an edited volume of 13 scholarly papers, which further demonstrates the museums commitment to research (Foller and Thorn 2005).

Plate 16 HIV dolls at the Museum of World Culture, Göteborg, Sweden, 2004
Source: Author.

Diverse Perspectives: Controversy and Culture Clash

Many of the artworks, which present challenging and radical political perspectives in *No Name Fever*, are controversial. I would argue the explicitly political stance is necessary, to comment on the rightwing views expressed by successive Catholic popes for example, which causes such hardship especially in poorer nations. Cajsa Lagerkvist tells us that the most controversy arose from a rather quiet figurative painting, one of two by Louzla Darabi, in the Desire section of the exhibition (Lagerkvist 2006, 2007). MWC received approximately 600 emails from Swedish Muslims that were mostly sad and polite requests to consider removing, Darabi's 'Scène d'Amour', from display. This painting depicts a naked couple embracing each other with a small inscription of Quranic verse, Surat Al-Fatiha at the bottom – a combination that is odious to Muslims. Darabi, who is a Muslim of Algerian heritage living in France, volunteered to remove her original painting and replace it with a less offending image, to which the museum agreed. A number of the 600 emails praised the museum's effort to collaborate with and welcome its Muslim audience but a tiny proportion of the 600 emails, no more than a couple, were rather aggressive in tone.

One email noted the fate of Theo van Gogh, the Dutch filmmaker who a Muslim fundamentalist murdered in Amsterdam in 2004, as a part of jihad for the film 'Submission' criticising the position of women under an oppressive fundamentalist regime in Iran. A Göteborg newspaper reprinted this email in large text that covered the whole of one edition, which provoked criticism from pro-free speech and anti-Muslim groups, who equally strongly objected to the museum's replacement of the offending painting, with one woman protesting outside the museum every weekend for more than a year. In this instance the museum was able to act as open forum but in doing so exposed the difficulty of attempting to maneuver a satisfactory position between opposing groups, which leaves us with some questions. Is it not usually the older men in the protesting group who wish to oppress younger women? We wonder how would the museum react if Darabi refused to bow to the demands? Lagerkvist, who has documented this incident thoughtfully, holds the view that controversy is not only inevitable but also desirable if museums are to fulfil a new role as agents of social change in the twenty-first century (Lagerkvist 2006, 2007).

Lagerkvist's views here echo Timothy Luke. Luke notes the importance of museum practice that 'accept clash as civilizing' since it 'pushes received opinion out of the ruts cut by empty, settled certainties' (Luke 2006: 24). He further contends that some of the museums 'best work' can be achieved by unleashing the civilizing clash of community self-reflection, debate and revitalisation. These ideas echo in *Advantage Göteborg*, which is located in a second opening exhibition – *Horizons: Voices from a Global Africa* exhibition, to which I turn to next.

Horizons: Voices from a Global Africa

Each of the letters in the title of the word 'Horizons' are split horizontally with blue ocean waves at the bottom and light blue sky at the top, presenting a meeting of the sea with the sky and preparing the visitor for other meetings, meeting cultures and returning to meet oneself at ever-new horizons (Gadamer 1981).

The introductory text panel notes the 'diverse multitude of peoples, languages, lifestyles, climates, landscapes and cultures' that comprise the African continent. In addition to the complexity within Africa the museum highlights 'Africa' as a 'political concept and the dream of a homeland' held by millions of people, who over the last five centuries, have left 'as slaves, due to poverty or political oppression, or of their own free will', taking forms of 'cultural expression' that have helped shape societies around the world. The exhibition promises 'stories' and 'life histories of women and men, objects, art and music' that will 'testify to ways of living and surviving, to the heartache and thrill of exile, to oppression, violence and resistance, to love, joy and hope.'

Visitors turn from this panel into the exhibition hall, where a variety of voices resound in the MWC narrative – a particularly challenging historio-political story of imperialism and colonialism – the oppression of a white elite over Black 'others' and the legacy of this in racism and inequality today. It is the strong Black voices from the past and the present that permit this story to be presented in an uplifting light with an optimistic view to making a brighter future for global citizens of the world. The voices are organised spatially together with historical and contemporary objects under seven key themes, which take us on a historical journey from the 'Past' and 'Resistance', through 'Power and Survival' and 'Gender', to 'Urban Voices and 'Voices from the Horn of Africa in Sweden', while the voices of contemporary fine artists in the 'Polyphonies' theme provide points of critical thought that comments throughout the other sections.

'Voices from the Past' highlights the richness and diversity of Africa – second only to China with respect to population and land mass – from the ancient Egyptian civilisations in the north, the mighty kingdoms of the east and west coast, through the trade routes of the Sahara to the prosperous Great Zimbabwe in the south. Here MWC selects 500 years of achievements, specifically focusing on the migrations of people to other parts of the globe, where they have made an extraordinary contribution to the cultural expression of their adopted societies through their creativity. Jette Sandahl comments on 'the enormous impact that African culture has had on the rest of the world', which 'was never based on military conquest or financial power, but on a fantastic innate quality and life force!' (<http://www.worldculture.se/smvk/jsp/polopoly.jsp?d=877&a=4533&p=0> accessed on 16.03.2005) These are glorious and positive stories that need to be told to counter the prevalent one-dimensional image of Africa in the world media as simply impoverished.

Additionally MWC does not flinch from telling negative stories that might account for present day suffering and inequality. For example, 'The Atlantic Slave Trade' tells the horrific history of enslavement from the fifteenth to the late nineteenth century, when 'between 9 to … 20 million' people were forced to make a gruelling crossing as 'chattel' in ships across the Atlantic Ocean. Over one whole wall of this display the visitor sees a projection of the blue-sky meeting the horizon of the ocean and hears the crashing of waves against the shore. Just a few well-chosen sentences of text are projected below the image, which takes us through the history of 'the slave trade', 'slaves in the new world' and 'the legacy of colonialism and slavery'. Before this projection, set into transparent display boxes at irregular intervals, raised from the floor like oblong coffins, visitors see some of the appalling instruments of restraint – the terrible iron shackles used to constrain bodies at the neck or the ankle – like animals. The display boxes are strongly spotlit and clustered together at the centre of the projection with space for visitors to walk around as Plate 17 shows.

**Plate 17 Slavery projection at the Museum of World Culture,
           Göteborg, Sweden, 2006**
Source: Author.

Beyond this space it is possible to sit at a computer terminal to look up at the
sea, down at the floor and use the touch screen user-friendly programmes to learn
more about the history of the slave trade and its legacy. At each computer screen
the visitor touches an active bar to select a slide, which is split vertically into
two, showing an image on the right and a brief text on the left; a mix of word
and image, which works well. Particularly successful for me were the personal
testimonies of Black freedom fighters. For example, Sojourner Truth (1979-1883)
who was born into a Dutch settlement in upstate New York, USA and given the
name of Isabella Baumfree. Sojourner Truth was sold from her family age 11 just
before slavery was abolished and eventually ran away with her infant son after her
master reneged on his promise to free her. She worked as a domestic for several
religious communes and had a spiritual revelation in 1843, when she began to
preach 'God's truth and plan for salvation' up and down the country. Truth went
to live at a utopian community, 'The Northampton Association for Education and
Industry', where she met abolitionists and fighters for women's suffrage, which

led her to add abolition and suffrage issues to her oratory. In 1851 she made her most famous speech to a women's convention in Akron, Ohio: 'Ain't I a woman?' which draws powerfully on her awful personal experiences as an enslaved person. Truth states:

> That man over here say / a woman needs to be helped into carriages / and lifted over ditches / and to have the best place everywhere. / Nobody ever helped me over mud puddles/ or gives me the best place / And ain't I a woman? / Look at my arm! / I have plowed and planted / and gathered into barns / and no man could head me / And ain't I a woman? / I could work as much as a man / and eat as much as a man / when I could get to it / and bear the lash as well /
>
> And ain't I a woman? / I have born 13 children and seen most all sold into slavery / and when I cried out a mother's grief / none but Jesus heard me ... / and ain't I a woman? That little man in the back there say / a woman can't have as much rights as a / man/ cause Christ wasn't a woman / Where did your Christ come from? From God and a woman! / If the first woman God ever made / was strong enough to turn the world / upside down, all alone / together women ought to be able to turn it / rightside up again.

To see a photograph of Sojourner at the right slide of two consecutive split screen slides humanises the life story that is told at the left of the slides. This portrait of a 'woman' – looking so smart in immaculate white cap, white blouse and shawl over a black dress – calmly fixing the viewer with a penetrating gaze adds to the empathy visitors feel, when later reading the third slide that speaks of her life story in the exceptionally powerful and moving poetic text 'Ain't I a woman'. Similarly the portraits of Olaudah Equiano, Harriet Jacobs and Sarah Gudger that accompany the selection of slides entitled 'Slave narratives', seems to increase the visitors' capacity to respond with fellow human feeling and raises a stronger admiration for the ways the enslaved 'summoned the strength to withstand oppression' than text alone.

MWC not only brings the 'invisible' and 'anonymous' to voice in the slavery exhibits but also presents a self-reflexive stance and accepts responsibility for past wrongs. Sandahl notes: 'It is essential for us Europeans to find a way of relating to our shared and interwoven history with the African continent, even when that history is at its most painful' (<http://www.worldculture.se/smvk/jsp/polopoly.jsp?d=877&a=4533&p=0> accessed on 16.03.2005). MWC offers an impressive survey of this field. Particularly well represented, are examples of those Black artists who speak of resistance through musical expression such as Bookman Experience from Haiti and Bob Marley from Jamaica, whose work is also available at computer stations and on the walls in the gallery, as well as in the shop. These Caribbean artists at MWC share a positioning of being 'nomads' between cultures, who celebrate the capacity of human beings to resist persecution and present a strong challenge to racism in their creative work.

Directly challenging racist perspectives is a persistent theme at MWC, quite unique in my experience of European museums. At the outset of the computer slide Racism and the Civil Rights Movement in the USA we read a statement in plain language 'Colonialism and slavery were based on a racist world view.' We further hear how despite emancipation in 1865 the 'struggle for fair and equal treatment is not over.' These emancipatory movements in the USA thread back to earlier, global Voices of Resistance at the computer consoles and on the walls of the gallery. The thought of Aimé Cesairé (1913-2008) celebrating Blackness to 'counter to the lies and distortions of racism' is heard here, alongside Franz Fanon (1925-1961) highlighting the connection of racism with white people's fear, which leads to objectification and the 'Negro' viewed as 'a symbol of sin'. These thoughts have a dramatic affect on visitors in this space, well-designed by Opera Ontwerpers, with projected waves and seashore on the far wall, we ponder the power of racist perceptions throughout the world today.

Strong Black antiracist voices abound at every turn of the gallery as we walk in a non-linear pathway between past and present. A reconstructed voudou shrine, enclosed in a cylindrical space highlights Bookman the voudou priest who was instrumental inspiring the Haitian revolution of 1791-1804. Bookman's words of resistance urge his followers to 'Throw away the symbol of the god of the whites who has so often caused us to weep, and listen to the voice of liberty, which speaks in the hearts of us all', a theme I shall return to in Chapter 5. These Black voices, do not dwell in any sense of passive 'victim-hood' but rather consistently emphasise active political resistance today, with for example Christiane Toubira-Delanon asking if Atlantic slavery should be condemned as a 'crime against humanity' and if 'former slave trading nations' should offer an apology for their involvement. It is clever design that permits 'high' academic Black voices of contemporary theorists such as Paul Gilroy's, to mingle well with Black voices from 'popular' culture such as Bob Marley's, which I consider next.

Culture as Resistance: Music, Religion, Politics and Philosophy

In a text panel entitled 'Resistance' MWC emphasises the persistent active resistance of Black people to the tyranny of the institution of slavery. The panel notes Black peoples' declaration of war on oppression in the fight for freedom and this idea is echoed in Bob Marley song, 'War'. Marley states:

> Until there no longer are / First-class and second-class citizens of any nation / Until the colour of a man's skin / Is of no more significance than the colour of his eyes / Me say war. (Marley 2004)

Marley's 'War' can be heard at a computer console with commentary from Paul Gilroy. Gilroy observes:

"War", Marley's uplifting rendering of a celebrated speech by Haile Selassie 1, remains a difficult piece for anyone who wants to contain or minimise the depth of his philosophical challenge to the racial ordering of the world. The song's militant stance is not military in any way. There is no exaltation here, only sadness, regret and sorrow at the damage done to all humankind by racism. (Gilroy 2004)

Similarly at this console Gilroy regards 'Burnin and Lootin' as part of the long struggle for civil and political rights. For Gilroy this song is a 'post-modern' successor to W.E.B. Dubois's identification of oppressed peoples' 'righteous rage' and 'moralising their bleak choices', which attentive listeners may come to see differently as 'responses to a divided world purged of hope and love alike'; while 'Concrete Jungle' highlights slavery as a key to the postcolonial present and the agonies of what Gilroy terms the Black 'ghetto life'.

Yet Gilroy points out that Marley's work is not negative. He uses lyrics and reggae rhythms to move listeners from looking at the horror of the past with rage to act in the present, so that we may move forward to a brighter future. For example Gilroy speaks of 'So much trouble in the world' as a force of oppositional counter-power, where Marley communicates the possibilities of engaging in a new 'political imagination', which is 'a cosmopolitan invitation to take responsibility for the things that have to be changed if the whole world is to be healed.' Again 'Get Up, Stand Up' speaks of 'human rights' and human freedom that respects no national boundaries and can be easily translated into every language.

Plate 18 shows a collection of musical instruments, displayed behind a vast glass wall that rises up towards the ceiling of the gallery and acts as a division, between the displays dealing with slavery on one side and cinema projection of Bob Marley's life story at the other. Marley's songs and words regularly echo around the wall of instruments. Thus while the musical instruments, which are silent on display and unlikely to be played again, may provoke melancholia, feelings of sadness and loss in the visitor, the effect in MWC is quite different. Sound here ensures the visitor's senses are not reduced to the imperialism of the visual and the use of contemporary music, with direct links to a rich African heritage, facilitates points of contact between peoples of the world today. Non-African peoples, of diverse ages during my MWC observations responded positively to the computer consoles, sound, film and fine art representing lived experiences of contemporary diaspora peoples.

It seems to be an open learning space, more attuned to the senses, which helps braid together the new 'knower with the known' here (Stoller 1989: 154-6). Next I shall consider how MWC imparts a sense of what it may be to 'live in other times and other spaces', through the experience of migration (Bhabha. 1995: 256).

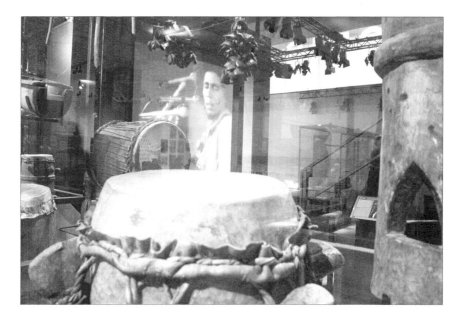

**Plate 18 Musical instruments wall and the Bob Marley video at
the Museum of World Culture, Göteborg, Sweden, 2006**
Source: Author.

Advantage Göteborg

One partnership project entitled Advantage Göteborg, the fruits of which are displayed at the Horn section of the Horizons gallery, comprising a rich display of objects, text panels and computer consoles with videos made by Horn people living in Sweden, justly deserves critical acclaim from fellow museum professionals (ICOM-ICME 2005). Cajsa Lagerkvist (from within the MWC staff) and Laurella Rincon (an externally contracted consultant) are two of the MWC project team who worked on the Horn project, which took place at the MWC for a period of 18 months from April 2003 to December 2004, immediately prior to opening (Lagerkvist 2005, 2007; Rincon 2005). The project invited 24 Göteborgians – Swedish citizens who have migrated from and retain contact with the Horn of Africa (Somalia, Ethiopia and Eritrea) – to both document and to reinterpret the Abyssinian collection through oral history.

The project is interesting for two reasons, firstly in demonstrating MWC's commitment to traditional museology, contextualising the collection through documentation. This was to be achieved alongside progressing the museum's social role and commitment to raising social justice, tolerance and inclusion at a local Göteborg level, through partnership project work with crucial international links (Sandell 2003). Advantage Göteborg is also intriguing for exposing professional power hierarchies that persist in the museum, despite the best conscious efforts of a radically principled management stance, to hinder full or 'Equal' access for groups who experience social exclusion (Rincon 2005; Lagerkvist 2005, 2007).

Two sources of funding sponsored the project: the Equal program of the European Social Fund and the Swedish government via the MWC exhibitions budget, which came with the express 'social' aim of breaking 'down barriers to accessing the labour market' that this group suffered, by using the museum collections and the exhibition process as a 'tool of empowerment' (Rincon 2005: 3; Lagerkvist 2005, 2007). For Lagerkvist, speaking from within the museum, major factors of exclusion from the labour force were considered to lie within the particular social group as low self-esteem, and also within the wider Swedish society as stereotypical, restricted and underlying racist perceptions of the Göteborg/Horn people by prospective employers. In Lagerkvist's writing it is because of these factors that the MWC team worked to increase a strong sense of identity and pride in home cultures with the Horn group and to establish equitable working relationships to present a more rounded picture to the future MWC visitor.

As a professional consultant, Rincon occupies a position at the borderlands between the museum and the Göteborg/Horn community. She foregrounds notions of struggles for power and control, over MWC ideas of self-esteem and empowerment that Lagerkvist highlights, and draws on Ames and Clifford to support her case. Rincon explores the metaphor of the glass box within a timely discourse of intellectual property rights and the World Intellectual Property Organisation (WIPO) and writes persuasively of MWC as 'cannibalising' or appropriating the disadvantaged community voices within their glass boxes primarily for their own study (WIPO; Ames 1992; Clifford 1997; Rincon 2005). Specifically she argues that 'the lack of relationships between people of different backgrounds outside the museum was reproduced identically inside', with MWC 'expectations on the sharing of intimate and personal experiences of displacement and discrimination' leading to Göteborg/Horn consultants feeling 'ethnologised' with their life-force reduced to 'their voices' that were 'to be captured in the glass box' (2005: 4). The compromise solution for some consultants was agreeing their particular end project 'be shown in the museum for a two year period' and further use 'submitted to their agreement', while all raw materials remained in their safe keeping.

Rincon further emphasises the subtle terminology to reinforce her views. The 'preferred term' for the Göteborg/Horn consultants was 'participants' rather than 'collaborators or consultants', with 'supervisors' rather than 'co-workers' within the MWC staff team. This terminology may be seen as condescending, pointing to the perpetuation of the traditional one way relationship and flow of knowledge from 'source' communities, or to use my preferred term 'originating' communities at the museum periphery, to the more powerful mainstream (Peers 2004; Dudley 2005). While some readers may regard all of this as a matter of semantic quibbling it highlights a set of underlying if unthinking assumptions made by those in power at the museum site, which need to be thoroughly interrogated if the museum is to relinquish some of its cultural authority and engage in genuine power sharing in the museum as part of an emancipatory social programme in the wider world.

In Lagerkvist's writing on the Horn project she foregrounds the value of specific cultural identities. She notes the importance of facilitating 'personally defined projects', which locate multiple subject positions for people in the local Swedish Diaspora, with reminiscence and reference to home countries around the globe. She hoped self-presentation and documentation might present richer views of the Horn of Africa to challenge media images of famine and lack, and considers the project broadly successful in fulfilling its dual aims of personal empowerment and more diverse representation. From the MWC position she agrees the weakness revolved around the questions of ownership and professionalism, over the fundamental 'rights' of interpretation, and she admits MWC held ultimate power, control and ownership.

Yet at the outset of the project Lagerkvist notes considerable discussion of what a museum was, is and what it might be, which is seen as a positive aspect. While these complex questions, give rise to responses that are dependent to a great extent on the particular socio-historical juncture in which they are raised, perhaps an appropriate definition of museum may be regarded as 'signifying certain kinds of cultural practice' with constructed rather than natural or 'contingent, not essential' relationships to originating communities (Lidchi 2003: 162). Notably the field trip to Hackney and Horniman Museums, where new exhibitions privileged African and Caribbean voices as we have seen led the group to question its own role, noticeable by its absence, in the Horizons steering committee, which included a number of external consultants.

In short the group felt unwelcome at MWC generally and a strong sense of exclusion to 'professional' areas. Lagerkvist admitted unintended exclusionary practice and gives a typically professional line of reasoning for this – the pressures of time, health and safety issues, as well as the difficulty in selecting a representative of the group. One fear, surely justified, is that a diversity of views may be 'filtered' through lens of a single spokesperson, most probably an elder man within the group. We may rightly question the ability of any single person to speak on behalf of the whole group whereas regular group discussions might enable a better telling of the different stories participants choose to present.

Yet, I discern a real desire for balancing museum professionalism with greater inclusion and the development of a stronger social role at MWC. For example, group dissatisfaction with the project room office was rapidly settled by MWC agreeing to an office move from the initial site in the basement. A misreading lay at the heart of group dissatisfaction with the original underground spatial location, which symbolically echoed the social marginalisation of the group in the wider world, yet was actually selected because of proximity to the object stores. There is also a genuine feeling of sadness in her report of the group encountering racism from MWC staff. A third of the staff had ethnicity outside of Sweden and anthropology degrees, which we may agree denotes an abiding interest in cultural diversity.

Overall Lagerkvist describes MWC 'openness' and the allocation of adequate 'time for dialogue and reconsideration' to characterise their new ways of working and power sharing. From her position within the MWC staff structure she reinforces the importance of embracing controversies, which we noted earlier in *No Name Fever*. She considers dissent as an essential part of a mutual learning 'process' of sharing 'ownership' that helps create a more inclusive institution. Yet she cautions against regarding the MWC work as a universal model applicable to museums and their communities the world over. She rather urges us to view the task as essentially to 'keep the dialogue alive, to negotiate and renegotiate and thereby to find a balance and move positions forward in each separate case of community involvement' (Lagerkvist 2006: 60).

The Horn People's Exhibition

The fruits of the dialogue Lagerkvist describes were available at the opening of MWC. At the far end of the Horizons gallery from the Marley exhibition, visitors could hear the authentic voices and see the faces of Göteborg citizens with roots and links to the Horn, at a series of computer consoles. Here Horn participants documented through video, aspects of 'Identity', 'Religion' and 'Family' in a highly personal manner to compliment the museum text panels in this section. While the labelling throughout MWC rarely minces words and is largely written in an engaging conversational tone, these videos were especially riveting. Video helps us to read the body language of the speakers, on subjects such as the veil and marriage from the perspective of individuals within the Muslim community, and we are thus transported to a position that is closer to them than a simple text panel, however good that may be. Certainly during my research visits the videos consistently attracted attention.

Overall the Horn exhibition makes a brave attempt to explore the Diaspora experience from the perspectives of Horn people living in Sweden today. A series of diverse Diaspora voices examine 'what is it like to live in a country that is still unable to integrate and make use of the expertise and wisdom that has arrived from beyond its borders?' (Lagerkvist 2004: 9). In this question Lagerkvist highlights the vital social role embraced by MWC, bringing the Horn Swedes to voice and their political position to visibility in the exhibition space.

Starting with 'The Horn of Africa in the World' text panel in the Horizons gallery, visitors can learn about the Nation states of Djibouti, Eritrea, Ethiopia, Somalia and Sudan in the peninsula region known as the Horn of Africa, which stretches geographically from the Gulf of Arden to the Indian Ocean, and is home to a rich diversity of peoples, languages and religions. Once again MWC text notes a vast area of Africa subjected to colonisation *and* the distinguished resistance of Ethiopia to the power struggles between France, Britain and Italy in the colonial period. Colonisation left internal political conflicts in its wake throughout the twentieth century, which coupled with famine plaguing the region, led to several millions of refugees and economic migrants moving to other parts of Africa, Europe and the US, with 48,000 currently making their home in Sweden. These Swedes with roots in the Horn keep contact through the internet, which helps link a sense of identity positively to Africa, without bounding it there. As the museum text panel states 'No longer is a person's sense of identity, kinship or citizenship necessarily bound up with a single country or part of the world' (MWC Horn text). Yet affirmative images of the home country are vital to strengthen positive identity construction, in the face of discrimination, prejudice and racism experienced in Sweden, which can only have a negative impact on new immigrants who suffer high levels of unemployment.

Said Abdullah's personal reflection on identity noted at the outset of this chapter and his subtle storytelling, which subtly highlights the political situation that forced his 'unwilling' journey to Sweden, provides richer and more emotionally valid images that provoke empathy in the viewer. Said's words pay moving tribute to the ways in which notions of identity are attached to childhood experiences and homelands. As the text entitled 'Identity' here states: 'A person's identity is the product of many factors: family gender, nationality, language, religion, sexual orientation, physical and mental makeup, education, skills and experience.' This text further speaks of the alienating impact of 'constantly having to face racism and discrimination' in contradistinction to the empowering 'sense of identity and belonging', which arises from encountering 'respect' and feeling 'at home in more than one culture and social context' (MWC 2004). We are reminded here of Homi Bhabha's notion, borrowed from Freud, of the 'uncanny' the unhomely or umheimlich and the need to develop 'homespaces' in the museum that CWWA recognised in Chapter 2 (Bhabha 1995).

The Horn voices also provided rich interpretation of material culture. One item, an exquisitely beautiful beaded 'Bag', measuring 33 x 12.5 x 5.5cm and originating from Mensa culture, North of Eritrea, is remarkable and speaks of homespace. Collected in 1909, this bag 'had served a 'metaphorical purpose' for a new bride, who used it for the safekeeping of her dreams for the future, while today its significance lies in the preservation of 'family bonds' through the matrilineal line between grandmothers and granddaughters, as well as the 'longing for and the hope of return' (Lagerkvist 2002: 47). Thus this object illuminates overlapping notions of family, gendered and political identities past, present and future. It shows the contemporary museum and community voices reinforcing the interpretive possibilities of the historical objects from the ethnographic collection.

Next I shall examine a global voice whose art intervention expands the interpretive potential of another historical collection and the MWC collectors in South America. I turn to Fred Wilson.

Artist Interventions into Museum Space

In his installations the artist Fred Wilson consistently draws attention to the value systems, the philosophy and politics underpinning western displays of the 'other', through visual means. Echoing traditional ethnographic exhibition practice, and reclaiming the human space of the 'dehumanised' other, he works primarily though juxtaposition, such as the wrapping of French and British flags around a collection of African masks, in the section *The Colonial Encounter* within his installation *The Other Museum*. Thus Wilson shows the masks as 'hostages' of the museum and dramatically raises questions of restitution to original owners or retention by the holding museum. Similarly his label 'stolen from the Zonge tribe, 1899. Private collection' at this exhibition is considered more accurate than the 'Acquired by Colonel So-and-so in 1898', which was more commonly observed at the time of the installation, in the early 1990s (Karp and Wilson 1996).

Wilson states 'I like to place things side by side, because objects speak to one another and speak to you about their relation to one another' through placing. Throughout his career, Wilson makes new juxtapositions to call into question the older, hierarchical, and seemingly 'natural' orders of the world that traditional displays of western museums speak of, and remain silent about. Notably, he reveals the museum silences and the hidden histories of object that are relegated to basement stores, by incorporating them into the public displays. In his 1992 seminal work, *Mining the Museum,* which was constructed at the Maryland Historical Society, Baltimore, he plays on the word mining – digging up, blowing up and making mine. Yet, like all play, Wilson's wordplay is serious. In his Maryland work he questions the very notions of 'truth' in the museum and points to the question of 'whose truth' throughout. Right at the entrance he displays a silver advertising globe from the 1870s with the word TRUTH inscribed. Also at the entrance, by locating three empty plinths with the labels Harriet Tubman, Benjamin Banneker and Frederick Douglas, who are all Black people with local Baltimore connections; alongside the existing plinths with busts of Napoleon, Henry Clay and Andrew Jackson, who have no connection with the area. Truth in this context is related to hidden histories that resonate in Wilson's personal identity, which has complex roots, with his African-American father and Native American mother as well as his training in the western art academy.

Wilson consistently poses a complexity of biographical questions to the museum objects. In this questioning he asks audiences to consider issues surrounding the objects such as: 'how did these object get to be displayed here thus and so, by whom were these objects collected and why?' He attempts to achieve a questioning stance in the viewer through juxtaposition, for example his 'Metalwork 1793-1880' label eloquently emphasises the economic basis of the silverware collection in slavery. By putting 'horrific' slave shackles from the basement stores amongst the 'beautiful' silver he forcefully shows how the production is determined by the subjugation of 'others'. Other novel exhibitionary techniques are used in the painting gallery. Wilson displays a damaged portrait from the stores, of a mixed race person (Benjamin Banneker) and highlights the physical damage – rape by the master to increase production, of chattel – inflicted on Black women during the times of slavery. Similarly in this gallery he employs exhibitionary devises to highlight those Black others marginalised in the picture frame. Covering lithographs with glassine paper to expose the Black person in the corner of the picture, or spotlighting the Black child in a painting when the visitor enters the gallery space, marks an attempt to make the viewer aware of those who existed in the shadows of the painting and in the wider society. Through such media devices, the viewer is able to reflect on and empathise with the historical pain of the subjugated and to re-experience this in the present (Corrin 2004).

Site Unseen: Dwellings of the Demons

A decade after the exhibition in the Maryland Historical Society, Baltimore, Wilson created an installation *Site Unseen: Dwellings of the Demons* at MWC, which was intended to probe that which lies hidden 'under the surface' of the museum institution's foundations, specifically 'the pillars of colonial power, evolutionary assumptions, racism and sexism', according to Sandahl (<http://www.worldculture.se/smvk/jsp/polopoly.jsp?d=877&a=4543&l=en_US> accessed on 14.01.2008). Wilson's work at Göteborg followed a similar path to his Maryland undertaking. He surveyed the stores for silences and gaps in the museum narrative to take the visitor on a journey through the museum, which is at once emotional and intellectual. First climbing the stairs we see a large desk in a glass case with a label stating.

> This desk is thought to have been used by the esteemed ethnographer and former director of the museum. This desk has been saved as a memento, though its provenance and true value as an artefact of museum history is unclear. (MWC 2006)

Thus his desk piece sets the scene for an imaginative engagement with history at the Göteborg museum. As the visitor climbs the stairs the route leads off the staircase into the installation and through a number of artistic interventions into this museum history. The museum has a long history of archaeological work in Argentina, notably Stig Ryden's excavations in La Candelaria in the 1930s. In the stores, Wilson found a collection made by Ryden in 1932 of huge burial urns, the largest one of which he tells us was partly broken in order to be transported to Sweden. Wilson addresses this find through juxtaposed labelling. He also offers information in the more usual 'museum voice' at the sides of the open topped glass case. The title here is 'Burial Urns', and the label informs the viewer how the largest urn contained the 'remains of three adults', while 'the skeletal remains of a child were found in one of the smaller urns.'

Wilson's response to this discovery goes further than the standard provision of information in the dispassionate or scientifically distanced museum tone – to give the silent and damaged urns a voice – literally. In his labels printed directly onto the surface of the walls, the urns are permitted to speak of cultural power – of time and place. For this viewer at least the urns really seem to speak – poetically. The urns make statements:

> You don't know enough about me to forget me. … What I share with you I share with many, but there are some things I share with no one … Don't forget me. … Some care about me, most do not. … I am out of place, but not out of time. … I was broken, but still whole. … Remember me.

This is a direct quotation. It clearly highlights for me the keynotes of memory and forgetting; an African ethics of care; a hermeneutics of part and whole, of time and place. Yet, my writing gives little of the emotional power originally felt at the site in 2004 and again, equally strongly in 2006. As Sandahl notes Wilson's 'interpretations serve as emotional bolts of lightning', which have a lasting affect by conveying 'insights that forever remain a part of the recipient's world view' (<http://www.worldculture.se/smvk/jsp/polopoly.jsp?d=877&a=4543&l=en_US> accessed on 14.01.2008).

Perhaps it is in part the graphic location of the labels – the concise and potent sentences in white letters running across the creamy coloured wall, with ample empty space between – the space between that performs the role of the silence, the pause like the breadth in speech – perhaps the speech so vital to African oral tradition (Stoller 1989). Wilson's spacing also somehow seems to mirror the shoreline with the waves crashing against land in the Slavery Gallery on the ground floor below. For me it is certainly the spacing between the sentences that add weight to the urn's 'speech'. In one section the urns state:

> You have filled my emptiness with your expectations.
> I am complete, though you know only parts.
> Understand me and understand something of you.
> I'm beautiful to those who know me well,
> unimportant to others.
> Though you only see parts, you imagine more.

As the visitor passes through this gallery where the floor disorientates walkers, tilting 70cm in two directions, a case of many fragments of ancient pots and small labels comes into view. These fragments, like the urns are likewise brought to speech through the considered placing of word and objects spread out in shallow pits, excavated objects are allowed to be 'reburied', rather than carefully positioned up on shelves. Labels sit with the fragments and pose questions on breakage 'Broken by ethnographers … Broken by war … Broken for science … Broken on purpose … Broken by looters … Broken in transit … Broken for transit'. Walking on we see a splendid case in more traditional display style of Nazca pottery from Peru. In this case Wilson shows his appreciation of pottery skills, which he experienced in Ghana. He shows this pottery, which is extremely finely potted and painted in earth coloured slips (liquid clays), very simply.

Next the installation draws attention to a 'Collection of numbers', which has humorous overtones. A sea of tiny pots are displayed upside down all over the floor of a glass case, all the better to see the museum numbering, the marks of ownership and careful cataloguing. Nearby a selection of archive photographs are re-labelled, one stating 'one pot, four men' and on the wall next to it another stating 'four pots, one man', which comments on the status and roles of the men in the picture, four diplomats and one security guard.

At the exit to the installation Wilson brings to the surface of display another set of untold stories – the notebooks of Ruben Perez Kantule, a Kuna Indian from Panama who made a visit to the old Museum of Ethnography in the 1930s. Wilson displays pages from Perez's notebooks, which contain remarkable drawings depicting Kuna images of the supernatural world, including the 'dwelling of the demons', which provide Wilson with part of the title for this installation. This title echos, for Wilson, more than the world of the drawings themselves, it refers to the 'demons that dwell in the museum itself – the exhibition hall in particular' (MWC 2004). For example, one set of six framed images shows a collection of drawings and photographs under the title 'How do you capture a Kantule hat?', which expresses this notion of collection/captivity inherent in museum practice precisely.

Conclusion: Artistic Intervention and the Audience

Thus, and so it seems to me, Wilson presents the Museum with an opportunity for reflexivity. However, this view is not universally shared, even among highly museum literate people. There was a wide diversity of opinion on the success of Wilson's installation at Göteborg amongst my MA classes for the Museion, Göteborg University cohorts of 2004 and 2006. The Swedish archaeologists in the student group were particularly upset by Wilson's 'cavalier' attitude to the museum's work with the Kuna, which they thought was exemplary for its time. They argue forcefully that the archaeologists were working directly with the Panama people in a highly charged political context where their very existence was threatened. While this view may be reminiscent of the ethnographic quest to 'save' the last fragments of a dying 'tribe' it continues to be echoed in professional circles at ICOM-ICME and perhaps raises the question once again of who may be permitted to speak for whom.

Should the artist be viewed as the gifted 'genius' of western culture, with full and inalienable rights of free and imaginative speech, since the creative view of the artist genius casts a true light on reality? What if this free speech disparages the real achievements, the gathering of knowledge and truth, by the archaeologists? What does achievement for the archaeologist here entail from the perspective of the present-day originating or source communities? For the Museion students questions such as these give rise to notions of essentialism and progress a questioning of the pernicious tendency of traditional ethnographic displays to fix the 'other' culture securely behind the glass cases of the museum.

The installation proved popular and useful to starting a 'dialogue on the theme of memory, objects, identities, diaspora', moving some visitors from ethnic groups to tears as Sandhal notes. Head of education, Pernilla Luttropp, also recalls first-time visitors sitting and talking 'about memories and power structures and about whose memories society thinks are worth talking about' (cited in Gascoigne 2005).

To conclude this chapter, the notion of arbitrary movement, objects becoming disconnected, or broken in transit offer the museum a potent metaphor for migration and it is to the representation of forced migration in South Africa that I turn in Chapter 4. Overall the degree to which MWC exhibitions have been constructed in power-sharing collaborations with local and international communities is commendable for a national institution and it is heartening to see new projects maintaining the 'political and poetic' ethos that has proved so attractive to young people. In the next chapter, I shall explore the greater control over representation and staffing that a smaller community museum is able to achieve. In Chapter 6 we shall observe the advantages and disadvantages of this position.

Chapter 4

Control: Shifting Relationships
in the Whole Museum

Introduction

The opening extract from Toni Morrison's novel *Sula* alludes to the balcony areas of white churches, cinemas, theatres and opera houses where Black people sat during the time of segregation in the USA, which were referred to in the 1900s as 'nigger heavens', reflecting a spacio-cultural distance and the separate experiences of Black and white communities. Morrison states:

> In that place where they tore the nightshade and blackberry patches from their roots to make room for the Medallion City Golf Course, there was once a neighbourhood. ... It is called the suburbs now but when black people lived there it was called the Bottom. ... [because of] A nigger joke. ... the kind folks tell themselves ... when they're looking for a little comfort somewhere. ... [originating from when] ... The master said, "Oh, no! See those hills? That's bottom land, rich and fertile. ... High up from us ... but when God looks down, it's ... the bottom of heaven-best land there is." ... So ... The nigger got the hilly land, where planting was backbreaking ... white people lived on the rich valley floor ... blacks populated the hills above it, taking consolation in the fact that every day they could literally look down on the white folk. (Morrison 1991: 3-5)

For me Morrison's text also chillingly echoes the 1966 declaration of the ethnically diverse District Six area of Cape Town in South Africa, stretching from Table Mountain down towards the sea, as a 'White Only' area. In 2006 I witnessed the warmth and generosity of the museum professionals throughout Cape Town actively healing the traumatic memories of the apartheid years. As Ciraj Raassoul and Sandra Prosalendis note, quoting the 'Johnson family ex-re-residents inscription on the memorial cloth' at the District Six Museum (D6M):

> Someone said memories are weapons. Let's think of them as tools. (Rassool and Prosalendis 2001: I)

While *Sula* is 'fiction', it reminds us here of the racism during the Apartheid years of South Africa, which led to the complete destruction of a Black community (Foucault 1980). Morrison's *Sula* also highlights the power of words, language and the imagination that we hold in common as human beings as well as power of community united to withstand oppression, to grasp power and control over their lives and the representation of their her/his/stories, which is evident in the story of the District Six Museum (D6M). I select D6M for attention here as it exemplifies how a determined body of people with a range of different skills can come together with the wider community to develop a new museum paradigm, a liberartory praxis, which while specific to the local history of the place has lessons for progressing museum learning around the world.

The small, independent D6M, echoes aspects of the post-apartheid new democratic narrative that is exemplified at the vast national Robben Island Museum (RIM), site of imprisonment for Nelson Mandela and other freedom fighters during the apartheid decades. Both museums, located at historic sites of oppression, privilege the voices of the previously subjugated, but direct painful recollection positively towards the future harmony of the whole country that Archbishop Desmond Tutu's optimistic metaphor the 'Rainbow Nation' so aptly describes. Two examples will illustrate this. Firstly part of Ahmed Kathrada's speech made at the opening of the RIM, which is widely reproduced on postcards and at the main walkway to board the ferry for Robben Island. Kathandra notes:

> While we will not forget the brutality of apartheid, we will not want Robben Island to be a monument of our hardship and suffering. We would want it to be a triumph of the human spirit against the forces of evil. A triumph of wisdom and largeness of spirit against small minds and pettiness; a triumph of courage and determination over frailty and weakness; a triumph of the new south Africa over the old. (Ahmed Kathrada was imprisoned for 26 years, prison no. 468/64)

These sentiments are mirrored throughout D6M. An introductory text panel first locates the destruction of D6 within the context of other instances of forced removal across South Africa and the need to '... Remember the racism. ... which sought to steal away our humanity', while also recalling that 'which marks us as human beings: our generosity, our love of justice and our care for each other.' The text continues:

> In remembering we do not want
> To recreate District Six
> But to work with its memory:
> of hurts inflicted and received,
> of loss, achievements and of shames.
> We wish to remember
> so that we can all,
> together and by ourselves,
> rebuild a city
> which belongs to all of us,
> in which all of us can live,
> not as races but as people. (Memorial Text, Digging Deeper D6M 2006)

I focus on D6M rather than RIM in this chapter because it details the resistance of a community, not well known heroes. I was also able to dwell there in longer private reflection and social engagement.[1]

I first outline the South African historical background to D6M. This section is crucial to readers who will be unfamiliar with the ways in which racism can permeate, utterly, the social fabric and divide communities; while fresh ways of working in the museum setting can point to new unity in diversity. Next I ponder the specific features that determine the success of the D6M. I highlight the prompting of memory and narratives or the imaginative recollection processes, which Peggy Delport's aethetics-based curating facilitates. In the main I consider two public exhibitions: 'Streets' which explores the visible exterior social lives of the D6 community and 'Digging Deeper' which considers their interior private worlds. I also engage with the notion of education for democracy and outline the Ambassador's youth programme. In addition to observation and dialogue with D6M staff, my selection of creative curatorship premised on community dialogue is drawn from published sources (Rassool and Prosalendis 2001; Goodnow 2006).

Finally in this chapter, I shall refer to UK and Japanese outreach projects that similarly highlight the value of recollection and the notion of 'mapping memory', still on a relatively small scale albeit in a different national context, which may prove useful to the profession around the world. Specifically I note the work of Age Exchange in London, Linda Sargent in Oxford and the Edo-Tokyo Museum in Japan.

Brief Historical Background: The South African Population and the Post-Apartheid Development of Iziko Museums of Cape Town

In 2007 the population is estimated at 46.9 million with 37 million Africans constituting 79 percent of the whole, white Europeans 4.4 percent, coloured 4.1 percent and Indian/Asian 1.1 percent (<http://www.ststssa.gov.za/keyindicators/mye.asp> accessed on 24.10.2007). The 'Rainbow Nation' metaphor describes the diverse population of S Africa today and marks a creative attempt at healing, linguistically, the centuries of colonial oppression and miscegenation that culminated in the abominable Apartheid (literally the state of being apart) system of Boer-dominated government in 1948. Under Apartheid people were strictly segregated into four groups according to skin colour: white, black, coloured and Asian. These old apartheid and racist terms linger and their roots require some explanation for non-South Africans.

---

1   This was simply not possible at RIM – declared a World Heritage Site in 1999 – where coach loads of tourist visitors need to be efficiently moved through the fascinating 'cell story' displays to cater for the phenomenal demand. I refer interested readers to Deirdre Prins's excellent discussion of intergenerational work there as well as Annie Coombes's detailed overview (Prins 2005; Coombes 2003).

Briefly the indigenous peoples who have a 40,000 year history in southern Africa, were semi-nomadic hunter-gatherers and pastoralists. Europeans knew these people, the San and the Khoikhoi, as 'Bushmen' and 'Hotentot' respectively. Crop-farming peoples with domesticated animals originating from West Africa, including Xhosa and Zulu speaking groups, appear to have settled during the third century. There are several hundred of these groups who are the 'Black' other of the 'white' European heritage settlers. Many of their languages have a common root that the derogatory word 'Bantu' describes.

While there is evidence of Portuguese traders at the beginning of the sixteenth century as well as British and French Huguenots in the seventeenth, it was a group of approximately one-hundred and twenty traders from the Dutch East India Company (VOC) who began settling the tip of the continent, the Cape, in the seventeenth century, notably building a fort and the Botanical or Company's Gardens in 1652. In the mid eighteenth century the free Dutch 'trekboers' (trekking farmers) gradually claimed the rich fertile lands and the mineral wealth of the interior. The British gained control of Cape Town at the beginning of the nineteenth century in 1814 and aided Britain during the Anglo-Boer War (1899-1902).

The UK Abolition Act of 1808 eventually brought some legal protection and human rights in 1828 for the South Africans who were enslaved by the first VOC settlers, although in practice new laws rapidly introduced exploitative labour systems, curtailing the free movement and even the criminalisation of 'Blacks' without work and a pass. However along with the indigenous Khoi-San peoples it was the VOC who first transported people from the colonies in Indonesia, Madagascar, India, Ceylon and Malaysia, to work under conditions of slavery and it is these forcibly removed groups who were classified under Apartheid as the 'Asian', and the 'Coloured' peoples whose numbers were swelled by miscegenation, the sexual exploitation of women and intermarriage.

From the outset of Apartheid in the 1940s people of all 'colours', creeds, ages and gender, inside and outside of South Africa united in diverse anti-apartheid movements of resistance, from international trade sanctions, the increasingly violent battles in the Townships, to the legal battles in the Courts of Law. One notable legal battle, following which Nelson Mandela was imprisoned in Robben Island for 'life', is the Rivonia Trail of 1963. At one point, defending himself, the lawyer Mandela made an impassioned statement, part of which is reproduced on a postcard from Robben Island Museum. He declares:

> I have fought against white domination and I have fought against black domination. I have cherished the ideal of a democratic and free society in which all persons live together in harmony and with equal opportunities. It is an ideal which I hope to live for and to achieve. But if needs be, it is an ideal for which I am prepared to die. (Mandela 2000: 438)

Mandela was imprisoned for 27 years. Imprisonment of the ANC (African National Congress), PAC (Pan African Congress) and Communist leaders merely served to strengthen Black resistance, such as the fierce Soweto student uprisings in 1976 and throughout the 1980s. Eventually in 1990 President F.W. De Klerk began to dismantle the discriminatory regime, repeal Apartheid laws and release the political prisoners at Robben Island, including Nelson Mandela. The first democratic elections took place over four days from 26 April 1994. Mandela was elected president and the long march to democratic freedom continued through government legislation.

Notable dates for the museum sector post-apartheid include firstly: 1996 when the TRC (Truth and Reconciliation Commission) opened and the Department of Arts, Culture, Science and Technology produced an important White Paper on arts and cultural heritage, which set out government policy for funding institutions involved in the creation, promotion and protection of South African Arts. Next the 1997 SAMA (South African Museums Association) conference *The Way Forward: Harnessing Cultural and Heritage Tourism in SA*, which led to the 'Tshwane Declaration' that highlighted the vital role of local communities in the museum and other heritage industries. Then in 1998 The Cultural Institutions Act created a flagship structure, for the Northern and Southern areas of the country, which provided subsidy payments to selected cultural institutions under the Governing Council that was established for all Museums in 1999. Thirteen museums were included in the Southern Flagship area of Cape Town in 2000 and these became IZIKO, Museums of Cape Town. Ciraj Raasool notes how D6M made a case for inclusion in the Southern Flagship, which was rejected and it is to this history that I now turn (Raasool 2006).

D6M History and the Notion of the Museum for Africa

The name District Six referred to one of the twelve areas of the municipality of Cape Town, which was designated in 1840. District Six was located close to the city at the time and linking Table Mountain with the sea and the Docks, attracted migrants from all over Africa and the world. Generations of families had made their homes in the area when The Population Registration Act classified the rigid racial categories noted earlier and The Group Areas Act of 1950 imposed a spatial system of Apartheid, segregating 'White Only' areas across the whole country, which led to the forced removals for Black and coloured residents in District Six and elsewhere where diverse populations, united in degrees of economic poverty, had long intermingled peacefully. In 1966 District Six, along with many other regions across South Africa, was classified as a white zone and over a fifteen year period the area was completely razed to the ground. The streets were bulldozed and between 55-65,000 people were forcibly removed to 'Townships' on the Cape Flats. Their place was taken with just 3-4,000 state employees, Afrikaans speakers, from the lower middle-classes.

The District Six Museum Foundation, which included academics, artists and community activists, was established in 1989 from the Hands Off D6 campaign committee, which itself arose from the Friends of D6 protesters against redevelopment in the late 1980s. Eventually in 1994 the D6M opened in the old church of the Central Methodist Mission in Buitenkant Street (Raasool C 2006: 286, 314). At the time of opening the Museum the Mission had a 120 year history of opposition to racism and in involvement in social justice issues. It continued to offer a site where the local community could meet and to challenge the white supremacism that deepened during the Apartheid years and which led to the total destruction of a community from 1966 to the 1980s (Prosalendis 2001: 10).

Peggy Delport explains how the decision to employ the term 'museum' exercised the Foundation (Delport 2001: 12). There is a history of museums in South Africa since the 1800s but the relevance and value of these institutions built during Imperialism to contemporary Africa has been widely questioned and contemporary academics have cast doubt on whether the traditional notion of the museum and the museum philosophy of collecting and laying out of objects in static sequences is universally appropriate (McLeod 2004; Corsane 2005; Pieterse 2005; <http://www.africom.org> accessed on 16.01.2007). Yet Malcolm McLeod notes the case of the Manhiya Palace Museum, Kumasi Ghana, which opened in 1995 as part of the celebrations for the king's silver jubilee that holds 'old authentic' and 'new replica' material, plus high quality 'fiberglass effigies' kings and queen mothers authentic gold regalia treasure (McLeod 2004: 458-9). He highlights the twin benefits of this modern museum – local and international – for the African context. For local communities the objects resonate with significance during regular ceremonial events outside of the museum walls and this mixed approach – display and ceremony – holds unique appeal for paying visitors to coastal towns.

McLeod's example highlights a sense of ownership, mutual respect and shared values as vital if visitors are to benefit from the museum experience. This community ownership is a great strength of D6M, which supports Corsane's argument that 'the traditional museum is a western concept' that demands to be 'redefined and situated in an African paradigm' (Corsane 2005: 26). Mandela reinforces this view on Heritage Day at the opening of Robben Island Museum in 1997, when he highlights museums as part of the national fight for 'Democracy, Tolerance and Human Rights.' He further notes the need to transform museums that were 'often seen as alien spaces' by the majority population, since they had long 'glorified mainly white and colonial history', excluding and marginalising most of the people and depicting them 'as lesser human beings' (<http://www.anc.org.za/ancdocs/history/mandela/1997/sp0924a.html> accessed on 15.03.2008).

Visitor survey confirms Mandela, showing that in colonial times, right up to the end of the apartheid era, museums were representative of and visited by less than 5 percent of the population, the white minority (Mathers 1993: 17). In contradistinction the National Museum at Robben Island and the independent D6M have shown themselves to be relevant to the lives of all human beings, the local South African people and the wider international community, an achievement resulting from deep thought and dedicated action.

Delport illuminates how the notion of the museum that was originally problematic for the D6M Foundation, with the static collections and displays, was countered by an underlying vision and ethos of D6M as a 'living space' for working with memory, on painful issues of displacement and loss, but also celebratory themes of human survival. Furthermore, since museum also suggests 'solidity, a continuity and a permanence that could withstand even the force of the bulldozer and the power of a regime committed to the erasure of a place and a community', the unique work of the D6M began (Delport 2001: 12).

Now I shall examine D6M in the light of this historical outline. First I shall consider the notion of memory that lies at the centre of the museum work. Then, with reference to the Truth and Reconciliation Committee, the ways in which memory is facilitated through 'aesthetics' will be explored, through a consideration of specific exhibitions and educational programming.

Memory: Contested Notions of Place and the Politics of Restitution

Mary Warnock's thought illuminates the value of memory work at D6M, as I shall briefly outline. In Warnock's analysis of memory she highlights the term 'person', as a 'reflective, self reflective human being' whose humanity and identity are interlocked and who has persistence over time (Warnock 1987: 59, 63). She highlights both physical and metal aspects of memory – how the reflecting person is essentially embodied and the body can trigger the reflective mental aspect sensually – most famously perhaps by Proust's taste of the Madeleine cake in lime flower tea. For Warnock the value and pleasure in remembering is attributed to human agency and ownership of the self or the part that survives through time, which is seen in the way mind seems able to detach itself from the past, has the freedom to reflect back on past experiences and to make plans to look forward into possible futures. Warnock notes this reflective recollection process is one of story telling, which involves creation or recreation of the fragments of a life linked into a narrative structure. Memory then is like imagination, it has subjectivity but can be shared in telling a story of the past and this telling and listening can lead to understanding the lives of others, to empathy.

These notes on memory take us to the heart of D6M and indeed RIM's success. At both museums the memory is attached to place and the voices of the previously subjugated are raised. D6M is a site of contested heritage and the museum space reflects the complexity of this political tension in not presenting a singular, linear narrative, but rather overlapping real and imaginary zones, articulated by diverse people with attachments to the site, to offer what Tony Bennett regards as new forms of civic self-fashioning (Bennett 1996, 1999). New conceptions of post-apartheid citizenship are associated with retributive reallocation of land and D6M has been involved in land restitution processes since its inception. Rassool notes the 'memory politics' at the centre of the museum mission that aimed to 'mobilize the masses of ex-residents and their descendants into a movement of land restitution, community development, and political consciousness' (Rassool 2006: 293-4). D6M has offered a political forum space, attempting to balance land restitution claims and the desire for a 'scorched earth' memorial to the past. Notably the land restitution process was finally launched at D6M in November 2000 when 40 hectares were restored to claimants to ensure the return of 17,000 ex-resident families (Rasool 2001: xi).

Truth and Reconciliation

Reality politics is vital to D6M, which the memory work supports and yet an equally important aspect of the D6M mission is a notion of reconciliation highlighting the imaginary. The artist curator Peggy Delport outlines the mission of D6 Museum when it was first established, which was 'To retrieve the scattered fragments of evidence and to piece together the wider narrative about this and other instances of forced removal in South Africa, not only to reclaim a hidden history, but to facilitate processes of reconciliation' (Delport 2001: 37). In Delport's words on the development of the D6M we discern echoes of the Truth and Reconciliation Committee (TRC). She regards reconciliation as vital if survivors of atrocities are to find healing and not remain fettered to the horrors of the past. In other words, healing can afford some sense of closure, but this must begin with remembering the painful past, then the wounds of loss can be made bearable.

At the TRC the healing of painful histories was connected with forgiveness, which had different aspects, positive and negative, for victim and perpetrator. Perpetrators were required to tell the Truth about past crimes, but not to apologise to earn immunity from prosecution. For the perpetrator, forgiving was associated with 'forgetting which severs the remorseful tie fettering authors of evil to those they have harmed, so that the latter no longer haunt the former' (Holiday 1998: 44). A great deal seems to be expected of the individual victims and their families here. However, Mandela notes the importance of the TRC remembering process for the whole nation, who he contends was a 'victim' whose 'dignity' needed to be restored, through a 'healing process' that might permit the nation 'to redeem and reconstruct itself' (<http://www.anc.org.za/ancdocs/history/mandela/1996/sp0213.html> accessed on 15.03.2008).

A major premise of the TRC was to redress the power of the perpetrator over the victim, calling on the power of the court over the perpetrator and the power of forgiveness to aid healing of victim and perpetrator. Yet there are tensions between memory and forgetting that stand in the way of reconciliation. Memory can offer a means of making loss survivable but closure may be difficult if not impossible in the face of painful memories and the economic inequalities that are legacies of racism. Outside of the national body, the TRC that dealt with major atrocities, but still within the public domain, I would argue that the D6M can provide what Barbara Misztel terms a 'high-prestige' location. D6M is a site where 'mnemonic communities' of 'the family, the ethnic group and the nation' that 'socialize us' can 'decide on what should be remembered and what should be forgotten' and most importantly we might add at D6M, 'how' (Misztel 2007: 381-384).

At D6M the site is imbued with the emotion of a traumatic past, the history of enforced removal, not only from place but also from a deeper sense of self, of humanity in the spatial system of apartheid that affects truth telling. The museum is popularly regarded as a prime location of truth and authenticity, which is important for the new democracy in South Africa. However D6M does not wish to present the past totally through a lens of victim-hood and their commitment to truth is again rooted in politics. Political commitment is seen in the desire to flatten traditional hierarchies of curatorial power and control, to facilitate the expression of individual and community voice in diverse ways, most importantly through 'aesthetics' or a poetics that underpins display (Delport 2001).

Next I shall explore the ways in which memory is prompted through aesthetics at D6M. The richness of D6M exhibitions is extraordinary and I have selected just two in an attempt to analyse the power of this place.

Collaborative Aesthetics and Interpretation: 'Hands-on' Methodology, 'Streets' and 'Digging Deeper'

A unique 'hands-on' methodology has been developed at D6M. From my perspective this is vitally 'minds-on' and characterised by a determined attention to level power hierarchies that is expressed in the African terms 'kanala' or sharing and 'kanaldorp' place of sharing from which the 'aesthetics' of D6M emerges (Hein 1999: 54). Most importantly I perceive an African 'ethics of care' that underpins D6M as a museum appropriate to the context of South Africa and resonates in my own work within a 'feminist-hermeneutic' framework (Hill-Collins 1991). This ethics is seen in Delport's idea of community dialogue as the 'tap root' of the aesthetics, guiding the hands-on collaborative method to develop 'interpretive vehicles' for the post-apartheid South African situation. Delport further highlights this as an ongoing interpretive project whose aesthetic form acts as a '*catalyst* or *generator* of meaning', which is not simply 'fixed by historians, curators or artists', nor by the diverse groups of local and international visitors, but is layered and open to continual shift and subversion (Delport 2001: 32, 159).

Aesthetic forms at D6M developed in active partnership from the earliest exhibition in 1992 of ex-resident's photographs, which was also marked by a direct craft-based approach when 'a length of old calico curtain was pinned' to an office wall, felt tip pens were provided and visitors were invited to inscribe names and messages (Delport 2001: 12). The calico became the 1.7 metre 'Name Cloth', which is an on-going method of recording community voices that now contains many thousands of penned messages embroidered over by Revina Gwayi in black chain and blanket stitches. The Name Cloth hangs from the gallery in the main hall and is one example of D6M's human, dialogical, and craft basis of aesthetic practice.

The aesthetic hands-on practice is evident in the initial discussion with ex-residents over the making of 'Streets' in 1994, which D6ers (ex-residents) decided 'should not mourn' but rather celebrate the 'cultural diversity' that once characterised the area (Delport 2001: 38). A main feature of 'Streets' is a simple but boldly painted map of the original D6 area before demolition in 1966. This street map on a white tarpaulin, covering the entire central floor space, is painted in warm earth and ochre tones that are reminiscent of an earlier community mural on the front wall, where the aesthetic colour decisions emerged in discussion and were inspired by D6er memories of the red clay earth that appeared to 'bleed' during bulldozing. Rather than designing a perfectly finished object of silent passive worship hands-on aesthetics offered an open arena for active working with the memory of ex-residents who were invited to write their names, addresses and articulate their memories directly onto the transparent plastic surface layer, which now contains many contributions including some from creative writers and artists who number among the ex-resident community.

Ex-residents have been able to externalise their heartache at loss of community on this map and it seems to be the street structure that acts as a powerful museum vehicle to remember a painful past. For example Donald Parenzee's poem 'Oh City' ends 'And you'll not call your children back / to a void / where your heart / used to be'. Other texts are taken from freedom fighters and poets in other parts of the globe, which adds to the international, outward looking stance of the museum and permits visitors around the world to approach the experiences and empathise with the loss of other human beings, of humanity itself. Sorrow abounds. Yet D6ers also remember the painful past in ways that look to the future as is evident in the Black American Langston Hughes's words that are inscribed at the corner opposite Parenzee's: 'Hold fast / to dream / for if dreams die / life is a / broken-winged bird / that / cannot fly'. Thus the map would appear to heed Toni Morrison's advice in another context, on remembering enslavement she states:

> There is a necessity for remembering the horror, but of course there's a necessity for remembering it in a manner in which it can be digested, in a manner in which the memory is not destructive. ... The collective sharing of that information heals the individual and the collective. (Morrison 1992: 247-258)

The main focus of this map project, the individual and collective healing through sharing, was on facilitating the everyday memories of 'ordinary' citizens, which contrasts with the 'Cell Stories' at the Robben Island site where the great leaders of the anti-apartheid struggle are commemorated. The D6 map has an extraordinary dynamism that is seen in its widespread continuing use as a site for sitting, dancing, meeting and sharing stories amongst the community today. There is a strong sense that the process of including the local community audience in the processes of visual construction results in a richer picture of the area than could be achieved by any curatorial team alone, however experienced and sensitive. The living community work marks a powerful reclamation of personal and community identities that the spatial apartheid attempted to destroy along with the buildings and it is perhaps this aspect of human resilience, local and international cooperation that continues to touch visitors I observed, and certainly touched me profoundly.

In addition to the intangible memories that are made concrete on the map and the embroidered name cloth that continues to grow, 'Streets' displays objects. At the far end of the map a collection of historical street signs are scaffolded into a tower that soars upwards in the church space, which Delport likens to tree of life. These objects were salvaged from demolition and stored in the basement of a council worker who disobeyed the order to 'dump D6 in Table Bay' during the demolition and later donated them to the museum. Other donations include photographs some of which are displayed as larger than life portraits of ex-residents, reproduced on translucent paper and suspended from high up in the gallery space, where they look and smile down on us. There are also archaeological finds now sited on the balcony, fragments of daily life pottery and samples of the earth and stones from D6 gathered during 'healing memory' programmes that are part of the educational work.

Overall 'Streets' symbolises in diverse ways the exterior community life of a place, of D6 prior to destruction. The highly creative curating of Delport offers a site full of symbolism, receptive surfaces for recollection, connections and interconnections, visual and textual pleasure, soft moving banners and hard metal street signs, diverse elements that work together to reinforce an optimistic message, one that points to the power of humanity to survive oppression, through co-operation (Delport 2001: 154). Delport notes how the D6M space mirrors the distinct topographical identity of D6 prior to destruction, where the district connected Table Mountain to the inner city docks the harbour and the sea through a series of slopes and different levels, which are echoed in the attention to high and low spaces, the feeling of openness in the main gallery with the material traces of the past that are linked by steps and passageways.

Visitors can move through 'Streets' in the main exhibition Hall to the community café and reading room into the rebuilt Memorial Hall, another open space that also offers an ideal site for meetings and workshops, where another mapping project has been located, the 'Writers Floor' that was part of the 'Digging Deeper' exhibition. Delport describes 'Digging Deeper' as building on the 'Streets' work of recollecting, which was largely concerned with the public spaces, to explore the 'warm interior lives' of ex-residents, the private world, the thoughts and feelings of individuals in greater detail (Delport 2001: 4). The central map feature here is constructed from durable ceramic tiling that is designed as an inner and outer circle with lines radiating out from the centre, four of them pointing North, South, East, and West. This ceramic map has large blank areas in warn honey and rust coloured hues, with blocks of fragmented colourful patterns that are reminiscent of the seventeen layers of linoleum excavated from a home in Horstley Street, and close to sixty small white tiles with cobolt blue inscriptions permanently fired onto their surfaces. The tiles act as 'notes' for the writer's reflexivity, and self-reflexive looking below surface appearances and public narratives to grapple with the complexity of meaning and re-examine that, which appeared to be certain.

Overall 'Streets' and 'Digging Deeper' marks the possibilities of working creatively with memory, providing a generative arena for historical retrieval, re-interpretation and re-articulation of identities. Next I turn from the visual to examine the oral testimonies more closely in this construction of new identities.

Narrative Truths: Emotion and Power

While D6M worked in tandem with land claimants Delport highlights Said's notion of imaginative return to, 'restore ourselves to ourselves', as of greater significance than literal return (Delport 2001: 40). Here yearning for place is seen as an act of freedom, of the imagination, to reaffirm and celebrate D6 communities, and '*making place* for tolerance, for the otherness' of different individuals and groups, for seeking out and affirming our common humanity (Delport 2001: 41). However, perhaps the act of imagination that is vital to recollection can cast doubt on the reality of the past events. Joan Sangster is helpful on this question of autobiographical truth. She points out:

> When people talk about their lives, people lie sometimes, forget a little, exaggerate, become confused, get things wrong. Yet they are revealing truths … all autobiographical memory is true: it is up to the interpreter to discover in which sense, where, and for what purpose. (Passerini quoted in Sangster 2003: 87)

While the notion of imagination can, like memory, be regarded as standing in the way of historical truth and the authenticity of the real thing that curatorial authority safeguards in the traditional museum, D6M provides a prime example of curators relinquishing absolute authorial control. Soudien and Meltzer elaborate upon this when they speak of narrative rights that emphasise the importance of ordinary D6ers taking control of their narratives, which are vital to the re-making of the identities that were shattered at D6, along with the physical demolition of the community spaces. They further justify their approach to value the people's or popular narratives and privilege their preferred ways of telling by questioning the notion of 'one true story', the dry and homogenising 'official' narratives that denigrate the D6 area of the 1960s as 'a festering sore in danger of infecting the moral fibre of the city', a slum with 'coloured' residents who are regarded as objects better relocated, elsewhere (Soudien and Meltzer 2001: 66).

In contradistinction the vivid 'popular' narratives 'work with different symbols and are motivated by the need to keep alive the meaning and memory of 'cosmopolitaness' at D6. Admittedly D6ers popular narratives are open to 'the power of invention and renewal', but this is regarded as part of the D6er's claiming agency and their narrative right to speak for themselves and retell their own stories. D6ers are empowered by D6M to 'talk back', to move from the silent object of narrative to the speaking subject (Morrison 1993, bell hooks 1989). Speaking strengthens a sense of self, of identity since it transforms the way individuals are able to reposition themselves in narratives of the past, which can make it possible to move on. Thus speaking is integral to the reflective process of knowledge construction, people come to know through telling, reflecting and most importantly engaging with a listener.

Listening seems to be a key strength of the D6M mission to empower audiences to speak of that which has lain in silence because it is too painful to articulate. The act of talking has positive benefits for speakers and this is enhanced by the knowledge that the prestigious institution of the museum is 'listening', thereby adding value to the recording of their memories for future generations. Listening and speaking are purposeful here. It is akin to the feminist-hermeneutic work of respectful dialogical exchange. In reclaiming the power of voice, D6 narratives permit some healing of a painful past, which they begin to repossess, in an imaginative sense. In other words subjects writing their own histories, can come to terms with their lack of historical power. They can find cause to celebrate their resilience and regain their humanity, within the process of democratic recollection. Such personal writing and telling inevitably has an ideological impetus, a tendency to include, exclude and romanticise.

Another vital element of this work is the sensual remembering that is evoked. Lalou Meltzer further describes the process of constructing narratives and remembering at D6M as a 'filtered and fine textured' entangling of 'then and now' to make an 'old-new thing' (Meltzer 2001: 22). She highlights the sensory qualities or strong memory senses, the smell of watermelon permeating fresh cut grass and remembering, not the actual 'flesh' of the past, but the ways the sensual memories 'hook thousands of tiny 'fleshy' acts in remembering. Toni Morrison supports Meltzer when she describes 'emotional memory – what the nerves and the skin remember, as well as how it appears' (Morrison quoted in White 2003: 179). Linda Fortune also highlights the emotional moments visitors experience at D6M. She recalls one visitor feeling 'too heart-sore' and needing to return when she felt composed, while another experienced opening memories that were 'too painful' and the need to return when he felt better (Fortune 2001: 48).

The point I want to make here is that while emotions inevitably affect what is recalled, which can discredit testimonies in the eyes of some historians, feeling and thinking is inextricably part of human recall. To take an example from another context, which Naomi Rosh White notes. A Jewish woman survivor, whose testimony noted 'four chimneys ... exploding ... people running ... unbelievable' event, contradicted the facts of the matter at the Auschwitz uprising where one chimney was blown up (White 2003: 173). Yet as White argues, the reality of an unimaginable event can require a survivor to understand and tell their stories of their individual experiences differently. Furthermore what is crucial is that these personal narratives are passed on, through listening and telling, for the sake of an ethical or morally responsible society. As Elie Wiesel states:

A moral society must have the strength to [hear] these accounts, just as the
authors have the strength to [give] them. For a moral society must remember ...
If we stop remembering, we stop being. (Wiesel quoted in White 2003: 181)

Next I turn to this notion of being, which as I note earlier is always becoming,
from the perspective of the younger generation. I consider how D6M engages in
the 'passing on' of histories.

Ambassadors

Dammon Rice writes on the contribution of the D6M Ambassadors programme to
the building of a new democratic nation, through widening access to community
heritage for the youth of the country, especially those from deprived economic
backgrounds. Rice speaks of the programme imparting a range of skills and
experiences to young people in a supportive, non-threatening and fun environment.
He tells us that enthusiasm and commitment, not proven intellectual ability, are
the only entry requirements to the programme, which trains Grade 11 teenager
volunteers to cascade knowledge amongst their peers, specifically to educate
school groups on the history of District Six using the museum collection.

    Diverse teaching strategies are employed during the training programme
including: role-play, group discussion and workshops, which encourages
participants to draw comparisons between their own contemporary lives, the local
history and the situation in the wider world. All these learner-centred activities
help to impart 'analytical, critical and creative thinking skills', leadership skills
as well as techniques for peer teaching (Rice 2001: 62-3). Ambassadors gradually
learn to develop their language skills and to organise their thought until finally
they are ready to use their own words and ideas in the delivery of their talks to
school groups, with a more experienced teacher taking a position of support in the
background.

    Rice celebrates the growth in Ambassador's self-esteem and confidence. He
notes, one participant's declaration that she would be the first member of her
family to finish school and another's contention that 'I can do anything that I put
myself to do.' Overall the Ambassadors programme results in transforming the
participant's limited perceptions of themselves and of museums, which were as
one young person remarked, 'not dull and boring ... not the elitist institutions I
thought they were', but 'for everyone' (Rice 2001: 63). This positive attitude is
clearly reflected in the school sessions as one Grade 7 visitor told an Ambassador
he would bring parents he had so much fun (ibid. 2001: 65).

    In addition to achievements learning and working in the museum, D6M
Ambassadors have succeeded through educational outreach activities. For
example, in the most economically deprived Mannenberg area where many
D6ers were forcibly removed to, an exhibition 'Mannenberg: young ambassadors
exploring a creative future' was held in the local library before touring the local

primary schools. This project enabled the Mannenberg youth to see and take pride in their heritage, which promoted an expanded notion of their potential and a more hopeful vision for their future lives. Noor Ebrahim's work at D6M also promotes an optimistic future. Let us turn to review this next.

Noor Ebrahim and Education for Democracy

Noor Ebrahim, was a former resident of D6 and is currently Education Officer at the museum. Ebrahim is a gifted storyteller and employs his considerable skills in the intergenerational work of education for democracy at D6M. I observed his talks over a week in October 2006, which kept groups of secondary school aged children transfixed during my visits, as Plates 19 and 20 demonstrate. He spoke with animated passion about living in D6 during apartheid, the good times as a young man with many friends as well as the terror of enforced removal. His talk was interspersed with great good humour and an abiding sense of reconciliation, which afforded relief to the audience, who were majority white. Ebrahim comments on forgiving 'But I always say, we don't hate them, we forgive them for what they did (Ebrahim 2001: 57).

There is a power to be derived in 'forgiving and not forgetting'. Ebrahim in forgiving has moved on from being defined solely, or primarily, as 'victim' and so he breaks the shackles of the past rather than perpetuating the inequalities and injustices of victim-hood. He has been able to recall the pain of the past removal and displacement as well as the ordinary and amusing instances of daily life. At one point he notes growing up and disobeying his parents, by performing in the 'Coon Carnival' with his friends. Although his band won this victory involved him lying to his parents and in his jubilation returning home he forgot to wash off the black minstrel makeup, which led to the uncovering of his lie (Ebrahim 2005: 42). Instances such as this, telling fibs, lying to parents and covering up misbehaviour, resonate today with children, and indeed adults, the world over.

The learning potential of D6M is phenomenal, with 'education for liberation, transformation and democracy' pervading every nook and every programme. Education and educators here stand in contradistinction to the 'education for oppression' that Mandela amongst others fought against, notably the intellectual '*baasskap*, which is based on the 'supremacy in all matters of the whites over the nonwhites', in the 1953 Bantu Education Act (September 2001: 23; <http://www.africawithin.com/mandela/bantu_education_0657.htm> accessed on 17.06.2007). Mandela deplored this Apartheid legislation that insulated 'African people within 'small tribal units' and fostered 'narrow outlooks and restricted opportunities for the Black and Coloured population (ibid.). D6M rather opens 'the doors of learning' not only locally but internationally. The Swedish government funded exchange entitled '*Balueka! Be Important Wes Belangrit!*', between young people in Cape Town and Malmö is an example of one such initiative (D6M Newsletter, Volume 8, No. 2: 1). In examples such as this, an educational aim in the 1956

Freedom Charter: '… to teach the youth to love their people and their culture, to honour human brotherhood, liberty and peace' is beginning to be realised at D6M (<http://www.anc.org.za/ancdocs/history/charter.html> accessed on 17.06.2007).

**Plate 19 Noor Ebrahim in dialogue with children on the map at
          District Six Museum, Cape Town, South Africa, 2006**
Source: Author.

Plate 20 Close up of young people on the floor map at District Six Museum, Cape Town, South Africa, 2006
Source: Author.

The inclusiveness in the Freedom Charter is extended around the world by D6M. I can attest to the willingness and generosity of D6M professionals, notably Benita Bennett, Mandy Sanger, Noor Ebrahim, Tina Smith and Chrischené Julius to engage in dialogue during my own visits. D6M exemplifies an inclusive approach as a founder member of the International Coalition of Historic Site Museums of Conscience, which is a global network spanning four continent. The common ideals and goals are to commemorate past struggles for democracy and to develop diverse methods for facilitating dialogue on contemporary social concerns. There is an emphasis on taking action to address major human rights abuses, thereby transforming site visitors from passive learners to active citizens and promoting democratic values (<www.sitesofconscience.org/eng/d6_how.htm> accessed on 11.12.2007).

Next I shall relate this South African memory work to the UK. First I offer some definition of key terms. Then I outline multisensory approaches that have successfully prompted remembering and returned some control of lives to elders during UK outreach with specific reference to intergenerational reminiscence (IGR) outreach activities, which will help connect us to the focus on sensory ways of knowing in Section 3.

Reminiscence, Oral history and Recollection: What's in a Name?

Senior citizens, old age pensioners, old people, grey hairs, wrinklies and elders are a few terms – derogatory and acceptable – describing people over 65 years old, which is the legal age of retirement from paid work in the UK. Elders, is my preferred term. This is taken from African Caribbean partners and is associated with respect derived from greater life experience and knowledge, which views elders as a resource rather than a burden. As one Horniman collaborator notes: 'we say in Africa when an elder dies we loose a library' (Kwappong 2006 pers. comm.)

Research sights grandparents as 'a precious resource for children' (Predazzi et al. 2000: 81). The valuable transmissive function and stabilising influences grandparents play in the family has also been recognised in a UK Government Green paper and the Dept of the Family (Home Office 1998, 2000). Yet in Britain, while people are living longer family relationships have changed as a result of increasing marital breakdowns (1 in 3) and the demographic movements caused by economic migrations around the world (ibid. 2000: 81). These factors can conspire and increase the risk of children becoming estranged from their grandparents and consequentially divorced from their cultural heritage, which highlights a need for intergenerational transmission in the wider social sphere. In other words there is a social value from engaging elders in sharing their experiences in IGR as knowledge bearers that extends their role within families to the school system.

Electing to take on a transmissive function as knowledge bearer is not universally appealing, but the elders who do engage in IGR find it rewarding, positive and life affirming. The keynotes for elders engaged in IGR with Age Exchange London appear to be: sharing; commitment to truth telling; being a bearer of special information and delivering a unique experience, value and self value; reflexivity; authority and confidence; negating stereotypes and false images (Schweitzer 1993: 7). Marwick's research reinforces this in Edinburgh. She notes children seeing beyond an impaired and frail body to glimpse something of the whole life of a person, which led one 10 year old to comment 'See these 2 old ladies over there? – they're great!' (Marwick 1995: 143). As they sit and discuss together people question: how were things then, how different are they now and why? This brings common sense beliefs to consciousness, so they can be consciously adopted, rejected or modified.

Tom Kitwood also observes there is a positive impact on the elder memory bearer in IGR, who is viewed as a whole sentient being, a 'unity' of body and mind, 'thought and feeling' and consequently a respectful process and value is highlighted that benefits the one remembering (Kitwood 1990: 205-6). Gaynor Kavanagh regards the focus on 'process' and value primarily to the memory bearer in reminiscence as distinguishing it from oral history, where the emphasis is on the 'product' and the sharing of knowledge to support historical research and interpretation in the museum. She notes how in the past the gathering of oral histories has led to memory bearers being regarded as a sort of filing cabinet or a crop to be harvested.[2] Certainly reminiscence may result in the production of oral history or resource packs for schools and oral history involves the process of reminiscence, yet the primary objective is regarded as 'giving' in reminiscence and 'taking' in oral history (Kavanagh, 2000: 118). It is also worth highlighting the term recollection, since it has positive connection with ideas of 'action and power' and 'success', it denotes the authority of the elders and can be employed to impart a sense of value to intergenerational reminiscence or remembering (COED 1976: 934). However the notion of writing history from below and stressing the recovery of subjective experiences in a mutually respectful way is common to reminiscence and oral history or life review and recollection, which are often used interchangeably in the literature.

In my experience of IGR this respectful work crucially involves the elder and younger person thinking critically together. For children, a change in the school routine and meeting new people is exciting in itself, which can lead to closer attention, to questioning and assimilating new ideas within the framework of prior knowledge. Engagement with real people and relating their words with objects, newspapers, documents and photos prompts pupils to gain new knowledge and develop skills of comparing, contrasting and evaluating the truth of evidence. Furthermore, the development of good new relationships 'scaffolds' an imaginative consideration of world change and an appreciation of present by locating the abstract past in reality.

IGR is motivating as children see elders in their multicultural communities as 'experts' and come to value the diverse histories of 'ordinary' people like themselves, which lie outside of the preferred narratives of British heroes and royalty that dominate the national curriculum for history. Age Exchange and the East Midlands Oral History Archive (EMOHA) worked in partnership with teachers to develop a broader range of national curricula material, including citizenship, based on reminiscence activities (Schweitzer 1993; <http//:www.emoha.org> accessed on 24.11.2007). Such IGR work initially challenges stereotypical views of elders, as the evidence of their eyes and their fruitful dialogical exchanges contradict any negative preconceived ideas, then by extension IGR aims to challenge prejudice generally. This is a large claim, which a brief outline of certain media tools such as resource boxes and citizenship teachers' packs employed during outreach activity may help to justify.

Age Exchange has produced more than 20 *Reminiscence Boxes*, which are carefully themed to structure dialogue and creative work around the interests of

---

2   Healy in Australia speaks of the interview process as a form of voyeurism, stalking 'the old' to 'catch history in a net of tape which scoops up words before the last breath expires. In its worst moments, the museum simply colonised and cannibalised the collective memories of the western suburbs in order to reproduce itself as an institution' (Healy 1991: 165 in Kavanagh 2000: 79). However in the best instances, such as in Liz Carnegie's work in Glasgow, Kavanagh suggests that greater empathy leads to richer records (Kavanagh, 2000: 75-78).

the group (<http://www.age-exchange.org.uk> accessed on 24.11.2007). Each box contains up to 12 objects, such as the 'Born in the Caribbean' box containing: cane sugar, bay rum, country chocolate, dominoes, charbolic soap herbs and spices, sasparilla, paraffin candles, traditional songs and a map of the Caribbean. These objects, or 'props' as Burnside calls them, act as 'tangible reminders of the past', which stimulate a remembering process for the elders who originally selected and work with them as 'points of departure, not arrival' (Burnside 1995: 155). At a basic level the simple act of 'holding' then 'passing' on connects people in a group and invites a sharing of opinions (Gibson 1994: 58).[3]

The *Living Memory in Education* programmes in schools, involves elders in schools demonstrating the objects and inspiring excellent writing, which is valuable for elders and pupils (Schweitzer 1993). The elders who I have worked with at Horniman are skilful storytellers, which enables pupils to gain imaginative access to the past based on the personal and subjective meanings associated with objects. In IGR elder storytellers also importantly encourage young writers to express multiple perspectives such as 'my point of view' and 'my nan's point of view'. The humorous ways in which the elders often tell their tales is extremely motivating and is often reflected in the young peoples compositions. I offer one example as typical. 'You may think that Nigeria is just a radiator with sand but you are absolutely wrong, wrong and even more wrong' (<http://www.brockleyschool. org> accessed on 05.03.2005).

I have begun to outline activities conducted during UK 'outreach'. A note defining this term will prove helpful.

Outreach: Developing the Social Role of the Museum in the UK

> The term museum outreach provision is usually intended to support "hard to reach" or "hidden" groups of people such as elders in residential homes and "involves going out from a specific organization or centre to work in other locations with sets of people who typically do not or cannot avail themselves of the services of that centre". (McGivney 2000: 16)

It was during the 1990s that professional museums, organisations and the new Labour government bodies asserted the need for museums to adopt a social role, which 'outreach' was a widely adopted means of fulfilling (Martin 1999; DCMS

---

3 Learning benefits, citizenship and identity issues, construction guidelines and evaluations for UK loan boxes are outlined at <http://www.museumse.org.uk/making_the_ most_of_museums/benefits_of_using_museums/Loan_Boxes.html>; <http://www.museums loansnetwork.org.uk/learning.htm>; <http://www.ucl.ac.uk/museums/loanboxes.html>; <http:// www.leics.gov.uk/moving_objects>; <http://www.objectdialoguebox.com/>; <http://www. gem.org.uk/grassroots/GR%20Resources/makeloansbox.html>; <www.mlasouthwest.org. uk/docs/Resource-Box-Report.pdf> accessed on 20.11.2008.

1999, 1996, 1999; DCMS 1999). David Martin provides a broad definition of outreach, which suggests 'an organizations involvement with or influence in, the community, particularly in relation to social welfare' that 'involves work with audiences which is related to museum subjects and collections but staged in non-museum' settings. He highlights typical venues including: 'libraries, schools, community halls, shopping centres, surgeries, old people homes and clubs, fairs and festivals, hospitals and prisons' (Martin 1999: 38). Martin regards outreach as 'fundamental to the process of changing the role of museums within their communities', since it can establish 'relationships with new audiences, and turn museums from inward facing to outward looking organizations' (Martin 1999: 38).

However, Peter Davies problematises this position. He denounces outreach that allows community access 'on a limited basis … separated from that community', and he further notes the term 'outreach or 'outstation' has etymological links to 'outcast', which reinforces this separation (Davies 1999: 32). Davis argues that while outreach can have truly transformational possibilities – offering the potential for flexible, plurivocal participation and responsive relationships and community empowerment through facilitating open dialogical exchange – it may have limited impact on the institution, its ethos and its wider priorities.

It is worth recalling that in the UK outreach seemed to instill a fear in some staff that museums might be taken 'beyond their natural physical and philosophical boundaries' (Anderson 1999: 69). The fear relates to museums engaging in areas of social provision unconnected with their traditional work of 'preservation, display, interpretation and education' as well as to their anxiety about public spending and accountability (Sandell 2003: 6). Nevertheless the benefits of outreach activity for both the museums and the participants can be considerable as the increasing evidence from case studies, research publications and evaluation reports demonstrate. Linda Sargent's work is notable here.

The benefits to Sargent's Oxfordshire project participants reinforce the D6M Ambassadors findings, which include enhanced social confidence and improved self-esteem as well as increased motivation and energy that is thought to arise from opportunities for self-expression. Sargent's outreach is notable in her emphasis on creativity, and in drawing on ideas from outside the discipline of museum studies, such as therapy as I shall outline next.

Building Bridges of Meaning: Mapping Our Place in a Safe Space

'Mapping Our Place' was one part of a larger reminiscence project entitled *Drawn from Memory*, developed by Linda Sargent for a target audience of 7 women aged between early 50s to early 80s who attended a weekly meeting during term time at their local Health Centre in rural Oxfordshire (<http://www.mlasoutheast. org.uk/assets/documents/1000033Cwordswings_last.pdf>; <http://lindasargent. co.uk/html/resources.html> accessed on 17.12.2007). Sargent begins her mapping sessions by showing and discussing her own sketch map of a 'favourite childhood place', which she tells us should not be beautifully drawn as this can intimidate participants. She explains the map details can range from a farm, a swing, a room, a den or camp, but must include the journey to the place and usually takes about 20 minutes to complete.

Sargent describes recalling 'the raw enthusiasm' and feeling for a place special to her in the Oxford session, and further notes how this personal sharing usually promotes an inclusive sharing atmosphere. She also observes how the mapping activity quickly absorbs people, it seems to touch 'a core, some piece of childhood recaptured' and the resulting memories were formed into stories of emplacement that were readily shared following the drawing exercise (Sargent 2002: 26). For example one member of the group recalls a childhood in London (ibid. 2002: 28). Her map represents her memories of 1934. She recalls feeding cart-horses 'carrots and sugar' at a diary with a Norwegian friend, then feeding fish at 'Golders Green Crematorium ... My friend went back to Norway before the war and I never heard from her again', she tells Sargent in conversation.

The success of this project as measured in evaluation seems to be due, in part at least, to the map work with the accompanying text crucially ensuring individuals had a personal textual space, which empowered them to extend the initial thoughts associated with recollection. Releasing personal creativity in individual production also appeared to be a vital source of pleasure and pride for all the women, while taking turns in the oral sharing of the stories following drawing permitted intimate connection amongst the group. The group leaders taking responsibility for setting a truly compassionate framework for people to share their memories/thoughts and feelings in 'a safe setting' was vital and this involved listening to the different dynamics of each group, judging when to speak and remain silent, when to be assertive and when restrained (Sargent 2002: 11-12).

Sargent points out that the work of recollection here has certain similarities with 'narrative therapy', which is a technique that allow therapists and clients 'to be light-hearted, humorous, and creative and yet surprisingly effective in resolving many of the problems that we face today' (White and Epston 1990). Narrative therapists recognise the 'idea of hearing or telling stories may seem a trivial pursuit', yet they contend 'conversations can shape new realities' by building 'bridges of meaning' together with clients, which helps 'healing developments flourish instead of wither and be forgotten.' In short, White and Epston note how it is language and creativity that 'can shape events into narratives of hope' (ibid.).

It is worth noting here that orality and writing are not mutually exclusive but may be complementary forms of recall. Furthermore, my own experience of conducting creative workshop activities, has shown that 'rationality' and the written word are not necessarily washed away, by some 'uncontrollable mass of fluid amorphous material' that constitutes the work of recall (Portelli 1999: 64).

Next I shall consider museums building creative and sensual 'bridges of meaning' in Japan. I briefly outline another mapping project.

Mapping for Health in Japan

In 2007 a team led by Yukiko Hashimoto at Edo-Tokyo Museum won a national award for their innovative memory work with elders who had lived before the second World War (WWII) in the area around the museum[4] (<http://www.edo-tokyo-museum.or.jp/english/index.html> accessed on 09.11.2007). 'Genki' [Health] was the title of the twelve month project that was conducted in collaboration with the University of Tokyo Dept of Gerontology, who issued each elder with a pedometer at the outset to measure cardio-vascular rates monthly and recorded a scientifically significant improvement at the end of the project.

The term 'genki' has a wider meaning than the translation suggests, including a whole mind/body attitude that pervades daily life, seen in the widespread use of 'O genki de?' as a greeting. It is also indicative of a desire to promote a 'healthy' relation, a sense of belonging and place, between the individual, the community and the land with its changing four seasons that is traditionally strong in Japan.

The Genki project aimed to bring a map archive held in the museum to life together with elder members of the local community, to increase the knowledge of the pre-WWII area and examine how the museum might contribute to improving the health of the elders, both physically and mentally. Edo-Tokyo Museum's maps showed the geography of the area prior to the devastating bombing in WWII over a period of many weeks that led to the complete destruction of many historical areas and a death toll exceeding the more rapid destruction at Hiroshima and Nagasaki.

The museum recruited survivors, eight in total, to volunteer for work with the map collection by issuing a small 'call for help' notice within the museum and placing a small advert in the local newspaper. Following initial consultation and negotiation in the museum of research themes the survivors choose specific aspects of the local area around the museum, such as entertainment and shops. The Genki project leaders encouraged engagement from a personal 'reminiscence' perspective to recall sensual and emotional knowledge, the smells, sounds and tastes of the past as well as finding factual material in the libraries. Elders actively researched every day, recording findings in notebooks and sharing them with each other in the museum once a month, when new directions for the next month were agreed. The traditional 1940s home, of wonderfully jointed wooden construction with tatami [rice straw] matting, rice paper windows, 'kotatsu' [low table heated with a sunken fire source and covered with a futon or quilt] 'tokonami' [alcove] and a more modern (for the time) ticking clock on the wall, was selected as an ideal site to promote sensual memory work during monthly meetings.

---

4   Japan has a tradition of holding the elders of the community in high esteem. For example notable artists and craftspeople can become 'National Living Treasures', whose knowledge gained over a rich lifetime is valued by the country as a whole and at the level of everyday life the 'ojiisan/obaasan' [grandparents], 'obasan' [aunties] and 'okasan' [uncles] are treated with considerable respect.

Next I shall make come concluding remarks. I shall outline the role of the senses in promoting recall.

Conclusion: Coming to Our Senses

Just as at D6M objects such as the floor map were seen to stimulate recall, a number of UK examples demonstrate objects working sensually in the process of recollection with the aging body. Alison McMoreland Director Living Arts Glasgow highlights the strong sensory component of museum object work. She recalls one previously silent woman in a care home, who had sung songs but not talked during earlier workshops becoming animated at the sight of a bobbin; her fingers 'remembering' the complicated 'weavers knot' from her days in the Jute Mill. Alison also notes taking Highland pipes for Angus, a piper and composer nearly ninety years old, who was partially deaf and totally blind. Angus, placing the reedless chanter to his lips and discovering the absence of sound, began vocalising 'diddle' while fingering one of his compositions 'dignity and authority.' When asked how he composed tunes; if he heard them in his head? He instantly replied, without stopping to think, 'I hear them in my heart' (McMoreland 1997: 112).

Eilean Taylor also speaks of sensory routes to recall. She explains how a bag of sweets can provide a complete multi-sensory experience to provoke memory through the five senses we usually count in the west. In *touching* the bag and selecting one sweet; *looking* closely at the chosen sweet; *listening* to the rustle of the paper bag and the crunching sound of eating; *smelling* the aroma; *tasting* the sweet past times can be re-imagined and communication of childhood, siblings and corner shops facilitated (Eilean Taylor 1997: 140-141).

The creative reminiscence workshops I have conducted along Sargent's and Taylor's lines have proved affective in building 'bridges of meaning' with MA students in Leicester as well museum professionals in Cape Town (2006) and Japan (2005, 2006) (<http://icom.org/ictop/2006> accessed on 11.11.2006). In the next Section I shall investigate the interrelationship between hearts and minds, embodied and sensual ways of knowing that I found exemplified at D6M, in Japan and in my UK examples. Specifically I shall consider these issues with reference to my own work with young visitors to Horniman Museum.

Section 3
Critical Collaborative Museum Pedagogy

New forms of museum practice centre on notions of collaboration and alliance. Audre Lorde is helpful here. She states:

> Change means growth and growth can be painful. But we sharpen the self-definition by exposing the self in work and *struggle* together with those whom we define as different from ourselves, although *sharing the same goals*. For *Black and white, old and young, lesbian and heterosexual women alike*, this can mean new paths to our survival. (Lorde 1996c: 170) [my emphasis]

In the last two chapters, I shall outline a creative research partnership entitled *'Inspiration Africa!'*, which aimed to progress the critical thinking and learning of London school children, to challenge racism through museum objects and to promote intercultural understanding. The collaboration I outlined with the adult members of CWWA earlier echoes in this section with young people in promoting a feeling that the museum is a responsive institution, one that listens and acts collaboratively.

In terms of facilitating opportunities for creativity and learning in the museum this section highlights the need for partners to fight against issues that arose in Section 2. Specifically collaborative practice during *'Inspiration Africa!'* was alert to signs of 'institutional racism', which was addressed from the outset of the project by attention to the ethnic composition of the team-leaders. Additionally any 'sense of superior [white] group position' was brought into the ongoing open dialogue, which was maintained throughout collaboration (Macpherson 1999: 6.18/22).

I open this introductory section with Audre Lorde, whose voice has informed the feminist-hermeneutic praxis that underpins the *'Inspiration Africa!'* projects I shall outline in Chapters 5 and 6. In addition to feminist thought the collaborative action underpinning these two chapters is reliant on broader frameworks such as Macpherson, which are crucial to the nurturing of children's budding identities and to the protection of their human rights that I shall briefly consider next.

Universal Human Rights and the Convention on the Rights of the Child (CRC)

In the context of the museum, the tenets of Universal Human Rights may be expounded alongside a study of objects. Museum objects have complex biographies and if educators draw attention for example to: the construction; indigenous meanings and use; travel to the museum, and the subsequent uses and meanings visitors may make there, work with objects can profitably draw attention to Human Rights issues today. Such object work, with a human rights focus, may be enhanced with reference to contemporary voices. I shall offer one instance to illustrate this point. Reflection on a Shona headrest c. nineteenth century that is said to inspire dreams, prompted one school group of autistic children to consider their own dreams, and also to look at the 'dream speech' of Dr Martin Luther King Jr., who raised his voice in resistance to tyranny for an optimistic future, as I have shown elsewhere. (King 1963; <http://www.usconstitution.net/dream.html> accessed on 30.11 2008; Golding 2009).

In Chapter 5 I shall expand upon this notion of pupil's writing object biographies during 'Inspiration Africa!' First let us consider the Horniman Museum's response to the United Nations Convention on the Rights of the Child (CRC), which underpins the multicultural-antiracist praxis I shall outline in Section 3 (<www.un.org>; <http://www.unicef.org/crc/> accessed on 30.11.2008). The Horniman Museum Education Department looked to the CRC, since it offers an ethical framework that we hoped might impart a sense of social responsibility to all children or young people, who are recognised as citizens. In addition to the outline provided in my Introduction, I emphasise the CRC applies to every child regardless of nationality, family background, gender, social status or racial or ethnic group as stated in Article 2. The right to education is noted in Article 28 and Article 29 declares the educational entitlement includes the advancement and respect for human rights and fundamental freedoms. In short children, who are defined as under 18 years old have rights of 'provision' including education and health, rights of 'protection' from harm and exploitation, and rights of 'participation' as seen in Article 12 that states their right to have their opinions given due regard when decisions will affect them. One example of practice illustrating these points occurred prior to 'Inspiration Africa!' and the construction of The *Hands on our World* Discovery Gallery for children at Horniman, when the Education Department worked intensely with a Children's Panel and independent consultants to ensure the exhibition themes and programming activities would be appropriately engaging.

At a practical level the UDHR and CRC Articles resonate with the radical feminist-hermeneutic pedagogy I shall detail presently as well the Songhay Peoples of Niger's advice that we 'must learn to sit with people … to sit and listen', which collaborative praxis during the 'Inspiration Africa!' project profitably took to heart (Stoller 1989: 128). It will be helpful here at the outset to outline certain features of this collaborative project work, which applies to both chapters.

I shall start with a demographic outline of the fieldsite. Next I shall consider the key team leaders. Then I offer an overview of the project. Following this brief account of 'Inspiration Africa!' I will be in a better position to highlight the structure of each subsequent chapter and the particular aspects to be covered.

'Inspiration Africa!' Field-site, Team-leaders and Outreach Work

The 'Inspiration Africa!' field-site I consider in the final two chapters is a frontier location between the Horniman Museum and local schools in the London Borough of Lewisham. The notion of a frontier field-site importantly dislodges hierarchical notions of museum as vital centre reaching out to promote creativity and learning in a subservient community at the periphery, which might be implied in 'outreach' activity, which we have considered. During 'Inspiration Africa!' outreach involved taking handling objects into school field-sites. Outreach was important prior to beginning the multifaceted 'Inspiration Africa!' projects to negotiate the most appropriate theme and activities across the curriculum together with teachers and pupils and to maintain momentum during the project with Lewisham schools, which were situated in geographical areas of 'deprivation' (Ofsted 1999). A brief outline of the demographics of Lewisham will illuminate this point.

Lewisham is a multicultural area of south London, which is disadvantaged by poverty. In 2002 the Index of Multiple Deprivation (IMD) shows that 16 percent of the population of Lewisham live in 'wards in the top 10 percent most deprived wards in England' (Lewisham Strategic Plan 2002: 19). This statement is based on 'six domain indices: Income, Employment, Health Deprivation and Disability, Education Skills and Training, Housing, and Geographical Access to Services', which are combined to form an overall score on the Index (ibid.). The Office for standards in education (Ofsted) made a report in 1999, which highlights the combined effect that these factors of economic deprivation have on creativity and learning in the borough. The report notes states that Lewisham is:

> ... the third largest London Borough and one of the most diverse. It is home to a *vibrant mix of communities*. In schools 50% of the population is black or from another minority ethnic group and 121 different languages are spoken. Between January 1998 and January 1999, 583 pupils new to English were admitted to Lewisham schools as casual admissions. Most of these were refugees. Though thus *culturally rich* it is *economically poor*, the 14th most deprived district in England according to the Department of the Environment, Transport, and the Regions index. 32.7% of its primary pupils and 39.1% of its secondary pupils are entitled to free school meals, there is a high proportion of lone parent families, youth unemployment is high, 30% of young people past school leaving age have no experience of work, and there is a high level of youth crime. *Levels of literacy* and numeracy amongst many of the population *are low*. (Ofsted 1999:4) [my emphasis]

The 'Inspiration Africa!' research team were able to build on the Horniman Museum's six years of collaborative experience dealing with the two contrasting factors of *cultural wealth* and *economic poverty* at the Lewisham field-site, which Ofsted highlights. Similarly the Cloth of Gold Arts Company and the visiting artists, musician and storytellers came to the project with an impressive track record of successful collaborative work in developing pupil's *literacy* and art skills, which in part at least determined the focus of work during 'Inspiration Africa!'

'Inspiration Africa!' Project Aims, Activities and Team-leaders

In September 1999 the Department for Education and Skills (DfES) approved 80 Museums and Galleries Education Projects (MGEPs) to encourage collaboration across institutions and across traditional subject boundaries. The DfES awarded Horniman Museum £72,000 to fund an innovative Museums and Galleries Education Project (MGEP) entitled 'Inspiration Africa!', which had four main aims to: explore and expand pupils responses to African Objects; encourage and stimulate creativity; develop skills in ICT (Information and Computer Technology) Art and language, and increase respect for African culture.

The DfES funding permitted twelve schools from south London to participate in 'Inspiration Africa!' and each school choose one class and one a key object from the African Worlds exhibition to base their project work on. Six of the twelve schools were located in the borough of Lewisham and six in the borough of Bromley, with two special, two primary and two secondary schools selected from each borough.

At each school the 'Inspiration Africa!' team-leaders comprised four people: Tony Minion as Cloth of Gold Artist/project co-ordinator; Jacqui Callis as website developer/artist; myself as Horniman outreach worker and Olusola Oyelele as Writer/director. Three other African Caribbean professionals were employed for some projects: Amoafi Kwappong as storyteller/musician, Ayo Thomas as musician/storyteller and Andrew Ward as rap poet/musician. Because the Cloth of Gold workers were white, a policy decision was taken at the outset of the project, before the funding application, that the poet, storyteller or musician should be of African or Caribbean heritage. In this way it was hoped that the people who delivered the curriculum would positively reflect the museum objects that formed the inspiration for the curriculum content, which research shows positively to impact on achievement (Gilborn 1995). It may be important to state here that the 'Inspiration Africa!' team leaders were not arguing that only African heritage people could adequately teach African themed museum projects. We believe that interest and commitment are more important than accidents of birth. Furthermore, the possibility of intercultural understanding determines a view that cultures are not fixed or hermetically sealed from each other. However, working in a multicultural society with African objects, and with an overriding concern for equality and social justice, it simply seemed logical to recruit team members with different skills and interests.

A non-hierarchical teamwork approach was adopted from the beginning of the 'Inspiration Africa!' partnership. At each school the teams of four always worked alongside the class teacher and the classroom assistants, pooling their knowledge and expertise to promote pupil learning through creative effort. The four person strong 'Inspiration Africa!' team took the role of project leaders and held regular meetings to ensure that everyone was clear about their particular responsibilities during the project, took ownership of the project work and felt committed to its success. These team leader meetings were held at the beginning, middle and end of each project. At the outset of each project a half-day brainstorming session was organised at the museum, where Jacqui Callis and I provided information on the particular artifact that served as the key object and the special cultural context that surrounded this artifact. These meetings were creative sessions where the team felt at complete ease in each other's company, sharing food and ideas for an appropriate key word and a sentence web that might inspire imaginative effort and raise the literacy levels in the particular pupil group. Perhaps it may be said that theoretically grounded practice was built around the kitchen table where the project activities were developed (Hill-Collins 1991).

The broad 'Inspiration Africa!' aims were achieved through a variety of project activities. The activities included: an In service Training for Teachers (INSET) with participating educators; an introductory visit to school – handling and discussing museum objects, story telling, working on Information and Computer Technology (ICT) and textile screen printing; a visit to the African Worlds exhibition with museum workshops; five days of workshops at school with a poet/storyteller/ musician, an artist and myself as Horniman educator – producing creative writing, music and artwork, investigating and contributing to the dedicated website and finally adding their own images to the virtual banner with the 'cogprog' media tool.

As well as the vital face-to-face interaction with each other and objects, experiences were virtually shared between participants via the website by creatively interacting and exploring the use of e-mail and the world-wide-web. In a sense the dedicated 'Inspiration Africa!' website provided a vital 'contact zone', for example to extend the discussion that artifacts prompted during the museum visit, by providing each participating school with an individual school space as well as a series of communal 'chat' spaces (Clifford 1999). In this way pupils from different schools could take pride in each other's achievements, which were professionally displayed on the school site promptly at the end of each 'Inspiration Africa!' session. This immediacy made each stage of the project work more meaningful to the students and aided reflection on the days activities by means of the visual, textual and aural prompts on the website. Seeing photographs of themselves with the unfamiliar objects and playfully engaged with each other also proved a motivating factor.

While pupils from the different schools were engaged in separate projects they could exchange ideas and discuss the progress of their creative efforts by leaving messages on the bulletin board. Callis notes how the web provided a 'safe' location complementing the museum visit and poetry composition. On the web pupils were able to express their 'very caring' self and share their more private feelings outside of face-to-face interaction (Callis 2002: 28). However while the pupils were impressed with the new technological aspects of the project, which provided a useful connection to their daily lives as twentieth century citizens and the museum objects from both ancient and contemporary Africa, it was the 'real thing', objects, which added the 'wonder and resonance' factors that lay at the heart of the project work (Pearce 1994; Greenblatt 1991).

Objects, ideas and issues from the *African Worlds* exhibition in the South Hall Gallery of Horniman (then only permanent UK gallery dedicated to African related Cultures) as well as the contemporary concerns of young visitors inspired the ambitious 'Inspiration Africa!' partnership project. An object-based route to affective learning was privileged during the project alongside the more traditional cognitive routes to knowledge, which the UK school curriculum must focus upon. That all of the project work was designed to spring from a close attention to museum objects and also the socio-cultural and political background from whence the objects sprang facilitated border crossing and creative linking of the curriculum areas – the new technologies of Internet/web-based learning with established textile printing processes, literacy, performance and music. This enabled pupils to produce an exciting, vibrant and diverse array of expressive outcomes stimulated by the 12 key objects from the African Worlds exhibition, which they were able to show off at the end of project exhibition.

The pupil's achievements were displayed for three months in the 'Inspiration Africa!' exhibition, which was hosted on the Balcony Gallery overlooking the *African Worlds* Exhibition in the South Hall of Horniman. At the well-attended launch some of the pupils performed some of their poetry to critical acclaim, which included members of the local advisory services. Additionally the public evaluation was overwhelmingly positive, importantly showing previously negative perceptions of a single stereotyped African identity might be challenged while the museum as a static boring space could be transformed (<http://www.clothofgold. org.uk/inafrica> accessed on 03.12 2008). A brief outline of research into the value of countering stereotype will illuminate this aspect of 'Inspiration Africa!'

Challenging Racist Stereotype to Promote New Identities and a Sense of Belonging

David Milner's seminal study into racial preference explored the preferences of 300 Black and white children for Black or white dolls and images, in which children were asked which dolls or image they preferred and which dolls most resembled themselves (Milner 1983). Maureen Stone has criticised this research as pure victim theory overemphasising self-hate and racial misidentification, while oversimplifying social factors including the stereotyping of Black dolls as the naughty 'golliwogs who no-one wanted to play with' in the literature of the time because they 'didn't like their black faces' (Stone 1985: 55-6).

Iram Siraj-Blatchford however has recently built on Milner and her research into Nursery children – under five years old – demonstrates that racist attitudes exist in some very young Black and white children. She cites a number of examples including white children who refused to put their boots into a bag with 'Packi' (a short-hand derogatory term for Pakistan) writing on it, which was upsetting for the children of Pakistan heritage in the class, but also she argues detrimental to the white children. Siraj-Blatchford notes Kutner's evidence in support of this claim, which demonstrates, 'young white children who are racist have a distorted perception of reality', and further that, 'their ability to judge and reason is also affected' (Siraj-Blatchford 1994: 8). She emphasises 'the need to offer all children guidance and support in developing positive attitudes to all people, and in particular black people' (Siraj-Blatchford 1994: 5). Following Milner, Siraj-Blatchford argues that some Black children and some white children can be severely damaged by the racist views, which surround them and strongly recommends teachers develop an antiracist-multicultural curriculum, to provide all children with the tools necessary to challenge racism in society.

Conclusion

Against a limiting historical background that tended to rather unthinkingly essentialise and fix very young children within a single ethnic identity, Horniman Museum has worked hard to represent a more complex picture of identities, of similarities and differences within as well as between socio-cultural groups (Golding 2007a). Next I shall examine the new theory-based practice at Horniman with reference to some success stories during 'Inspiration Africa!'

First in Chapter 5 I show 'Inspiration Africa!' tackling Black underachievement in school through holistic mind and body museum approaches including drama and language activities, which helped pupils construct more positive and essentially hybrid identities (Hall 1996). The project work here that prompts motivation and 'flow' learning is based on dialogical exchange with a Haitian Shrine and an Igbo ijele housed in Horniman (Csikszentmihalyi 1995).

Then in Chapter 6 I shall critically consider creative work with an Ashante stool housed in Horniman. The major themes of this chapter include the concept of active learning, which I address with reference to a feminist 'both and' notion of the 'power to' see, hear, move, and speak (Foucault 1980). These powers are linked in the chapter to embodied knowledge gained through handling that is most beneficial to the group of children with special learning needs.

Chapter 5
Identity: Motivation and Self-esteem

Introduction

Stuart Hall connects identity with active enunciation. He states.

> Or is quite a different practice entailed – not the rediscovery but the *production of identity*. Not an identity grounded in the archaeology, but in the *re-telling* of the past? (Hall 1996: 111) [my emphasis]

The museum frontiers provide an excellent location for the articulation of identity, which can be motivating for non-traditional audiences and especially for pupils in danger of disaffection. Young people of 13 and 14 years old who teachers note as troubled with hormonal changes that further de-motivates their classroom learning, can find it especially helpful to reflect on and write about the complex feelings that contribute to the production of identity. Let us look at one example of a pupil expressing her state of inner turmoil, which the teacher thought may have led to bad behaviour at school, and subsequently periods of exclusion.

> All I want is my independence. / *Free speech*, free *spirit*, free my whole *life*. / If that were to happen where would I be? ... I have a normal life but *deep down* its terrible. / I'm like a Gemini. / There are two sides to a story. / I'm happy on the *outside*. / And hurting on the *inside*. / For me to feel this way. / There must be something wrong. / ... What the hell is going on? (Year 9 pupil, Telegraph Hill School) [My emphasis][1]

This poem was produced during a museum/school curriculum that was informed by antiracist-multiculturalism and in this chapter I shall first consider the notions of multiculturalism and antiracism as well as the newer term interculturalism, which the UK government has recently been concerned with, and which is the subject of a 2008 Council of Europe *White Paper* (<http://www.coe.int/t/dg4/intercultural/Source/White%20Paper_final_revised_EN.pdf> accessed on 03.01.2009). I point to the distinguishing features of these concepts while arguing for the underlying value that lies at the heart of them all, with reference to recent government policy and research into the underachievement of Black pupils (Cantle 2002; Gilborn and Mirza 2000).

---

1 I protect the identities of the poets throughout for ethical reasons. I feel privileged that the poets have shared a deal of private and painful information with me, but this sharing was situated and not for wider publication.

Then I briefly outline elements of my theoretical positioning, feminist-hermeneutics, which grew out of antiracist-multiculturalism and determined the practical approach taken with museum objects during 'Inspiration Africa!' Next, I justify the rather large claims made for my particular theoretical perspective by demonstrating how the theory works in practice with personal reference to the Haitian Voudou shrine, which was the key object for creative effort around the key word 'spirit' for Year 9 pupils at Telegraph Hill Secondary School during their 'Inspiration Africa!' project. Following this I shall offer further justification by investigating the imaginative work produced by Telegraph Hill pupils. Then I shall expand upon the method which echoes in Freirian critical pedagogy with reference to work by Year 6 pupils at Christchurch Primary School whose key 'Inspiration Africa!' object was the Igbo ijele and whose key word was 'pride'.[2]

Overall, my focus on the Telegraph Hill and Christchurch projects will highlight the use or value of a theory, which is derived from a feminist-hermeneutic process, to interpretive educational work at the museum/school frontiers. I aim to show that such praxis can result not only in a wealth of creative outcomes, but also a more positive attitude to life for this museum audience. I further argue that theoretically informed collaborative praxis helped promote community cohesion by aiding pupils' critical thought and communication. In short I claim that feminist-hermeneutics brings to the centre of critical dialogical exchange, possible roots of inclusion and exclusion in social, economic, political and cultural systems, as well as the necessary actions to counter injustice. This is rather a large claim and some background information may prove helpful before proceeding.

Multiculturalism, Antiracism and Interculturalism

In the 1980s and 1990s 'race riots' according to much media reporting, or 'uprisings' in the words of some political analysis, was seen in UK cities including: my home Brixton, London (1981, 1985 and 1995); Liverpool (1981, 1985, 1995); Birmingham (1981, 1985); Bristol (1980) and Bradford (1995). These disturbing events occurred in multicultural and multiracial areas and involved large numbers of young people including African Caribbean youth.

---

2   These UK school year groups may need clarification for international readers. In the UK Year 6 pupils are aged between ten and eleven years old. Year 6 pupils are in the final year of Primary School and at the end of Key Stage 2, which starts for children aged between eight and nine years old. Year 9 pupils are aged between thirteen and fourteen years of age. Year 9 is the last year of Key Stage 3, which is of three years duration and starts at Year 7. These are key years for pupils. Year 6 is the year before pupils leave for Year 7 at a secondary school, which is determined by their progress in Year 6. Year 9 is the year before Key Stage 4 when UK pupils begin the two-year General Certificate of Education (GCSE) examination courses, upon which their future job prospects depend. The Qualification and Curriculum Authority (QCA) provide information online (<http://curriculum.qca.org.uk/> accessed on 22.08.2007).

In the first decade of the twenty-first century violent unrest continued to occur in parts of England, notably Bradford, Oldham, Leeds and Burnley (2001), where large communities of South Asian (Indian, Pakistani and Bangladeshi) heritage people lived. Ted Cantle's Report following these troubles notes extreme separation between communities as a major factor in the disturbances. He observes the 'physical segregation in our towns and cities and the depths of polarisation to which this led between communities', and goes on to state:

> Whether in respect of separate educational arrangements, community and voluntary bodies, employment, places of worship, language, social and cultural networks, many communities were operating on the basis of a series of *parallel lives*. Often, these lives did not seem to touch at any point, let alone overlap or promote meaningful interchanges. (Report of the Independent Review Team <http://www.oldham.gov.uk/cantle-review-final-report.pdfpage11> accessed on 12.12.2008) [my emphasis]

To address the culture clash arising when communities emerge from their 'parallel lives', the concept of 'interculturalism' was developed in line with the new labour government agenda on community cohesion. This highlighted the importance of nurturing a sense of 'belonging' to a wider national community and sharing 'common values', alongside the need for people to 'treat each other with courtesy and respect', so that communities are not 'disfigured by racism or other forms of prejudice' (Cantle 2002: 14). Interculturalism was heralded as a new idea, distinct from the older multiculturalism and antiracism. In the context of education Jagdish Gundara highlights the key issue of interculturalism as the promotion of a sense of 'belonging' and 'inclusion' rather than marginalisation, which is seen as crucial for the future of the wider community as a cohesive whole rather than a number of isolated social groups (Gundara 2000).

I take Gundara's remarks on school education to include museums and agree that museums cannot solve all the problems of the world alone but need to adopt a 'multi-agency' approach as Macpherson advised, as well as meaningful museum-community links, so that chauvinistic and fundamentalist parents do not undo interculturalist work (Macpherson 1999: 45.18, 45.20). Specifically museums need to value multilingualism; develop cross-cultural peer-group solidarities to help replace negative aspects with more constructive value systems; deal with xenophobic and racist behaviour; organise spaces and develop programmes so that children with different competencies can learn about each other and levels of cultural distance can be bridged, for example through clothing style, sport and music; develop a non-nationalistic curriculum or programme of studies respectful of diversity, welcoming of questions and criticisms to enable a negotiation of core values that must be held in common, which will recognise the dynamic hybridised culture of the UK that has for so long been enriched by outside (Gundara 2000: 65-81).

In this list we can observe considerable overlap between these interculturalist principles and 'antiracist multiculturalism', which the UK museum recognised in the last decades of the twentieth century. A brief background to the multicultural and antiracist debates may help readers plot the seemingly shifting terrain.

'Antiracists' criticised 'multiculturalists' during the late 1970s and 1980s for taking shallow and tokenistic approaches to diversity, which was exemplified by a single 'Diwali Celebration Day' or isolated events restricted to Black History Month in October. Antiracists argued against looking at surface details of 'exotic-other' cultures at set times on the margins of the curriculum and urged for extended and central attention to the historico-political framing and institutional structures of power within which racism functions. The debate was long and vociferous. Margaret Thatcher was our right-wing prime minister and her 'swamping' speech of January 1978 a year after Enoch Powers 'rivers of blood' speech made attempts to unite multiculturalism and antiracism urgent.

The fused notion of an 'antiracist multicultural strategy' that might potently reflect 'the diversity of cultures throughout the curriculum', so that 'insistent questions about justice and equality' remain 'in students' minds', was one attempt to heal the divide (Grinter 1985: 8-9). The hope was that 'sympathetic teaching of other value systems will weaken the hold of prejudices' and 'act as a form of inoculation against the future development of racist attitudes' (ibid. 7). Grinter echoed Stuart Hall's idea of, 'a kind of wager or bet that if we understand things better we might be able to unlock or shift them' (Hall 1980: 5). This optimistic view was widely mirrored by teachers working collaboratively with Horniman, 'understanding of other cultures is a challenge to racism, which feeds on ignorance and complacency', is a typical comment taken from a survey (Golding 2000: 157).

Understanding takes time. My 'Inspiration Africa!' colleagues distinguished 'antiracist multiculturalism' from racist 'tokenism' in museum education by: expanding the duration and content of the curriculum. Most importantly in museum school INSET locating similarity and difference at the heart of the learning process was deemed vital. Finding points of contact between the cultural lives of people and their objects at home and in the museum through dialogical exchange is the key here. In the museum we can draw attention to the human lives we lead: the clothes we wear and the foods we eat in different weather; our families and our friends in this place and around the world; the games we play; the music we listen to; the way we celebrate important events like birthdays, weddings, and mourn our dead; how we select our leaders; why we fight our wars; what kind actions are to be praised; what cruelties should be punished and how. All this is indicative of thorough and detailed museum/school teaching strategies, to challenge bias and racism by facilitating 'human empathy' and noting human similarities through differences, which I shall now outline with reference to methodology (Gilroy 1994b: 57).

Ethnographic Research at the Museum/School Frontiers, London

The 12 'Inspiration Africa!' projects resulted from the endeavour over two years of a small four-person research team, who drew on elements of contemporary anthropology to inform their method. As practitioners we operated from a self-reflective and feminist stance, which aimed to understand individual meaning or sense-making within particular social worlds, and most importantly to stand in a political position with the peopled field of research (Clifford 1994, 1997; Clifford and Marcus 1989; Bell et al. 1993). As researchers we were 'not satisfied with exposing power relations' but actively worked 'to overcome these relations' through facilitating an expression of deepening thought processes about museum objects, 'other' cultures and ourselves (Mascia-Lees 1989: 33).

Towards this end as team leaders we occupied subject positions that shifted between speaking and listening, teaching and learning that overturned the traditional power and voice relationships between museum and audience, teacher and pupil. The multiple voiced text at the website highlights the possibilities for a reflective 'thinking together' that was achieved during research listening to the peopled field of research (<http://www.clothofgold.org.uk/inafrica> accessed on 18.08.2008).

Feminist-hermeneutics entered into 'Inspiration Africa!' essentially to contest silences and invisibilities from the position of the pupils, who were multiply 'disadvantaged' according to the local government statistics cited earlier, largely through imaginative means: story telling, creative writing, music and art. Clifford contends, the methodological technique of writing a 'poetic collage' of various 'key informant' voices from the field-site, does not require abandoning 'facts and accurate accounting for the supposed free play of poetry', since 'poetry is not limited to romantic or modernist subjectivism: it can be historical, precise, objective' (Clifford 1986: 25-6).

Clifford's statement echoes the feminist-hermeneutic concept of new *verstehen* or understanding, which is premised on feminist ethics an, 'ethics of care' that prioritises notions of striving to achieve equality between researcher and researched (Hill-Collins 1991). In contrast with the distanced and hierarchical 'objectivity' of much traditional social science, feminist ethics strives for non-hierarchical collaboration in the construction of a 'poetic collage', and as far as possible joint ownership of the research study (Roberts 1981). This concept is distinct from the simplistic idea of an anonymous researcher 'giving voice' to the researched. The poetic Year 9 voices in this chapter arise from a theoretical perspective that demands and facilitates openness from the researcher and the researched. I shall emphasise this point with reference to a key object of 'Inspiration Africa!' project work, the Haitian Voudou shrine.

Plate 21 Haitian Voudou Shrine, *African Worlds* **at the Horniman Museum, 2004**
Source: © Heini Schnebeli.

Feminist-hermeneutic Dialogue Informed by Mindful Emotional Exchange

The Haitian Voudou shrine, which is on display in the *African Worlds* exhibition can be seen at Plate 21. Horniman Museum's voudou shrine houses a wealth of powerful artifacts, the strongest alcohols, the most pungent perfumes and the richest most vibrantly coloured objects. There is a fertile synthesis of elements from traditional West African and Christian religions as well as contemporary images from popular television and film culture such as Fred Flintstone and Darth Vader. Extreme levels of economic poverty, 70-80 percent of the population lives below the absolute poverty level, necessitate a highly creative approach to the construction of sacred objects for the voudou altars, which are often recycled from discarded rubbish by Haitian artists (Cope 1999).

This combination of objects hold multiple and complex meanings for visitors to this anthropology display as two examples will illustrate. There is a large construction in the centre of the shrine embedded with a collection of broken dolls that were initially read as aborted foetus by some visiting teachers during INSET, rather than the symbols of special children intended by the originating communities. To the right of this art work there is a small wooden cigar box that once contained the strongest Cuban Havana's and inside there are photographs of Reg Jones, my first love and myself, taken in 1971 when we were beginning life as art students at Goldsmiths College London and escaping our parent's working class expectations of secure but dull 'jobs for life.' The photos are wrapped in two sheets of poems written to Reg 12 years later by some children in his art class who were writing as part of a mechanism to cope with the shock of his sudden death in a mountaineering accident.

The cigar box stores a personal story of death and connection. It points to a way of gaining personal relevance from an anthropology collection whose history and meaning is remote from the lives of most people in the western world of the twenty-first century and my research partners asked me to share it with the Year 9 children beginning their '*Inspiration Africa!*' project. I was inspired to share this part of my history by Renato Rosaldo's moving account of his feelings – grief and rage – following his wife Michelle's accidental death, which powerfully illuminates the way emotional life can positively permeate intellectual explanations and cross-cultural understandings. It was through acknowledging the range of his own terrible grieving emotions that Renato Rosaldo came closer to the Ilonglot men's headhunting ways of dealing with grief, through feeling.

Michelle and Renato Rosaldo's accounts of the headhunters shame and rage are interesting from the perspective of embodied knowledge. Michelle Rosaldo's account of the headhunter's shame casts light on the notion of seeing as widely equated with understanding in the West (Rosaldo 2005). In her text we understand thinking as connected with weighing and knowledge as gained through looking, smelling and holding. She speaks of the 'hearts of Ilonglot men 'burdened with the 'weight' of insult, envy, pain and grief' being afforded some relief by tossing a newly severed head to the ground. Rosaldo notes how when on occasion an Ilongot appears paralysed with the 'heaviness' of the 'smell of blood', an older Ilinglot cuts a lock of the afflicted's hair and calls loudly for 'lightness' to affect relief. She points out that the feelings and emotions, notably shame that are evoked in describing this weight that enters the body freezing and sickening 'the heart' have socio-cultural roots, which are not to be equated with the English metaphor 'frozen with fear' but rather associated with the role of the individual men within, or most usually as bachelors outside of, the social family group.

The importance of this account for me lies in clarifying the ways emotion impacts on intellect and behaviour in the West just as in Ilonglot culture, where we see 'emotion is the fluid, motile part of an individual's conscious life, identity' and has an affect on 'decision making' (Rosaldo 2005: 206). I retell the voudou shrine, the Ilonglot and my narratives of grief here because they illustrate a vital part of the research team's theoretical location in feminist-hermeneutics, a determined breaking down of the *either or* inherent in dualist thought such as emotion *or* intellect, life *or* death. These stories indicate a rupturing of the hierarchies of power and control separating the lofty researchers simply gathering stories from the researched, through the opening up of a new truly respectful dialogical space between equal partners where both question *and both* answer. As I opened a distressing aspect of my personal life and showed a creative way of dealing with this – finding a place to put my grief – this presented pupils with the possibility of employing a similar coping mechanism. It certainly seemed to facilitate an exploration of difficult personal issues through the creative media of poetry, drama and art at Telegraph Hill.

The Telegraph Hill research team follow Paulo Freire's pedagogy here, which aims to promote pupils' critical thought. Towards this end we do not behave as teacher subjects simply imparting knowledge or sets of skills to students, who are treated as objects – empty bank vaults waiting to be filled with deposits of knowledge. We rather strive to turn the power relations inherent in teaching and research around and respect our pupils as equal subjects by listening and learning about their life-world, since it is only from this position of mutuality that research and teaching might increase understanding, by opening a space of dialogical exchange that is central to feminist-hermeneutics, as I shall outline (Freire 1996: 30).

Entering Dialogue and Combating Prejudice

Most importantly, feminist-hermeneutic dialogue in the museum describes a mutually respectful process of interpretation and understanding, in which each partner in the conversation exhibits openness and kindness, towards the interlocutor and the self. However it is not a simple matter for people from disadvantaged backgrounds to enter such dialogical exchange and so there is a 'pedagogical responsibility' here to 'ensure that the other person is with us' and gains a 'productive attitude', through gentle 'questioning responsiveness' to aspects of lived experience which arise (Gadamer 1981: 264, 330; Gadamer 1980: 46). Such questioning can shatter what appears to be negative 'fixed criterion' and make us aware that possibilities are 'fluid' (Gadamer 1981: 107, 330). In this Gadamer's position is not one of extreme relativism as dialogical work aims to reach understanding in language that we share in common. He states.

> Hence the meaning of a text is not to be compared with an immovably and obstinately fixed point of view which suggests only one question to the person who is trying to understand it ... We can see that this is the full realisation

of conversation, in which something is expressed that is not only mine or the author's, but common. (Gadamer 1981: 350)

However for Gadamer interpretation and understanding in dialogical exchange can be hampered by 'prejudices' that are also known as preconceptions or fore-knowledge, which comprise part of our lived-experience in a social world and are inescapably part of the language through which they are expressed. In the museum the 'will of our knowledge must be directed towards escaping their thrall' in language, which marks 'a central point' of convergence where 'I-Thou' and world meet (Gadamer 1981: 431, 446). Prejudices are only detrimental to the hermeneutic task of understanding objects and other people if they remain 'imperceptible habits of thought', alternatively they can assist the hermeneutical process if the interpreter uses 'one's own preconceptions so that the meaning of a text can really be made to speak for us', which is possible if we are prepared to truly 'listen' (Gadamer 1981: 236, 358). As Gadamer poetically elucidates.

A person who does not accept that he is dominated by prejudices will fail to experience the "Thou" truly as a "Thou", i.e. not to overlook his claim and to listen to what he has to say to us. To this end openness is necessary. ... anyone who listens is fundamentally open. ... Belonging together always also means being able to listen to one another. (Gadamer 1981: 324)

The process whereby 'foreconceptions are replaced by more suitable ones' is clarified with reference to the concept of the 'hermeneutic circle', which describes a structural movement of understanding; a state of perpetual motion between 'the whole and the parts and back to the whole' (Gadamer 1981: 236, 259). With the Haitian shrine our eyes focus in on Fred Flintstone, move to Darth Vader onto the cigar box with Viv's secrets. There is also a switching where our eyes move across the parts to take in the relationships in the whole display. This is a dynamic 'circle of understanding' and 'positive possibility ... of knowing' rather than a 'vicious circle', which applied to museum learning promises change and transformation of limited prejudiced views on voudou (ibid. 235-6).

Prejudices inevitably arise out of the traditions and belief systems into which we are born and for Gadamer it is 'the tyranny of hidden prejudices' which deafens us to the knowledge and broader understanding of ourselves, in relation to the traditions of others. Tradition here represents both the present-day 'horizon' of the interpreter in London, and the distant 'horizon' from which the object of interpretation originates in Haiti. The Telegraph Hill interpreters who aim to gain understanding of the other tradition, connect with its contemporaneity, its meaning 'for us', which I emphasised in my story of Reg's death. Understanding then is a creative process characterised by putting the beliefs of one's tradition 'at risk', in a 'fusion of horizons' with another tradition (ibid. 239). Furthermore the relationship of fused horizons involves a special recognition 'which does not leave him who has it unchanged' (Gadamer 1981: 89).

Tradition then is not 'something alien' but 'a part of us ... a recognition of ourselves', who are not fixed but capable of growth through dialogical engagement and understanding that is continuous (Gadamer 1981: 250). In the broad context of museum learning the lack of fixity in the face of tradition implies an increased faculty for self-development, a capacity for resistance and creative departure, as I shall outline in this chapter with reference to the pupils' creative writing. Thus philosophical hermeneutics as a discipline of radical museum education can bring interpretors to a 'state of new intellectual freedom' in the hermeneutic circle of understanding where 'horizons fuse' in an 'I-Thou' dialogue (ibid. 231). This is a borderland, an in-between location.

> The place between strangeness and familiarity that a transmitted text has for us is that *intermediate place between* being an historically intended separate object and being part of a tradition. The true home of hermeneutics is in this intermediate area. (Gadamer 1981: 262-3) [my emphasis]

To clarify the process of feminist-hermeneutic dialogue I have drawn the elements of a feminist-hermeneutic circle of understanding at Figure 5.1, which describes the circular process of increasing understanding. In short the circle shows all understanding is predicated on a notion of respectful *dialogue* with another: a speaker, or an object of art. For successful communication and understanding participants need an open *reflexive attitude*, to reflect upon *prejudices*, which inevitably arise out of particular world-views or personal histories and the wider *traditions* from whence these emerge.

The figure shows this process of understanding can never be completed, but only adjourned when participants decide to halt discussion, for there is always the possibility of resuming dialogue again on another occasion. It is in this sense that the *present* moment of understanding must draw elements of the *past* histories, including lived experience [erlebnis in German], and project elements of *future* perspectives or *horizons* into this circular location of understanding.

This viewpoint helps to increase opportunities for creativity, learning and intercultural understanding in a museum and community context because it does not elide and erase diversity but facilitates understanding in and through the complexities of difference. Furthermore Figure 5.1 shows how feminist-hermeneutics in the museum also requires us to pay careful attention to *artifacts* from our contemporary position in dialogical exchange, which ultimately involves *self-reflection*, a *transformation* of our prejudiced opinions in the light of continuing new knowledge and ultimately a perpetual *growth of the self*.

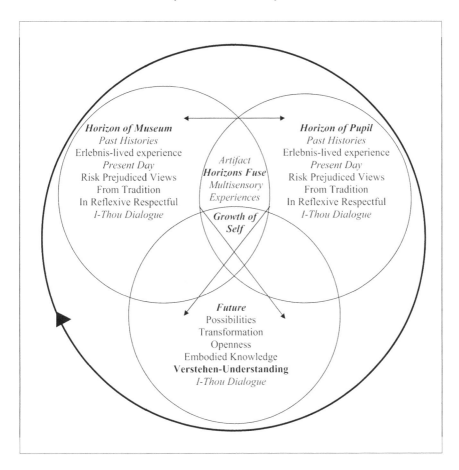

Figure 5.1 Feminist-hermeneutic circle of understanding

The feminist-hermeneutic circle of understanding is thus vitally empowering because it facilitates a re-construction of what counts as knowledge in the museum and extends this understanding to the wider world, which permits new identities to be formed and extended possibilities for future lives to be realised. Feminist-hermeneutic praxis shows the museum frontiers can be locations where individuals might risk their prejudices or comfortable notions of themselves and change their traditional group allegiances. For example, the nature of feminist-hermeneutic work at the frontiers between the museum and the school requires a more flexible approach, which may necessitate a movement from traditional groups that are established either by ability levels or by friendship sets. In these new positions individuals come face-to-face with the taken for granted prejudices inherent in their cultural traditions, which opens them to a transformation that is liberating because it constitutes a 'demolition and shattering of the familiar' way of perceiving the world and the peoples of the world. The new view widens individual horizons, by pointing to new aspects of the self in declaring 'this art thou' and also demanding that 'Thou must alter thy life!' (Gadamer 1977: 104).

A close examination of first Telegraph Hill pupils' creative activity and outcomes during 'Inspiration Africa!' will illustrate these points. Then an outline of the Christchurch pupils' work will reinforce this position.

Dis-ease and Denial

A poem can condense intense feeling and express complex emotions concisely. As one poet at Telegraph Hill wrote:

> *My heart, mind, body and soul are crying out* for love and compassion. / ... My life is like a big room with *nothing* inside of it, just *empty*. / It's like a *waste of space*. It's like an empty cup, *waiting* for the milk to pour. (Year 9 pupil) [my emphasis]

This poet was able to convey strong feelings of dread, being '*nothing ... empty ... a waste* of space' towards the end of '*Inspiration Africa!*' The project team leaders consider feelings of dread and low self-esteem, which were permitted to emerge gradually in Year 9 creative writing, point to one source of the pupils' negative school attitude and the subsequent poor performance that Ofsted highlighted. The local council were employing drastic measures such as exclusion alongside a series of cosmetic modifications to tackle the outward manifestations of pupil difficulties in concentration and learning, such as changing the school name from Hatchem Woods to Telegraph Hill in September 2001, during project work. In contradistinction the *Inspiration Africa* feminist-hermeneutic approach was premised on mutual questioning, listening and developing positive action.[3]

At the beginning of '*Inspiration Africa!*' Year 9 had little experience of using complex language and finding a range of words to express themselves. Their project keyword spirit conveys abstract ideas that can be difficult to discuss with the most articulate young people and Olusola Oyelele (Sola) began the first drama

---

3 As the underlying economic problems remained and were disregarded, it is not surprising that the pupil's unruly behaviour and low achievement largely continued, with the exception of the 'Inspiration Africa!' group although it must be admitted that the 'Inspiration Africa!' pupils did not always behave impeccably and act in a uniformly appreciative manner towards the team leaders, which resulted in Viv shouting 'BE QUIET AND LISTEN' for the first time in the research team's presence and Sola loudly exclaiming 'I AM ASHAMED OF YOU, I SEE ALL THESE BLACK FACES AND MY BLACK FACE IS ASHAMED' on one occasion. Yet over the course of the project work Year 9 exhibited extremely high degrees of motivation and produced exceptional work. The school was closed at the end of the academic year in July 2001.

session on the theme of spirit by reciting one of her poems, LOOK AT ME I'M SOMEBODY. This sharing of her work, in the open spirit of feminist-hermeneutic dialogue, rapidly established a respectful bond and strong rapport with the pupils. Sola's poem is based around the twice-repeated rhythmic phrase 'You see me, I'm somebody, I have S.P.I.R.I.T. You see me. I'm somebody. I have S.P.I.R.I.T.' The different elements that constitute a source of pride and selfhood for Sola are then inserted into the repeated phrase to build her individuality such as, 'You see my *SMILE*. I'm somebody. I have S.P.I.R.I.T.'

After Sola's dramatic recital the whole class had a brainstorming session around being somebody. They employed the 'frame sentence' technique, which provides a framework or scaffold for pupils to develop their thoughts and is useful for pupils who struggle to articulate in verbal language. Using the frames 'I am somebody because of ... (pupils complete the sentence)' and then 'We are somebody because of ...', they were able to produce this list of the determining factors that composed their individual and group identity that was linked to the key word spirit.

> We are somebody because of: the way we dress and the way we speak; our attitude towards people and the way we act and react; our different personalities; our religion and colour; the way we think and the way we believe in ourselves.

> The last thing is the way we are built, our spirit. Spirit means alcohol and it means somebody's soul.

The pupils found this frame poetry work a source of pleasure because in Csikszentmihalyi and Hermanson's terms it provided a rapidly achievable 'task that matched' and extended their existing 'skills', which involved some thought and gathering a group consensus of opinion through feminist-hermeneutic discussion (Csikszentmihalyi and Hermanson 1995). Sola also employed the form of acrostic poetry to provide another achievable expressive task for Year 9. Writing a word lengthways down the page begins the composition of an acrostic poem. The first letter of the word is then used to inspire the first word of each subsequent line of poetry. A spirit acrostic poem will illustrate this.

> Soul is your inner beauty or darkness
> Personality makes you what you are
> Intelligence, integrity, that's what makes you human
> Respect yourself, others and mother earth
> Identity is a cultural thing it represents who you are
> Trust yourself and life, you don't know what you've got until it's gone

Following this introductory work at school, Year 9 made a visit to African Worlds and a museum talk, which included my personal story about the shrine holding photographs that helped me deal with issues surrounding death. Pupils were then encouraged to brainstorm words to express feelings and to play with rhythm words, using specially designed worksheets asking them to look at the Haitian shrine and write down how it made them feel without worrying about spelling, grammar or correct answers. Here the museum/school pedagogy vitally counters the prevalent notions of value and absolute truth to include new Diaspora understandings especially the creative play with the rhythm of language at which African and Creole speakers can excel. Remembering that their keyword was spirit one worksheet required them to write rhyming words against their feeling words, which prompted the following pairs: strife/still life, amazing/aging, soothing/moving, jealous/fellows, potential/essential, relaxation/situation, sad/mad, complete/beat, crying/buying, fate/plate.

This playful activity was vital to maintain a balance between openly confronting sensitive issues like personal loss but not stagnating by excessive dwelling on this absence. It illustrates part of the 'to and fro' of feminist-hermeneutic conversation, much as the worksheets were intended to. For example one worksheet asked pupils 'what would you put in the Haitian shrine? Give your reasons why', which prompted the following remarks.

> A photo album because it would make me remember my family when they are dead.

> Something to represent every culture.

> My baby cousin's ashes.

> I would put a picture of my family and friends because without them I wouldn't know where I'd be, they are a real inspiration to me and I care about them a lot.

Family, friends and culture for this group were in London and around the world, predominantly in Africa and the Caribbean. Diaspora identities, especially a sense of 'doubling' were explored in performance activities that I turn to next (Du Bois 1999; Gilroy 1997).

Telling, Truth, Performance and the Body

At the third stage of the project back at school the class was split into two groups who swapped activities and team-leaders at lunchtime, so that everyone experienced a drama session with Sola and ICT work with Jacqui. In the Drama session pupils were asked to make tableau vivant or still picture sculptures with their bodies for the words SOUL, SPIRIT and POWER. This silent work with the expressive powers of the body proved helpful to expanding the notion of articulation. The body sculptures focused attention on body language and the extreme difficulties of enunciation when dealing with sensitive issues. Students were alerted to the suffering inscribed in certain positions that the body takes under duress as well as the fake bravado postures that they admitted to adopting when feeling fearful of 'getting shown up, looking stupid or making mistakes'.

Two scenarios were particularly helpful to pupils building an improvisation on the tableau vivant. In *Guardian Angel* (GA) pupils worked in pairs or trios with one student taking the part of the guardian angel to reflect on their lives. Sola gave a framework for the drama. She stated.

> Your guardian angel has come to tell you something about your life. To warn you about the way you are living your life. What does he/she say to you? What were you doing when this event happened?

In one pair GA was invisible but warned her subject to think with her mind and not only with her heart. She identified three areas of life needing improvement: going out with older boys, experimenting with drugs and staying out late on the streets 'looking for men' or 'fit boys'. GA asked her 'to think hard' and 'to change her ways'. The subject asks the guardian angel 'is this a joke?' as she watches TV, but the guardian angel answers her it is not. Another pair took the theme of trying to work in a rowdy environment. Trying to stay focused when there is disruption around and how hard it is not to join the crowd. GA encouraged the girl to stick to her principles, although hard, she would gain 'benefits later with better life prospects'. A third male and female student pair, a couple in real life, dealt with relationships in school and how they can be both enriching but also distracting regarding schoolwork. Here the female GA talked to the young man who was in love and unable to concentrate on anything but the girl. All the scenarios provided a vital focus for bringing the internal thoughts of young people and their perceived challenges in life to a verbal level and more objective consideration.

This drama session ended with a sit-down name game, re-establishing the dynamics of the individual students and giving them a dramatic opportunity to 'cut some style', as Sola observed. The name game lightly builds on the intense tableau vivant to extend the idea of body language as a potent means of communication. Pupils stand in a circle and everyone makes two loud handclaps and two silent handclaps in the air to a steady rhythm. In the gap or the silent handclaps the student must rapidly make a movement with their body to describe an aspect of themselves. Sola led this circle game calling out instructions 'in the gap' to the student response 'clap clap'. Sola's words and actions described how pupils could fill the short two silent claps of time 'say your name' and claim their space in the museum with their bodies. She emphasised the importance of making simple precise movements to articulate clearly rather than just wiggling all over and overstepping the two-clap time limit. Pupils joined in with the team leaders and revealed parts of their personality with a star jump, a thumb up or a cool shrug of the shoulder and head.

In the ICT sessions Jacqui and the team leaders moved the pupils' truth-telling aural work into writing, where new technology provided a potent means of sharpening thought and ideas. Jacqui also utilised a previous incident with a student to consider questions of truth and representation. Showing part of the website with a blurred out image of a student who had asked to be taken out of the picture she replaced this female pupils' image with another male pupil who volunteered to pose for the shot. This rapid and dramatic transformation from female to male student on the website demonstrated the possibility of adapting images or fabricating images and pertinently illustrated Jacqui's warning, 'don't believe all that you see'.

Technical ICT activities, like handling museum objects, provided essential playful release and maintained concentration for increasingly deep self-analysis. Such activity illustrates the diverse opportunities to examine underlying factors, or 'thoughts that lie hidden ... unsaid', often a complex mix of tragic life events resulting in emotional upheaval. Many pupils articulated feelings 'deep down', a 'happy outside' persona presented to the world, but concealing a 'hurting inside', as the poet noted at the outset of this chapter.

Year 9 pupils' suppressed anxieties varied. One poet was finally able to inscribe his feelings of intense love and gratitude to his father who he admires because, 'when my mum went he was there for me'. His poem acquaints us with a precise event that shatters the protected world all our children deserve. Another poet admits extreme loneliness stating 'I crave for some attention, for someone to notice me.' Confronting her dis-ease in creative writing and in feminist-hermeneutic dialogue she comes to realise that her attention-seeking 'bad-girl' behaviour is counter-productive and only serves to isolate her further. A more productive political attention is highlighted in some poems, as this example exemplifies.

> ... *How to speak, my thoughts are hidden, so much left unsaid.* / People say that colour counts but I think that it shouldn't. / Because *everyone is equal.* / Everyone has a *right to an opinion and to defend their case.* / Some people get into their minds that *white should stick to white, black to black and all other colours to their own.* / *But this is a multicultural society.*/ Some people say this is a white persons country. / It may be run by white people, but other *people still have a right to say what they want done.* / People still constantly ignoring us / but *they'll know we are speaking the truth.* (Year 9 pupil) [my emphasis]

This poem shows the value of bringing the root causes of pupil 'failure' and all the emotional baggage or feelings of worthlessness that accompanies this label to the political attention of the group. The young poet articulates an optimistic belief in multiculturalism and the importance of claiming equality through *speaking the truth.*

Next I shall expand upon these ideas with reference to Year 6 pupils at Christchurch Primary School. In the main I shall examine Christchurch work with reference to the critical pedagogy of Paulo Freire.

Christchurch School: Pride and the Horniman Ijele Mask

The Christchurch pupils engaged with the Igbo ijele as a key object and the key word 'pride' (see Plate 9, p. 70). I offer the first acrostic poem they composed as a group here at the outset, which highlights their initial ideas on the theme of pride, as part of their language work.

Pride comes before a fall
Race doesn't matter, it's what you are inside that counts
If you run before you can walk, you might end up falling
Don't throw stones if you live in a glass house
Everyone's proud of something

Connections, Disconnections, Inversions and Subversions in Dialogue

At Horniman Christchurch pupils heard about the Igbo people of Nigeria's rich tradition of expressive culture, notably the masquerade where the ijele mask, the largest in all of Africa carried by one person, features in the central performance. Ijele carries with it the authority of Igbo elders and ancestors who feature prominently in the lives of the whole community and to celebrate the opening of *African Worlds* in 1998 Horniman specially commissioned an ijele from Ichie Ezennaya of Achalla, Nigeria, which he constructed in brightly coloured appliquéd fabric and foam around a cane and bamboo frame, and assembled the following year at the museum.

Christchurch pupils were interested to hear of Ezennaya's long family history building the highly complex ijele, often taking a year to complete and involving contributions from the whole community in marking an important social and historic event. Thus community-owned ijele fosters a sense of collective ownership and community 'pride', the key word and focus for their project work. This theme held exciting possibilities for connecting with Igbo culture through cross-curricular work, for example pupils thought the idea of the ijele dancing to the 'music of kings' played on flutes and drums and taking regal steps in keeping with kings and elders, might be employed in a musical performance for the whole school, utilising the ijele they were going to make. There were however disagreements. In the to and fro of dialogue cognitive dissonance was strongly felt between certain of the beliefs and practices inherent in the Nigerian ijele and those of Christchurch. These revolved around what was perceived, as sexism. I shall explain this feeling that arose from two instances.

The pupils heard how in Igbo land a man carries the ijele mask by balancing it on his head and shoulders and performs dance movements in an open clearing in the centre of a town or village. The masquerade, which is likened to an elephant with its huge size and slow movements, occurs in rounds of only ten or twenty minutes at a time, since despite the lightweight materials its great size means it is extremely heavy. After listening with interest to the background information on the Horniman ijele and the tradition in Nigeria, Christchurch pupils commented: 'But why is it only a man that carries the ijele? Is that fair? I don't think so! I do! Can a girl carry our ijele? No! Yes!' While we called a halt to this heated, although important and highly interesting debate, we voiced our pleasure as team-leaders with the respectful way the comments were considered by the class and promised that we would all ponder this issue further over the next few days. Freire is helpful to pedagogy here. He states:

> I would recommend … each day be open to the world, be ready to think, … do not accept what is said just because it is said … reread what is read … investigate, question and doubt. (Freire 1985: 181)

It was eventually decided, by majority group decision, that in line with Freieian critical thinking – a girl would indeed perform Christchurch ijele – to break the 'glass ceiling', which the pupils had been discussing, at least in this local area of community life. The second instance where questions of prejudice and justice arose was during the first storytelling session at school, when a new storyteller-musician Ayo Thomas came to perform some traditional tales at the school with some of Horniman's handling collection. Ayo had been highly recommended by Sola Oyelele, who we had worked with on many projects, and he had performed extremely well at interview. However when Ayo travelled to the faith school with Jacqui it emerged that Ayo, a committed Christian newly arrived from Africa, held deeply homophobic views, which as team leader Jacqui strongly stressed were not acceptable to the project.

Ayo began his session at school by talking about the importance of names in Nigeria. He explained that his own name meant 'Joy comes to me' and why he was called this, without any homophobic references. Then he told the story of the 'Tortoise and the Elephant', which he performed with gusto and enthralled the pupils, especially when he – the elephant – comically wriggled his bottom at them to emphasise his pride! Ayo's story recalled how, one day, tortoise left his wife at home to save the village from a troublesome, rampaging elephant. His cunning trick to pander to elephant's pride and trap him in a pit was successful, whereupon he was able to marry the king's beautiful young daughter and inherit the kingdom. Pupils cried out 'Hooray! … But … wait … what of tortoise's first wife?' Again sexism reared its ugly head in conflict with the anti-racist aim of 'Inspiration Africa!

Discussion followed. Stories in Nigeria can be used to teach pupils about life and each story has many meanings. Year 5 pondered the meaning of the 'Tortoise and Elephant' story: 'Don't pay too much attention to strangers', 'Even if you are very small you can achieve great things' and 'Pride comes before a fall', which led to a general discussion about 'pride' and how it can have both negative and positive aspects. There was much concern for 'poor Mrs Tortoise, left at home alone' and so discussion turned to different endings, new beginnings, to what extent traditional tales might be creatively re-made in the telling and if this conflicted with the value of preserving an original – an authentic script. Questions immediately arise here. Who has the power of voice and should they retain this for all time? If a situation is unjust – leaving your old wife for a new one – should it be challenged as detrimental to the oppressed one, even if it was part of the traditional value system? Can we, in London, object to practices and beliefs in other countries? Surely some Africans, perhaps most especially older women, might object to sexist laws? Didn't many, many people around the world join Nelson Mandela's battle to challenge the old Apartheid laws of South Africa? Should good citizens the world over work together for social justice and human rights?

Freire is helpful in directing pedagogy here and as team-leaders in this dialogical exchange we adopted a position that was 'not impartial or objective', but 'rigorously ethical' (Freire 1998: 22). Educators aiming to promote critical consciousness cannot be 'neutral' since it is 'part of our human duty to struggle against discrimination', which 'transgresses our essential humanity and is immoral' (ibid. 60). However, the dialogical method demands team-leaders 'listen connectedly ... democratically ... *with* the other as a subject' (ibid. 107, 110-111). In the context of museum learning, this requires pupils unpacking taken for granted ideas and demystifying ideologies, including those of their teachers.

Imaginative Object Biographies and Dramatic Dialogical Pathways to Literacy

With all of the pupils questions resounding in our heads we worked on the idea of object biographies, as a way of empowering pupils through imaginative re-telling, re-naming and re-newing culture. The idea behind this interpretive exercise was to 'bring out both what is in the object and what is in ourselves', which as Pearce notes is 'a dynamic complex movement' (Pearce 1994: 27). This notion echoed in the feminist-hermeneutic concept of the respectful 'I-Thou' relationship and led us to introduce a session where the pupils worked in pairs and engaged in creative writing exercises to develop stories around particular objects from the handling collection. Using their imaginations they re-named the object and wrote about its birth, social life and subsequent journeying to England, from a feeling perspective, as the object, considering how the object might have been made for example, did it feel pain, joy, anxiety, exhilaration? In their creative writing these feelings were connected with wider issues discussed during the project. For example, 'The Greedy King' story featured the topic of human rights and royal responsibilities, enforced marriage and the power of the well-crafted object to become 'dull' or become 'completely golden and represent happiness and peace', which had been raised by Ayo's story. The 'Upside Down Drum' raised the question of value, specifically the financial issues underpinning the movement of objects in the global art market, as well as contested ownership that the 'museum' can best be entrusted to handle, as this extract of the object's imaginary biography shows.

In Benin City there was a family that was quite poor. ... One day a bowl fell out of the sky and the family used it as a kitchen bowl but it wasn't very useful so they put an ornament and shells on it and sold it to another family ... their baby played it as an upside down drum, music filled the air and everyone started to dance. The king of Benin heard about this splendid drum and was willing to pay a million pounds for it. But the England king was on tour in Benin and ... both kings were arguing – they were pulling it hard and they let go – they fell back and it dropped out of the window. It dropped into the stream and ... in London, a fisherman picked it up when getting some shrimps with his net. ... the fisherman went to the king and said 'For one thousand pounds the magic drum can be yours.' So the king paid the money and thought: 'If I keep it around the king of Benin City will come and take it, so I shall hand it to the most trusted Museum – the Horniman Museum.

The creative use of the handling object here permitted the pupils to play with the idea of knowledge as socially constructed and bound in ideological relationships, which 'show us a picture of ourselves' (Pearce 1994: 202). It is important to emphasise that in this exercise pupils were fully aware they were writing imaginatively, not employing museum documentation. Sparking imagination was vital to motivate the development of literacy skills in general throughout the museum/school project. For example in writing their musical drama, the writer director Sola Oyelele talked about scripting and the use of adverbs to increase the richness and range of the pupils's expressive powers for the school production. To show the difference dramatically between what people say and feel, body language proved helpful, for instance: 'Hello Sola', Tony said gloomily with a deflated hunched over stance, 'Hello Tony' Sola 'replied happily' beaming and bouncing about.

Pupils were split into groups and worked with an adult, either their teacher, classroom assistant, Ayo or two educators from the museum, to write scenes for the script re-telling the 'Tortoise and the Elephant' story, which were typed up and edited into the final script ready for the rehearsals. The quality of the final piece reinforces Vygotsky's notion of the ZPD (zone of proximal development) that children can be assisted to achieve a higher level of understanding together with a more experienced adult (Vygotsky 1996). At the ZPD the groups of writers were able to strongly reference African call and response in the script. For example at Scene 1, *The Temple*, Narrator states: 'Once upon a time' and the group calls out 'Time, time' in Response. Again, towards the end of the play, following on from the discussion of sexism, the class had elected for a split between boys and girls, with Sola leading the girls group and Ayo leading the boys group in the dance procession scene. To reflect a real village life the words and melody of Nigerian call and response songs and movements – one for the male procession, one for the female procession and a Coronation call and response song was enacted.

An extract from the end of the play will highlight the high quality of the drama writing. This section clearly shows the rewriting of a traditional tale from a humorous feminist perspective.

Table 5.1 The 'Elephant and the Tortoise': Script of the final scene of the play

Narrator:	The Elephant wriggled proudly towards his throne. As he began to seat his enormous rear, the floor gave way and he fell immediately into the pit.
	The Elephant falls into the pit.
	The Tortoise steps up and takes the hand of the Princess.
King:	You may now lift the veil and kiss your new wife.
	The Tortoise lifts the veil and shouts in surprise.
Tortoise:	What? My wife! How can this be? AH! I'm meant to be marrying the Princess – NOT YOU!
Tortoise's Wife:	Hah! It serves you right. Yes, I am the Princess and you were the King's in-law all along.
Tortoise (flabbergasted):	But, but, but …
Tortoise's Wife:	It serves you right.
Tortoise:	How?
Tortoise's Wife:	You shouldn't have got all excited about marrying a Princess when you were married to a wonderful Princess all along. You, Tortoise, should have appreciated what you had.
	THE END

The 'Inspiration Africa!' team-leaders saw that working with the professional writer/director Sola Oyelele, storyteller/musician Ayo Thomas and artist Tony Minion raised the quality of the pupils' own art, creative writing and literacy. The class teacher considered it was the professional contact and the way all creative effort was predicated on respectful dialogical exchange and provoking the pupils' critical thinking, which was motivating; a point that can be clarified with reference to the ijele art-work.

The Christchurch Ijele

Christchurch pupils worked with Tony to create their own brilliant ijele, which can be seen at Plate 22. The many motifs adorning Horniman's ijele including hands, elephants, police and eagle feathers, all hold symbolic meaning and were of contemporary interest for the pupils. For example, the python represents a powerful animal, a reptile that can swallow a human being, while the figure on a horse at the top of the ijele represents a human with power, a colonial District Officer or an Igbo king. The notion of power prompted discussion around members of the pupils' local community who held power and reflected aspects of their community life that they were proud of.

Plate 22 Christchurch Ijele, *African Worlds* at the Horniman Museum, 2004
Source: David Fortser.

Deciding what 'pride' images to place on the Christchurch's ijele, which was created in three main sections, was difficult. Eventually after discussion it was decided that the lower section would depict local characters and professions that were valued – 'people that make a difference' as one pupil said. Sola helped the pupils to think of people doing jobs they were proud of and these included: 'My mum, Teachers; Lolly-pop people; Police; Actors; Shop-keepers; Writers; Pilots; Mechanics; Cooks; Ambulance-workers; Builders; Priests; Nurses; Doctors; Caretakers; Security Guards; Parents; Firefighters and Lifeguards'. Each child took responsibility to draw up one of the figures cut it out and screen-print it onto a fabric panel.

The centre section featured animals from proverbs and followed on from work carried out with Sola and Ayo around proverbs from Nigeria and the follow-up encouraging pupils to ask about proverbs from their own culture back at home. All this work informed the middle section of the mask with shapes standing out as bright, colourful images that feature animal proverbs such as: brave as a lion and wise as an owl.

The roof of the mask was made from fabric that the pupils had painted with patterns and marks that they had sketched from various objects at the African Worlds exhibition. Since Christchurch is a faith school the fact that Ijele motifs represent the interconnection and harmony between animal, spiritual and physical worlds that prevails in Igbo communities was also of primary interest and abstract representations of spiritual beliefs, intangible feelings of connection, wholeness and well-being according to the pupils, featured prominently at the apex of the school ijele. Finally four figures representing children from different cultural backgrounds – two boys and two girls – were drawn, printed, cut out and stuffed with wadding to go on the top of the piece. These figures were chosen by the pupils in the class to reflect the pride that they shared in their differences and were linked together to show the friendship that they all share.

As a whole 'Inspiration Africa!' at Christchurch draws on pupils' lived experience, while calling them 'out of and beyond' themselves and their community to make contact with another. Specifically the pupils' stories, their musical drama and their ijele demonstrates an ethics that is essentially 'relational to the world and others' (Freire 1998: 25). I shall examine this idea in a little more detail before drawing some conclusions

Christchurch and Telegraph Hill: Partial Connection in Metaphor and Story

This language and story work reinforces Alfred Gell's note on being 'partially connected', pointing to the possibility of communication and understanding across cultures, through an appreciation of objects (Gell 2006: 230).[4] Seeing in

---

4   He stresses the importance of context and acknowledges 'partially connected' as Marylin Strathern's (1991) term.

the Igbo ijele a metaphor of personal and social 'pride', which while rooted in the world and building on elements of daily life was motivating and acted as an inspiration to excel. Similarly seeing in the voudou shrine a metaphor of 'spirit' was empowering for Telegraph Hill pupils, permitting them to soar above the trappings of the everyday to wider realms where they might fulfil their potential.

The ijele and voudou shrine as Gell asserts of the art object, acted as, 'thought traps', holding the viewer for a time in suspension, to give them pause for thought by halting them in their hurried passage through daily life. In this chapter I have attempted to confirm Gell and focused on showing that looking closely at art, listening, speaking and thinking about it deeply through making art and engaging in creative writing can induce pupils to take ownership, of their own stories and their own lives.

Margaret Meek emphasises the universal importance of storytelling that she regards as 'part of our common humanity' since 'as far as we know all cultures have forms of narratives'. She further notes the value of stories and narratives that form part of human conversations, enabling us to better express our 'hopes, fears, actions, feelings and motives', which is so vital for the pupils (Meek 1991: 102). Bruno Bettleheim reinforces this point when he speaks of traditional stories providing a safe route to imaginatively work with deep feelings, fears and anxieties of loss and abandonment, which we saw in the Telegraph Hill poems (Bettleheim 1991: 117).

There seems to be a sense of safety in the imaginative story space that collaborative team leadership can build on by establishing an open framework for dialogue and sharing stories. Furthermore encouraging pupils to actively focus and contribute ideas helped to render 'otherwise shapeless, chaotic events into a coherent whole, saturated with meaning', which proved pleasurable and motivating (Rosen, H. in Rosen, B. 1988: 164).

Conclusion: Multisensory Motivation with Artifacts

The tactile exploration of objects appeared to offer an especially rich set of opportunities for learning through the senses, which are not limited to an individual's skills with the written word, although as team-leaders we directed considerable attention to developing these language skills, which was the focus of this chapter. Artifacts, especially handling objects, which included textiles and costume, sculpture, musical instruments, masks and toys during 'Inspiration Africa!' seemed to loosen the imaginative faculties of the participants by providing a unique sensory threshold that the 'whole body ... whole brain' can engage with (Falk and Dierking 2000: 10). Handling allowed all pupils, including less assured ones, to participate and make a contribution to the learning environment, which provided increased access to the arts and humanities curriculum and was an especially important tool to increase the confidence of children who were considered 'failing' or 'weak' academically. This provision of direct experiential learning was vital for all students, especially those who prefer a kinaesthetic approach to knowledge and struggle with the more traditional routes of reading, writing and mathematics that are prioritised in the National Curriculum.

The handling element of the project work was not regarded as a simple end in itself, but was essentially connected to individual interests and concerns. Handling artifacts while engaging in feminist-hermeneutic dialogue about them and their relationship to the lived experiences of the pupils was crucial. In feminist-hermeneutic terms handling was viewed as one *part* of a *whole* journey towards a greater understanding of the unique self and its potential, which constitutes the rich frontier experience. Figure 5.2 describes this part/whole concept as it relates to creativity and learning through handling during issues-based work.

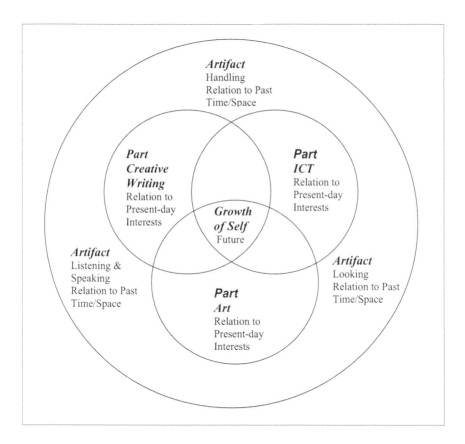

**Figure 5.2 Part/whole concept describing the
 'Inspiration Africa!' curriculum**

Figure 5.2 highlights the importance of the tactile provision, which offered an immediate 'hands on' encounter that the team leaders ensured was also a vitally 'minds on' discursive involvement to facilitate learning and growth (Hein 1993: 31). The figure shows how the pupils' minds were engaged by the questioning approach of feminist-hermeneutics governing the project work, which made clear at the outset that there was no single right answer to be found, as in maths lessons, but rather a whole complex range of new individual interpretations that should be examined in detail, in relation to the past time and space that the artifact sprang from and the contemporary world of the visit.

In other words, 'Inspiration Africa!' participants were expected to look for connections between individual interpretations, beliefs and opinions in the social circumstances from whence they arose. This approach demanded a weighing of evidence from different cultural contexts as well as an evaluation of what counts as evidence or fact in different cultures. In this way the project work was intended to promote intercultural respect and understanding. The questioning approach also enabled the project teams to present a powerful challenge to stereotypical or racist views, which media coverage of poor, starving Africans in war torn lands continues to promote.

These ideas will be developed in Chapter 6. In particular I shall further explore the sensory routes to meaning, including touch, which is key to progressing the disabled pupils' learning that I consider in the next chapter.

Chapter 6
Towards a New Museum Pedagogy: Learning, Teaching and Impact

Introduction

I have drawn extensively on Black feminist thought to theoretically ground more inclusive learning practice at the museum frontiers. The educator bell hooks speaks of such work as 'liberatory pedagogy'. She notes:

> ... as a black woman, I have always been acutely aware of the presence of my body in those settings that, in fact, invite us to invest so deeply in a mind/body split ... you've got ... to remember yourself ... see yourself as a body in a system that has not become accustomed to your presence or to your physicality. ... one of the unspoken discomforts surrounding [how] a discourse of race and gender, class and sexual practice has disrupted the academy is precisely the challenge to the mind/body split. Once we start talking in the classroom [museum] about the body and about how we live in our bodies, we're automatically challenging the way *power* has orchestrated itself in that particular institutionalized space. ... *Liberatory pedagogy* really demands that ... one *work with the limits of the body.* ... *Both with and through and against those limits* ... move out beyond the desk ... walking towards the students, standing close to them, maybe even touching them ... Acknowledging that we are bodies ... disrupt[s] the notion of the professor as omnipotent, all-knowing mind. (hooks 1994a: 135-138) [my emphasis]

Chapter 6 further examines the possibilities of teaching and learning within a framework of critical or *liberatory pedagogy*, which was outlined with reference to feminist-hermeneutic praxis and Paulo Freire in Chapter 5. Here I want to mine the roots of my theoretically grounded work, which I hope may point to other ways of developing new museum pedagogy. In other words I am not trying to sell a ready made product – feminist-hermeneutics – for universal museum education, but rather aiming to inspire critical thought in readers of this book, which might lead to a myriad of new pathways to learning mutual respect and intercultural understanding at the museum frontiers.

Colleagues around the world have recently been considering the body and in Chapter 6 I draw on bell hooks's notion that addressing the 'mind/body split' is crucially important for Black people – professors and students, museum curators and visitors alike. Additionally, I contend this problem of Western thought needs to be considered not just for Black people, but to develop new, more inclusive museum pedagogy for all. Towards this end, some temporal and geographical perspectives of the mind/body problem, specifically more holistic cross-cultural views of knowledge construction as these apply to the context of the museum, will briefly be explored first (Classen 1993).

Then learning as importantly an active 'power to' in the Foucauldian sense will be examined. In short Foucault's 'power/knowledge' couplet is employed to expose the 'cracks and gaps' in the museum discourse for ways in which individuals might insert new knowledge(s), which I shall argue can be profitably based on multisensory ways of knowing (Foucault 1980). In this initial mapping of the power/knowledge terrain, I shall interrogate the museum as a site where more than one sense might be employed together with mind, to produce embodied knowledge. Following this critique of the hierarchically classified five senses and the overriding visualism of the traditional western museum I shall begin to outline new relationships between embodiment, experience and perception across culture and time, arguing for a more multisensual museum learning experience that is vitally embodied and promotes an enhanced apprehension of unusual objects in a space beyond pure spectacle.

Next the culturally naïve view of learning in the western museum is considered from a cross-cultural perspective; specifically the complexities of an African, Anlo-Ewe perspective is addressed, to enhance learning possibilities about material culture from Ghana. These Anlo-Ewe concepts are related to collaborative work that I carried out during a particular 'Inspiration Africa!' project with a 'difficult' audience, children aged between five and eleven years old, with special educational needs attending New Woodlands School, London, who were engaged with an Ashante stool as their key object and 'respect' as their key word (<http://clothofgold.org.uk/inafrica>; <http://www.newwoodlands.lewisham.sch.uk/> accessed on 12.12.2008).

Here I demonstrate how the experience of the body in space can be enhanced through touch, which can affect the relationship between proprioception and the construction of meaning. For example, balancing the body on an Ashante stool exaggerates an awareness of the body in relation to the ground, which presents new challenges and makes new demands on a body more used to upright chairs or sofas. Furthermore voicing these feelings in the social space heightens a sense of conviviality and aids meaningful communication among pupils, since aural and tactile encounters seem to open the participants to deeper emotional engagement.

The museum audience considered in this chapter had Educational Behavioural Difficulties (EBD) and some socio-historical context to these specific learning needs is provided. The particular audience, who as Cole notes might historically have been regarded as 'feeble minded', comprise largely Black boys, and the 'Inspiration Africa!' team leaders were acutely aware of a setting that invests deeply in a mind/body split and finds them 'lacking' mind (Cole 1989; Cole et al. 1998). In contrast I show how intensive work with this group opens feeling routes to knowledge construction – listening, imagining, creating art, making music –

inspires pupils' sense of wonder, joy and the desire to repeat the successful embodied engagements that are initiated by African objects.

Overall the chapter demonstrates the value of considering knowledge from a global perspective as essentially embodied and makes an argument for embodied learning, in the widest sense, as a broadening of the museum-school space and a global curriculum. Promoting embodied knowledge will be shown to represent a state of wellbeing and wholeness, which, as I shall argue, characterises human knowing, understanding, and meaning-making in the museum and in the wider world.

Viewpoints and Worlds of Sense

At the risk of oversimplification it may be helpful here at the outset to outline the roots of the mind/body split in western thought, which we can trace to the Ancient Greek philosophers, who demonstrated that our senses are not to be trusted. Vision offers a prime example of sense deceiving rational mind. A great artist such as Parrhasius produced such a lifelike image of a curtain that he was able to fool even the trained artistic eye of Zeuxis – whose painting of grapes deceived only the birds (Gombrich 1968: 119, 173, 346). For Plato it is reasoning through questions in dialogical exchange – the to and fro of living spoken language – that human beings can access Truth. It might be argued that the 2,000 year history of western philosophy since the Greeks has increasingly esteemed mind and reason with a consequent devaluing of the body and the senses, resulting in the linear reductive reasoning behind Descartes's famous statement 'cogito ego sum' in the seventeenth century, emphasising reason coupled with an extreme mistrust of the senses.[1]

The rise of visualism has been said to characterise the birth of the age of Enlightenment in the eighteenth century and in the nineteenth century museum, when the 'visualising scientific paradigm' prohibited museum visitors to touch, eat or even speak loudly, and imperialist power and domination was reinforced with every visitors' gaze. (Edwards, Gosden and Philips 2006: 208). In the late twentieth and early twenty-first centuries we have witnessed a reaction in the museum to the hypervisualism of contemporary culture, with adult exhibitions such as *Touch Me* and *Shhh* at the V&A, encouraging haptic interaction and sound long recognised as vital in children's museums around the world and at the Horniman Museum (Pearce 1998; <http://www.vam.ac.uk> accessed on 24.03.2008).

Furthermore, it is worth noting here that while we have traditionally counted just five senses in the west, they have been ordered and combined differently

---

1   Today, since linguistic philosophy and the philosophy of mind recognise Descartes' ultra-sceptical statement 'I think therefore I am' presumes an, 'I' that thinks and fails to reach the logically limiting statement 'there is thinking', we might assume the poverty of this position is exposed, or do we detect some aspect of this doubt still lingering in a pessimistic hermeneutics of suspicion.

through the ages. As Classen observes to hear is based on a root meaning to look, to see on a root meaning to see and say, taste originally meant touch, while the meaning of the Latin terms sapient and sagacious are derived from sapere to know and sagacis keen-scented (Classen 1993: 56). What remains constant is that we apprehend the world through the body, the senses. Additionally our relationship with the tangible world of objects, including museum objects, is intimately bound up with and affected by intangible factors, by emotion and memory, as we noted in the last chapter (Wulff 2005).

Working with 'Inspiration Africa!' participants visiting the *African Worlds* exhibition at Horniman we wanted to highlight the unique ways of valuing, combining and ordering the senses that different African cultures have, which is embodied in their material culture. Our aim was to introduce visitors to different 'worlds of sense', contending that the senses need to be re-valued cross-culturally to enhance museum learning (Classen 1993; Classen and Howes 2006; Stoller 1989). We considered a richer embodied learning environment might prove particularly profitable for the EBD pupils at New Woodlands, facilitating them with new 'power to' access knowledge(s).

Embodied Knowledge and a New 'Power to'

To begin explaining how the key concept of embodied knowledge might nurture a new 'power to' at the museum frontiers I shall present a view of the mind *and* the bodily senses acting in a socio-political world. In short, embodied knowledge is viewed as a necessary mixture, of intellectual activity inevitably arising out of bodily experiences in a relational world of objects and others (Braidotti 1994a, 1994b; Lennon and Whitford 1994).

The importance of this idea to the museum lies in developing pedagogy, which understands learning to be predicated on the properties and limitations of the body, or as proceeding in sensual *and* intellectual ways. To achieve embodied knowledge at the museum frontiers a certain sort of *activity* is essential and the Foucauldian discourse proves pertinent here. Foucault centrally distinguishes active and passive bodies in his histories of the prison and asylum (Foucault 1991, 1995). He notes how the 'capacities and forces' of the body are severely curtailed in the classical age when techniques of power over the body make totally 'docile bodies' (Foucault 1991: 137-8). We are reminded of the private museum spaces where knowledge is actively produced and framed in the glass cases of the public galleries, and passively consumed by docile visitors under constant surveillance.

Yet Christopher Falzon's recent reading of Foucault on the disciplinary society highlights the power of active human beings who have the capacity to transform their world, to revolt and 'transgress existing limits', which is useful to museum pedagogy (Falzon 1998: 52). He notes how relationships of power are not passively reproduced from generation to generation but, surface within particular historical communities and can be subjected to change. Falzon also notes how changes in particular relationships of power can occur by opening up concrete spaces of embodied freedom, of corporeal capacities and forces where a human power to act can be facilitated. This power to activity is essentially creative and involves experimental processes of play with different possibilities, it is not an elitist thesis of the artist genius or super-hero but one which emphasises the 'creativity present in all active humans' (ibid. 55).

Facilitating this new power to activity demands an imaginative reconstruction of museum knowledge and priorities. It demands a change in focus: from the static display of museum knowledge about the material objects in the glass cases of our public galleries; to a continual cycle of creative investigations into how new embodied knowledge(s) might be constructed *with* the museum audience. To clarify these ideas I shall consider specific human capacities and corporeal forces, or the role of individual senses in the construction of knowledge.

Power to See

Ludmilla Jordonova has examined the assumption that looking at objects can offer knowledge, not merely about the object itself but also about the wider processes in which it is embedded. As she further observes 'objects are triggers of chains of ideas and images that go far beyond their initial starting-point' (Jordanova 1993: 23). Jordonova's notion begins to offer a corrective to the eye that masters, and sight that predominates over the other 'lower' senses of touch, hearing, smell and taste. This is not to dismiss vision. But to regard it as a vital component of a mixed discourse, a poetry and politics, which constitutes learning and enables museum visitors to construct their own knowledge(s). The important point for museum education is to distinguish an active power to see from a passive looking or 'mind*less* gawping' (Vergo 1993: 58) [my emphasis]. A new power to see is mind*ful*, it requires students at the museum frontiers to take account not simply of the visible features of objects displayed in a linear way, but of the socio-historical world, the more complex narratives and the broader philosophical context, the discourses or 'articulatory practices' from which the objects emerge (Hooper-Greenhill 1990: 60).

A history of vision can be illuminated from a Foucauldian perspective, within a socio-historical framework of shifting 'epistemes'.[2] In short Foucault notes Renaissance notions 'intersect, overlap, reinforce, or limit one another on the surface of thought', recognising similarities in neighbouring things in the world, which seem to be joined like links in a chain for Renaissance thinkers (Foucault 1994: 17, 19). This view shifts during the Classical age when observation is linked to knowledge that guarantees Truth but excludes 'hearsay, taste, smell and touch'

2   The term episteme refers to the socio-cultural construction of knowledge in different historical eras.

(ibid. 132). Such scientific understanding persists until the nineteenth century when the corporeality vision and a more abstract optical experience are conceived.

Foucault regards the nineteenth century optical experience, which is characterised by a new regard for human temporality and finitude, as a movement towards modern thought, where we come to appreciate the anatomical, physiological, historical, social and economic conditions of knowledge that is formed in the 'relations woven between' people (Foucault 1994: 319). In other words, vision emerges as an, irreducible complex of factors that belong both to the observing body and the information received from the exterior socio-political world (Crary 1995: 70-71).

Contemporary feminist thought on vision elaborates the relevance of Foucault's analysis to contemporary museum education, by arguing for a new postmodern and post-colonial movement of knowledge construction to take account of the difference and similarity between knowers. Specifically 'Nomadic' travel beyond the Modern episteme and a lingering Classical concern for prioritising the visible enables a more fluid reconstruction of knowledge at the museum borderlands (Braidotti 1994a).

A Feminist Analysis of Vision Applied to the Museum

Rosi Braidotti counteracts the ancient dualism of mind and body, with the concept of thought as essentially embodied active experience (Braidotti 1994b). Her nomadic movement acknowledges 'the corporeal roots of subjectivity' while denouncing the equation of the visible with truth as a male fantasy (ibid. 18). She elucidates this fantasy that renders woman's bodies intelligible by the technology of camera and microscope, pointing to contemporary pornography and anatomical studies in medicine as areas where men reign powerfully in domination over women's bodies that are treated as fragments, almost dismembered parts of a whole object. For Braidotti it is through an intense focus on the visible under patriarchy that a hierarchy of power is maintained, with the active subject behind the lens observing and controlling the passive woman as mere flesh.

Perhaps the security cameras in our museums can similarly be viewed as instruments for rendering the male and female visitor a passive object, of the distant but dominant gaze (Hooper-Greenhill 1989: 63). Such rendering passive can be read as a 'feminisation' in psychoanalytic terms since women under patriarchy are subordinated. This notion reaches a climax in Foucault's account of male prisoners in Bentham's panoptican, where men are feminised by the state of extreme passivity and observation to which they are subjected. Braidotti sees psychoanalysis as providing a positive revaluation of subordinate positioning and she cites Freudian psychoanalysis as adequately addressing this problematic of knowledge and the body within a political space for women. She states 'psychoanalysis has developed into a philosophy of desire and a theory of the body as libidinal surface, a site of multiple coding, of inscription – a living text' (Braidotti 1994b: 18).

The contribution of psychoanalysis for Braidotti lies in a re-theorisation of the body to admit the bodily roots of all knowledge claims. Her psychoanalytical focus usefully suggests a space and a technique to assert alternative knowledge, truth and representation on an affective and corporeal ground, which is denied in strict logical terms. In the museum Braidotti's analysis reinforces more attentive 'listening' and truly cooperative action with audiences to construct 'three-dimensional, philosophical links between the objects', or in other words to facilitate a new power to see.

The thought of Donna Haraway also clarifies museum educators facilitating a new power to see in the museum. Haraway has explored the 'cyborg' as a 'political myth' that points to imaginative possibilities or 'potent fusions' (Haraway 1991a: 149, 154). Her postmodernist reading of cyborg technology permits vision to be reemployed for the feminist discourse. Additionally envisaging new cyborg relationships between mind and body offers creative ways for subjugated people to explore and gain greater visibility in the museum, which furthers the political work of increasing equality.

Haraway also offers an important redefinition of objectivity for feminist epistemology in her idea of 'situated' knowledges. This notion repossesses ethics and politics by acknowledging 'irreducible differences' and a 'radical multiplicity of local knowledges' (Haraway 1991b: 187). The ethical and political achievement of 'situated knowledge' lies in making the museum community involved in the presentation and perception of this knowledge responsible, accountable or 'answerable for what we learn how to see' (Haraway 1991b: 190).[3] For museum learning a new power to see would regard knowledge as a process of 'passionate construction', radically opposing the 'cannibal eye', of single-point perspective (Haraway 1991b: 191, 189). In contradistinction, partial perspectives would permit the constant unfolding of multiple and complex viewpoints by pupils and teachers, who would be presented with limitless possibilities to learn from museum objects without reaching a climactic or final end point.

We have begun to consider personal and political knowledge informed by feminism in the museum context. Next we will explore the relationship of knowledge with the sense of touch, which will help to illuminate these ideas.

Embodied Knowledge as a New 'Power to' Touch

Luce Irigaray has contributed to the theory of embodied knowledge as essentially including feeling and emotion. Irigaray speaks of 'the passional foundations of

---

3   In this sense Haraway echoes the Hill-Collins's 'standpoint' theory as well as Falk and Dierking and Hein's constructivism, which prioritises the visitor's personal viewpoint or construction of knowledge.

reason' (Whitford 1991: 10). The 'double gesture' in Irigaray refuses the binary oppositions of western logic and insists on the linkage of 'both at once', which prefers a 'creative fertile partnership' and rejects the elevation of either male or female readings. Irigaray also emphasises the importance of acknowledging differences within woman as well as between women, and locates relationships between the 'global' and the 'specific' by drawing connections between theoretical positions (ibid. 24-25). Most importantly Irigaray emphasises the power of the sense of 'touch' in opposition to the power of the gaze. She argues for the concave surface of the speculum to counter the flat reductive model of the human psyche seen in Lacan's image of the mirror that is his 'other', woman. Women, she states, need a surface that will reflect and validate them as autonomous subjects 'for-themselves and not just in their *exteriority*, for others' (ibid. 142) [my emphasis].

I have employed Irigaray's work alongside museum objects with groups of adult women to reflect on this 'exteriority'. The beautiful image taken from the body of woman, which Irigaray offered to us in '*the sex which is not one*', has been the source of some creative response in feminist discourse at Horniman (Irigaray 1981). In this seminal text Irigaray speaks of a womans' vulva as one set of her 'two lips', and perhaps it is the poetic structuring of her semiotic here that seems to assist a high degree of clarity, for the feminist semiotic to be envisioned and *felt,* which feeling objects further progresses. For example cowry shells are traditionally seen as mirroring woman's distinctive anatomy, her vulva, and I have employed headwear and musical instruments that have cowries as decoration as well as the units of cowries historically used as currency in parts of West Africa, to reflect on the body of woman with groups of adult feminists and inspire creative writing. In creative writing workshops Irigaray's thought was seen to proceed in a sensually theoretical way, and feminist speculation imaginatively achieved at the margins of discourse, which thereby evades the dominant phallogocentric world-view. There are repetitions, circling and refusing any closure of meaning in her work, which opens up a semantic space for 'active' readers to discern a plurality of meanings. Her writing also constitutes a 'healing text' since it marks out such a range of alternative possibilities without the violent forcing of the psyche into a position where it must choose 'one' (ibid. 172). I quote her here:

> A woman "touches herself" constantly without anyone being able to forbid her to do so, for her sex is composed of two lips which embrace continually. ... The *one* of form, the individual sex, proper name, literal meaning – supersedes by spreading apart and dividing, this touching of *at least two* [lips] which keeps woman in contact with herself, although it would be impossible to distinguish exactly what 'parts' are touching each other. (Irigaray 1981: 100-101) [my emphasis]

Irigaray, highlighting the sensual and intellectual link with the sexual, points to the sense of touch as extended over the whole surface of the body. If Irigaray's ideas are translated to the world of the museum; to be touched by a museum object is to be moved psychically and physically. The experience of active touching in the museum does not leave the museum visitor 'unchanged' to recall an aspect of the Gadamerian discourse. Using the 'handling collection' is an important part of a successful museum visit during which students are facilitated to construct their own knowledge, as teacher' testimonies demonstrate (Golding 2000). Teachers highlight the importance of this direct physical contact with the materiality of museum objects to expand pupils' horizons; their views of others and the possibilities for their future lives.

School pupils visit the Horniman Museum to 'look and learn 'from 'other' cultures, but my research team of teachers argue that knowledge cannot easily be constructed by looking in isolation from other human senses (Bennett 1996: 98). Perhaps an important lesson to be 'learnt' from the focus on 'looking' in many western museums is one of 'civics' to 'respect property and behave gently', since the British school system is rooted in a western politico-philosophical tradition a museum-visit seems to provide us with as much 'knowledge' about this tradition as the one displayed (Bennett 1999; 1996: 49, 102). We contend that wider lessons of 'respect' and 'care' for 'other' cultures can be learnt from touching or handling sessions, which the New Woodlands 'Inspiration Africa!' project I shall outline presently will furnish evidence for.

In western cultural forms touch has long been considered an important vehicle for proving and transforming reality: Pygmalion animates his statue through touch; Carravagio's Doubting Thomas sticks his finger in the wounds of Christ; Michelangelo's God creates Adam with the gentlest brush of a finger. Today, only a tiny hierarchy of museum professionals can share these powerful sense impressions with the original makers and users of museum artefacts. The sensual pleasure of touch and its role in the construction of knowledge by museum curators, is a factor rarely acknowledged in the exhibition texts for visual public consumption, although Mr Frederick John Horniman permitted visitors to touch and keep pieces of cartonage from one of his Ancient Egyptian mummies following a public lecture (Horniman Museum Report 1898).

Today the admonition 'Don't Touch' in our public spaces denotes a rigid segregation, which removes this important category of affective responses from ordinary visitors, who are expected to rely almost entirely on the visual. The touch and care afforded to the object by the makers is reduced in the framing of the glass case, but democratically restored in an educational handling session at the Horniman Museum, alongside the 'power to' speak and listen, which we will examine next.

Power to Listen and Speak in the Museum

Audre Lorde developed a notion of genuine communication, which is predicated on the possibility of really 'listening', that is central to the notion of 'dialogue' in philosophical hermeneutics (Lorde 1996; Gadamer 1981). Listening for Lorde does not entail passivity but is rather an *active* opening up of one's 'subjectivity' to another so that further questioning of each subject can occur. Listening also imposes the responsibility of increasing self-awareness and ultimately self-knowledge. In a reference to Paulo Freire, Lorde notes how it essentially requires recognition of an outer world, where the real conditions of lived experiences can be investigated as that internalised 'piece of the oppressor planted deep inside each of us' (Lorde 1996c: 170).

Thus Lorde's 'listener' makes a movement towards 'realism' in her vital connection of personal 'knowledge' and ethical responsibility to the external world. She is not condemned to a passive wallowing in mysterious internal processes but moved to take action against the horrors of 'racism and homophobia' for example. This manner of listening for Lorde points to ways in which 'the personal as the political can begin to illuminate all our choices' (Lorde 1996b: 161). Listening to Lorde and Freire as an education worker in the museum, a professional responsibility is highlighted; to listen closely to the 'piece of the oppressor' lodged deep in the museum discourse, a discourse of extreme realism and rationality which silences unreason. Perhaps a short outline of Freudian and Foucauldian thought will begin to clarify this idea.

Listening to the languages of reason and unreason is central to Freudian psychoanalysis, as Foucault and Derrida both emphasise. Foucault notes in *Madness and Civilisation*, that Freud began 'once again to *listen* to this language [of unreason]' (Foucault 1995: 262). The language of madness was condemned to silence during the enlightenment, where it occupied a position of banishment outside of discourse. Foucault in his 'archaeology of that silence' discusses earlier times when unreason was at least able to occupy a place in the margins of discourse (ibid. 1995: xiii).

For example in the middle ages the insane were not totally suppressed but 'kept at a sacred distance', in the way that lepers were living with a certain freedom within the lazar house just outside of town (Foucault 1995: 6). Neither was exclusion from the wider community considered detrimental to their ultimate achievement of 'salvation', a form of 'divine knowledge' according to the thought of the time. Foucault rapidly moves his discussion to consider the 'Ship of Fools,' during the 'imaginary landscape of the Renaissance' where it seemed to 'occupy a privileged place'. The ships also had an existence in real or historical time when madmen, 'led an easy wandering existence' (ibid. 1995: 7-8). 'Listening' would appear to grant a corporeal 'power' of some movement for the insane at this time.

It is not until the Enlightenment that 'rational' thought becomes totalising and suppressed difference and otherness. In the absolute rule of reason thoughts were ordered in a perfect symmetry of 'either or', and 'madness was torn from that imaginary freedom' which previously allowed it to flourish and flounder in 'broad daylight' (Foucault 1995: 64). In short, the dichotomous thinking that post-modernism argues against, reduces madness solely to its inscription on the body, to a visible 'spectacle'. Foucault tells us:

As late as 1815, if a report presented to the House of Commons is to be believed, the hospital of Bethlehem [the present day Imperial War Museum in London, UK] exhibited lunatics for a penny, every Sunday. ... the madmen at Bicentre were shown "like curious animals, to the first simpleton willing to pay a coin" ... One went to see a keeper display the madmen the way the trainer at the Fair of Saint-Germain put the monkeys through their tricks. (Foucault 1995: 68)

This passage has resonance for the museum whose business revolves around display. In Foucault's historical analysis the insane becomes the absolute 'other', and their consequent distancing from sane humanity to a closer proximity with animals is redolent of a historical, racist organisation of museum knowledge. The idea of relegating as 'other' or to a category of sub-humanity: mad; poor; disabled and Black people for example, was reinforced by a morality which equated such 'others' with 'beasts' in the discourses of the asylum and the museum (Foucault 1995: 63; Bennett 1996; Coombes 1993) Movement between categories, from insane beast to rational being and from savage slave to saved Christian was later deemed to be possible, but only by the imposition of a new totalising order of rationality which overtook the old. This was not achieved by 'active listening.' The meanings of insanity were unheard as were the traditional African belief systems of the displaced slaves whose material culture continues to be housed in western museums of anthropology. It will be profitable to consider the contribution of contemporary anthropology next.

Anthropology and the 'Sensual Revolution'

In the *Empire of the Senses*, David Howes has gathered together an astonishing collection of interdisciplinary essays on the 'sensual revolution', which elucidate human thought and ways of knowing that centre on the body (Howes 2005). Howes and his contributors examine a vast range of sensory experiences across diverse cultures, geographies and times that contrast strongly with the hierarchy of the five senses in the West. Constance Classen for example, describes the high valuation attached to the sense of smell amongst the Ongee. She states.

In a little Andaman Island in the Bay of Bengal live the Ongee, a hunting and gathering people who have little contact with the outside world. For the Ongee smell is the fundamental cosmic principle. Odor is the source of personal identity and the reason for communal life, a system of medicine and communication, it determines temporal and spatial movements, it produces life and causes death. (Classen 2005: 153)

Classen's richly detailed account of embodiment is intimately connected to location, emplacement, which emphasises the social nature of knowledge construction. In other words the different spaces in which people live and gain embodied knowledge are social spaces where individuals communicate through performance or utterance in social groups. I offer one more illustration from Howes of this point.

Kathryn Linn Guerts demonstrates the culture-bound Western perspective with reference to the Anlo-Ewe group of people, who originate from the land around the Volta coast and the Keta Lagoon, although they also live in other parts of Ghana, Europe and the USA today. In 'Consciousness as 'Feeling in the Body'' Guerts contrasts the privileging of individual sight and the use of cinematic metaphors in the West, with the Anlo-Ewe theory of consciousness, which is intersubjective, phenomenological and processual in character. Specifically one Anlo-Ewe concept, *Seselelame*, which translates as a generalised 'feeling in the body', links emotion, sensation, perception, cognition etcetera without distinction, including internal senses (i.e. balance, proprioception) and external senses as well as other perceptual, emotional and intuitive dimensions of experience (Ameka 2002 quoted in Guerts 2005: 165). *Seselelame* describes 'hearing or feeling emotions' such as happiness and sorrow, physical sensations such as heat and cold, and the embodied presence with others in cultural settings (Csordas 1993: 139 quoted in Guerts 2005).

It may help to clarify this point if we consider the cross-cultural significance of the clothed body in a social ritual in the context of a museum handling session with textiles, which the New Woodlands pupils I discuss presently experienced. For example, the diversity of attire we observe mourners wear at funerals around the world: black in the west, white in China and Adinkra cloth (a bright orange/red background with black stamped designs that have auspicious meanings) in traditional Ashante society Ghana, might imply different emotions are attached to the experience of death. Yet a closer examination reveals similarities. In the west, while black is worn to express sadness and loss of the mourner, we may understand the feelings attached to white in China if we think of the iconography surrounding the lily, a symbol of purity, as well as the associations of vibrancy, life and death with red in Africa. The point here is that we can teach pupils to read the African adinkra symbols as any sign system, it is a matter of learning the codes.

Individual and social balance/equilibruim and adaptability is emphasised in the Anlo-Ewe account of consciousness. The idea of supple, balanced and flexible persons in a physical, emotional and moral sense is seen in the image of the baby in the womb as sitting, poised and balanced on a stool. As the New Woodlands boys saw stools seem to invite the body to balance in a certain way, to centre the body physically on the earth, at one with the forces of gravity, which is quite different from the western chair with a backrest that almost seems to encourage fidgeting. In other words, the sense of balance I am considering here connects the individual physical body and the individual character, with concern for the balance or harmony of the wider social group.

New Woodlands pupils who experienced difficulties in society found complex notions such as these could be more easily accessed through objects, for wrapping themselves in the range of kente, adinkra and other printed cloths, balancing on the stools and headrest while, most importantly verbalising their feelings about these experiences. The Anlo-Ewe regard speech as a sense and emphasise similarities and relationships in the experiences of eating, speaking, drinking, breathing, kissing and so on. They consider spoken words to convey information and meaning through the physical force of sound that operates not just in the ear but through whole body. Therefore speaking is viewed as 'feeling in the mouth' and speakers must take care as children can absorb animosity through the power of adult words. There is a richness in the Anlo-Ewe philosophy of the senses, which are rooted in shared feelings and shared ways of life that challenges the culturally naïve Western view of 'one body, one self' that echoes 'one person one vote'.

These points will be illuminated with reference to New Woodlands pupil's reflexive work on their key word 'respect' presently. First since this final case study in the book concerns children, deemed to have Educational Behavioural Difficulties (EBD) at the time (2000) I shall first offer a little background information.

Educational Behavioural Difficulties (EBD) History and Definitions

In the first year of the new millennium, educators in the UK saw the term Educational Behavioural Difficulties (EBD) widen with the revision of the special educational needs (SEN) Code of Practice, to include the term 'social', and to place an emphasis on 'development' as opposed to difficulties. Social development is one of four areas of 'needs and requirements' laid out in the 2001 Code, alongside three others, which are 'communication and interaction', 'cognition and learning' and 'sensory and/or physical' (DfES 2001: 87, para 7.60). However, at the time of writing in 2006, this extended definition is not in universal use and EBD often remains as a descriptor. Since our precise use of language and taking power for naming the world has proved critical throughout this book, it will be valuable for future museum collaboration to define terminology in a socio-political context before proceeding.

Children have presented challenging behaviour to the educational setting since Victorian times, when a 'medical model' was in operation. The medical model firmly locates 'problems' requiring medical-leaning 'treatment' at an individual level 'within-child.' This model is evident in the imprecise term 'maladjustment', which was a 'catch-all for children showing a wide range of behavioural and learning difficulties', and legally enshrined in the category of 'maladjusted children' with the 1945 Regulations following the Education Act 1944 (Cole 1989; Cole et al. 1998). In the UK the individual or medical model, with its false notion of 'normality' and its deterministic emphasis on biology, was prevalent throughout the spectrum of education for special needs until the 1960s, when the 'social' model entered the literature, via the pioneering theoretical work of disabled people, most notably Oliver and Barnes (Oliver 1996; Barnes et al. 2002). This social model highlights the wider social context in which terminology reflects prejudices within the minds of non-disabled people, influencing human interaction and professional practice, too often with the effect of disabling individuals. The newer social model is more appropriate for progressing inclusive learning agendas in the museum/school context since it recognises many difficulties or barriers to learning individuals face may, in part at least, be reactions to social barriers and environmental factors.

The UK struggle over appropriate definition reverberates in the USA, where a similar social perspective seems to be predominant in contemporary disability discourse, although theorists tend to speak of 'disorders' rather than 'difficulties.' In Kaufman's seminal work he states. 'An emotional or behavioural disorder is not a thing that exists outside a social context but a label assigned according to cultural rules'. Kaufman further highlights the subjective nature, 'at least in part', of defining terms when he notes that 'typically' a 'disorder is whatever a culture's chosen authority figures designate as intolerable', because it 'is perceived to threaten the stability, security, or values of that society' (Kauffman, 2001: 22-23).

This point was underlined for me following work on INSET[4] at Horniman with the Ghanaian musician/storyteller Amoafi Kwappong during the 1990s. Her input into the 'Multicultural Musical Traditions' INSET courses helped to sensitise all the participants, myself included, to culturally diverse behaviour in one role-play. She recalled a teaching assistant to a class of 25 children aged between seven and eight year-olds, angrily shouting at a small boy who had misbehaved, 'look at me by when I'm talking to you!' while the lad's gaze seemed to bore ever lower down into the ground. In Ghana children who recognise they have behaved badly with an elder demonstrate their apology with their body, casting their eyes down in a sign of respect to the elder person. If this situation occurred in the museum, educators could draw attention away from the child and defuse the situation. They might beat a drum at great speed, moving towards the teaching assistant and child smiling broadly. Then, briefly explain the polite practice concerning adult-child eye contact in Ghana. Finally the whole group might begin to discuss and to construct: angry sounds, happy sounds and sad sounds as well as the silent expressions of anger, happiness and sadness, which we can actively make with our bodies.

The best way of tackling problematic pupil attitudes is to adopt a more positive presentation of appropriate behaviour, a non-threatening and ultimately more instructive manner (Mayor's conference 2002). What needs to be drawn out here is the importance of creating 'an atmosphere', in which our 'own position' as museum/school educators is allowed to 'emerge without people feeling over-

---

4   At Horniman we organised INSET sessions for teachers in service almost every week. The themes would be related to the collections, allow the teachers to be creative and may result in a qualification. For example, teachers following a ten week 'multicultural musical traditions' course could be awarded a certificate from the Trinity College of Music on completion. INSET would be held during the 'twilight' time 4.30-6.30pm so that teachers could attend after they had completed their days work and the school did not need to find money for agency teachers to cover their work. A nominal £5 fee was charged, to pay for the services of a professional musician, writer, storyteller or artist.

weighted by its authority' (Hall 1980: 3-4). Hall does not ask us to deny our opinions, or prejudices to use Gadamer's terminology, but he does highlight the importance of open and reflexive dialogue that enables vital connections with the wider socio-political world to be made. This as he says, 'becomes a great deal more complex because it requires putting together explanations from different areas of knowledge', and it is here that a great strength of museum/school collaboration lies (Hall 1980: 4).

Although just one example has been sketched here my experience indicates that a range of educational partnerships can be forged in the museum, which most importantly increases the number of 'significant others' that research suggests is vital to effective learning, or 'joined up' practice for pupils with EBD (Ofsted 1999; Cole et al. 1998). Ethos is critical. Educators who take joint responsibility for providing a 'flexible' teaching and learning space, a 'safe and supportive environment', who listen to and clearly value all the pupils' contributions engender appropriate role models for 'positive interaction' amongst pupils and behaviour that is conducive to learning (DfES 2001: 87). In short we strongly advocate a collaborative approach to teaching at the museum/school frontiers. Collaboration can assist us in helping EBD pupils to break out of negative cycles of pessimistic thinking in which they may be locked. This requires us developing our teaching skills, maintaining high expectations of our pupils, and providing a variety of activities, which build upon the individual capabilities rather than highlighting weaknesses (Ofsted 1999a; Cole et al. 1998). In other words, project team leaders at the museum/school frontiers should work in 'effective partnership' to facilitate activities disabled pupils might 'do with support', rather than focus on 'what they can't do' (Valuing People 2004: 14).

A number of large claims and rather abstract points have now been made, which I shall attempt to justify with reference to 2 case studies. I shall detail work with New Woodlands School (labelled EBD at the time of collaboration and now simply SEN), London. At this school, the museum team leaders who included Sola Oyelele (writer/storyteller), Tony Minion (artist), Jacqui Callis (ICT specialist), and myself (museum educator), worked alongside the class teachers to develop educational programmes, which recognised that while disabled pupils may take longer to learn new skills and grasp complex information, as much 'choice and independence' over their project work as possible should be enabled (Valuing People 2004: 14).

New Woodlands School: Year 6 Boys Learning Respect with an Ashante Stool

I shall introduce this section with an acrostic poem on 'respect', which was the key word for the Ashante stool project:

Running about
Exhausting my body
Started my life over again
Perfection that's what I am
Excellent that's me!
Courteous – very respectful
To my elders I'm very respectful

This poem expresses a power of the body, a possibility of changing lives for the better through transforming negative attitudes, a belief that excellence can be attained and the importance of respect. The poem was written by a group of boys attending New Woodlands School during six weeks of museum/school collaboration. It represents a huge achievement.

New Woodlands School is a primary age school (for pupils of four to eleven years old), catering for fifty-two boys with special educational needs (SEN), including those with 'behavioural, emotional and social difficulties' (<http://www.lewisham.gov.uk> accessed on 21.04.2006). The attractive single-story school building is newly built (1998) and nestles in secluded grounds surrounded with mature trees that gives almost a countryside feeling; a small haven located within a densely built up area of old and rundown council housing stock, in Downham, the London borough of Lewisham.

The multiple levels of economic deprivation noted at the introduction to Section 3, which clearly impact on the learning opportunities of children in the borough, are compounded at New Woodlands by the special educational needs of the pupils. The teaching staff strove to provide the children with full access to the National Curriculum for England at Key Stage 1 and 2, and welcomed the opportunity to work in partnership with the 'Inspiration Africa!' team. After three initial meetings and some intensive discussion over the telephone, at the school and at the museum, the specific needs of the pupils emerged and we selected an 'Ashante Stool' from Ghana as the key object and 'respect' as the key word to focus project work. The respect theme was designed to aid the pupils who experienced difficulties learning in the core curriculum areas of English and Maths, which was frustrating and led to further difficulties in terms of behaviour, to approach the curriculum in new and more creative ways through a range of holistic multi-sensory experiences, as I shall detail. Specifically the New Woodlands project will help to demonstrate the thesis of gaining embodied knowledge and cross-cultural understanding, which I have been exploring, in action.

Introducing the Respect Project at School

Due to the small size and unique nature of the school it was appropriate to involve all the pupils in some part of the introductory project day at school. This ensured that everyone, pupils and staff, got to know the team of artists and educators and understood what they were going to be doing in their school over the next few weeks. The introduction day started with an outline of the project, some warm up games and a handling session for the two Year 6 classes, totalling thirteen boys. While New Woodlands pupils clearly enjoyed playing some of the musical instruments, listening to a tape of African drumming and trying on some of the African garments from the Horniman Museum's handling collection, it may be helpful to examine their learning here at the outset of the project. I shall argue that handling assisted these very disadvantaged pupils to begin to engage in aesthetic education – in the mystery of perception.

When we engage pupil's imaginations in the particular West African patterns by asking them to 'describe this shape' and 'imagine, what does it remind you of', we are employing Wittgenstein's concept of 'seeing as'. In this idea Wittgenstein refers to the way a certain combination of lines on a paper can denote a duck at 'this' moment and a rabbit at 'that' (Wittgenstein 1974: 194). The related concept of 'hearing as' is also highly relevant to the context of the museum frontiers, if we consider the idea as essentially referring to the cultural context within which aural perception holds meaning and value. In terms of Western classical music, 'hearing a melody' from Mozart, in all its complicated nuances rather than a dissonant series of sounds, requires extensive work, both teaching and learning. Similarly, in my experience, with time and effort some appreciation of world music – 'hearing as' musical relationships from 'Other' cultural traditions – can be achieved.

In the New Woodlands case, practising a simple dance, a drumming rhythm and a call and response song uses the voice *and* the whole body, which helps provide a more fully embodied deep learning experience that is both more pleasurable and more memorable than a simpler observation exercise. Of course it should be emphasised that mimicry alone is of no value in furthering understanding. It is the special context of the teaching and learning situation, which permits 'hearing as' enduring knowledge and understanding of the particular Ghanaian musical forms and this new embodied knowledge of another cultural form can only be provided by active human beings open to learning at the site of the museum frontiers. I shall now turn to briefly consider the theme of music.

Musical Engagement

On day one of musical engagement at New Woodlands School pupils played an active song-game about caring grandmas from Ghana. The first verse states:

> Grandma, grandma, sick in bed. She called for the doctor, the doctor said "Grandma, grandma, you ain't sick, all you need is a walking stick."

> Chorus: Hands up, shake, shake, shakedy shake. Hands down, shake, shake, shakedy shake. To the back, to the front, to the si-si-side.

The pupils found it quite easy to repeat each line after Sola and I and clearly enjoyed using their bodies for 'shakedy shaking', although sensory engagement was enhanced when they held small shakers to mark out the space 'to the back, to the front and to the sides' around them in space. Singing also helped the pupils with timing when to take a breadth, since the rhythm of song and speech as Classen notes, is dependent on the rhythm of breathing, the breadth of life itself (Classen 1993: 107). Paying attention to the breath and shaking the body while singing was seen to connect the inside of the body with the external world in an amusing manner. Furthermore singing the grandma song, which was active embodied fun for all the pupils permitted those who were linguistically less able to reinforce literacy work on upper and lower case letters in the alphabet, as they were motivated to note 'G' and 'g' are for grandma at the beginning, middle and end of sentences respectively.

Following the song activity pupils had a quiet period of resting their bodies while listening to tapes of African music. This aimed to impart a sense of intention, of musical form as distinct from simple sound and to introduce the musical instruments from the handling collection. At the outset of this relaxation hearing gentle tracts of music played on the thumb piano or mbira, the xylophone, the antelope horn, bells and a range of drums also appeared to provide a sense of emotional freedom, which seemed to visibly relax the pupils further. Whether this freedom occurred by virtue of music's transitory existence in time and space, or is due to the power of the musical sounds to enter the body and deeply move or 'touch' emotionally but without the physical human contact that many pupils found difficult is unclear, but the emotional affect was strongly seen in the body. It seemed the pupils could not be 'unaffected' by the power of musical sound to penetrate and promote positive emotion (Stoller 1989: 109).

Perhaps there is a certain sense in which the pupils experienced a 'sensual wraparound of sound', as well as smell, touch and the visual delight in the colourful African textiles here, which helped to promote bodily feelings of 'togetherness' and ease in the social space that may be similar to the forest dwelling Kaluli people of New Guinea's ways of knowing that Steven Feld describes (Feld 2005: 184). What was clearly a major contributing factor to the pupil's increased calm and embodied receptivity according to the teachers was the power of the objects and Sola's professional direction, her pace and timing. Sola helped to promote embodied knowledge by working sensually with and through the body – engaging the embodied mind and emotions – and bringing special objects to life through her musical skill and her sensitivity, which heightened the emotional appreciation and communicative skills of the pupils. Sola dressed in traditional costume and dramatically employed her own powerful live voice alongside the instruments in the musical activities she developed for the pupils. This seemed to provide a new key to unlocking positive emotions and a compelling sensory route to the communication of ideas, moods and feelings, of self and of others in the school group, as well as those represented in the musical forms.

These communicative aspects of music are of special significance for its connection with bodily sensory interest. Just as timing is key to music so pace and rhythm are vital to progress museum/school learning, and after the morning break the boys were introduced to screen-printing. By lunchtime they constructed one half of the introductory day banner on the theme of chairs and seats to mirror the key object, the Ashante stool. They created a variety of shapes including benches, stools and upright chairs, seats from the dentist, the barbers and an impressive looking electric chair! At the end of the day the pupils posed for a photo with the completed 'Chair Banner.'

Working on Respect at the Museum

New Woodlands School visited the Horniman Museum on day two of their project. Seated around their selected key object in the *African Worlds* exhibition, the day started with a review of their introduction day, which had taken place at the start of that week. It is important to reinforce learning for all pupils and especially so for this group of pupils with special educational needs. Holding up their 'Chair Banner' in front of their selected key object the Ashante stool permitted connection with prior knowledge and provoked exclamations of pride in their creative abilities. This positive feeling was attached to the subsequent days work.

While New Woodland boys worked with the key object 'Ashante Stool Museum number: 34.136', which is intricately carved from wood by an, 'unknown' maker, they were also able to observe a large range of material culture, as well as historical and contemporary video material on display in Horniman's *African Worlds* exhibition. As team-leaders we were able to work with the richness of the exhibition, which helped prevent any tendency to 'fix' African peoples and their knowledge, in a timeless past behind the glass cases. We also all adopted a feminist-hermeneutic or respectful dialogical approach with the boys, which permitted us to draw connections between people and processes, past and present times, the distant and local practices that sustain human lives and culture within specific socio-political contexts.

Additionally, while walking around to observe, talk about and draw the beautiful aesthetic displays of museum objects certainly inspired awe and wonder, use of the handling objects permitted greater understanding for this group. Handling objects, including a specially carved Ashante stool and two plainer stools made for Ghanaians with less finances helped the boys to see how in addition to royalty, individual stools were specially commissioned to relate to personality and spiritual states as well as social position – for use by many different types of people – people like us. This is a crucial point, educators must be alert to the complexity of difference and similarity within and between cultures to counter the racism that paints the 'other' as an undifferentiated mass.

To illustrate this point, in conversation the Ashante handling stool as a symbol of power, authority and respect in Africa could be pertinently compared with the

Royal Throne representing power in the UK. The boys could really experience these feelings of power and respect in their bodies, since sitting on a stool without a conventional chair-back demands good balance as we saw in the examination of Anlo-Ewe thought. Sitting in a certain posture, gracefully, appropriately dressed in kente cloths, and respectfully attended by classmates, the boys seemed to be transformed into kings. The pupils took turns to sit on the handling stool and then Sola facilitated the expression of their feelings in poetic form using the writing frames 'This chair is for …', 'When I sit on this chair' I feel … and 'I must have …'. Some of the pupil responses include:

> This chair is for (a king/ sitting/ a royal person/ a rich person)
> When I sit on this chair I feel (respect/ happy/ important/ special/ comfortable)
> I must have (respect/ a crown/ drinks/ authority/ protection/ food/ happiness)

Following this activity the boys were asked to find and draw one of the key objects they had looked at on the Internet with Jacqui previously. Their favourite objects included the Egyptian Coffin and Mummy, the Midnight Robber's Headdress and symbols from the Voudou Shrine. In addition to seeing the actual objects, 'the real thing', the boys welcomed the opportunity to form new relationships with volunteer guides during this tour. The male guides were popular. According to the teachers this was probably because a number of the boys felt the lack of male figures in their home lives, and consequently the names Ben and David featured alongside the artefacts in subsequent recollection of the museum visit, including some of the poetic expression. Making a new relationship with a male figure in the museum and reflecting 'together with' with this new figure permitted 'scaffolding' of knowledge in the ZPD that we noted in Chapter 5. In partnership with a more experienced adult the pupils were asked to find two different shapes or patterns, to draw them and to write about what they might represent. There were symbols of strength, the sun and God. With adult help, one young boy was able to compose an elegy, to express a sense of loss for a beloved member of his family beneath his symbols. He commented:

> A grandfather passes on
> To another relation in his family
> I will always love you.

The pupils also had an opportunity to work with their adult guides on writing down some feelings about the stools in the exhibition. Some stools have intricate carvings of leopards and elephants, which are understood to represent the greatness and fierce nature of a King and prompted the following remarks:

> The leopard is kind.
> He doesn't bite.
> The leopard thinks it is a King

This stool looks like a face.
This stool helps me think of home.
I feel happy about my stool.

Next Sola told the boys the myth of the 'first stool', covered in gold, reputedly sent from heaven to the first Ashante King and passed from generation to generation, which was believed to contain the soul of the Ashante nation. Even the king never sat on this sacred stool. It was so precious that on state occasions it was placed on another chair during the ceremonies and protected from the sun by a large umbrella, called a kyrinie. Following this story the boys were better able to appreciate how differing stool designs show levels of social power and authority, such as the addition of silver and gold to denote royal use, the carvings of leopards and elephants to represent the greatness and fierce nature of a King, as well as the various support shapes, which distinguished male or female use in past times. This led to some disgruntled expressions that our special handling stool had none of these distinguishing gold or silver features, and the familiar questions about the price of this object arose.

To the question 'how much does it cost' I could honestly answer 'it's priceless to us in the museum.' In this instance not because of the materials, it is not golden, but because it was a gift from a dear friend who has since died. Knowing the owners of the handling stools provided useful human prompts to ground the pupils' talk. My Ghanian friend who died wanted the pupils who visited Horniman to use his stool and we remembered him warmly with each new use. Clearly I could not replace this stool with any amount of money, as I could the Pokeman that the boys were agitatedly collecting at the time. Then we contrasted the museum handling collection with the boy's own collecting practice and the idea that certain objects are connected with prestige at different times and in different places emerged.

Next Sola was inspired to narrate two short stories – a myth of origin and the historical story of Ya the great queen ruler of Ghana, which connected talk with women as power figures in our lives today, mothers, grandmothers and aunts (important primary carers for a number of the pupils), teachers and head teacher at New Woodlands, as well as a return to the theme of respect, offering equal respect for all: men and women, elders and youth, Black and white people.

Stories permitted discussion of the key concept, respect, and in the to and fro of conversation some critical thinking on the associated notions of power and authority in contemporary and historical societies emerged. In Ghanaian society today the Ashante King maintains prestige as an important symbolic figure, escorted by chiefs during ceremonies. Historically the king's own stool was a symbol of his power, his authority and commanded respect, but this was provisional. Royal authority, inherent in the stool, was dependent on maintaining the respect of the people during the ruler's lifetime. The stool of a respected ruler could be placed in a shrine after death and subject to acts of commemoration and remembrance. On the other hand the people could withdraw the stool from a king who lost their respect. This point prompted us to the related ideas of losing or gaining privileges at school through good behaviour and how many individual extra points the museum visit might lead to, since a trip to eat burgers at MacDonalds was the much desired reward at the end of each month.

Additionally the storytelling process provided an opportunity for the pupils to calm down and to rest, which was essential for a number of this group who suffered from Attention Deficit Syndrome (ADS). A moment of stillness importantly 'balances' the child in Anlo-Ewe terms, which permits focused thought and is not an antithesis to the active subjectivity that characterises learning at the museum frontiers.

Creative Work Back at School

During the four days of subsequent project work at school each of the two Year 6 classes screen-printed two ceremonial deck-chairs and a large ceremonial umbrella representing those used in some West African state ceremonies, which can be seen at Plate 23. The seats were specially made to denote respect for their teachers and for their use in the playground area.

In addition to the artwork the project started each day with a brainstorming session, looking for keywords around respect, power and authority and referring back to the frame poems the pupils had written with Sola and during their Horniman Museum visit. First of all the boys wrote acrostic poems using their names and indicating their special interests. Two examples from Luke and Anton are typical in revealing the 'inner mind' lying 'underneath tough skin'.

> Likes Maths and English
> Underneath his tough skin he's lovely
> Keeps playing football
> Even when I am sleepy I still play football
>
> Anton likes flowers on a summer's day, flowers in his mind
> Now he thinks he's going wild
> To and fro he sniffs the rose
> Only on his birthday
> Now he must go home

The boys worked very hard on their writing and considered what power and respect might mean to individuals and how respect is gained. Brainstorming for ideas and words prompted 'respect' and 'power' acrostic group poems. I offer just one example:

Respect makes people feel nice and loved. Respectful people listen and pay attention

Education is fun. I like Maths and making my own choices

Silly people do not gain respect. Sensible people do not butt in on a conversation

Power to the people!! Affection to the people!! Kindness to the people!!

Energy gives you life and adds strength to your body – body power

Calm voices, command and control, showing our brain education, showing our leadership to the world

Taking turns, giving everyone the ability to move, we don't make anyone feel worse because it is disrespectful.

They also composed individual lines of poetry using the frames 'respect/power is ...' and 'respect/power is not ...'. Here are some of their ideas:

Power is what makes you strong

Respect is what you give and do

Respect is sharing

Power gives you ENERGY

Respect is when you help people

Respect is not making someone feel worse about something. Feelings.

Respect makes people feel NICE AND LOVED

Power means leadership, body power and BRAIN power

You get respect by being nice.

Based on their initial responses two phrases were discussed further and completed individually. One pupil wrote:

I command respect by:

being good

helping someone

being kind

saying please and thank you

my inner feelings

I demand respect because:

I helped you

I listened to you

I did as you wished

I helped you when you were sick

I took you out

I made you food

Plate 23 New Woodlands Respect Stool and Kyrinie
Source: David Forster.

Conclusion

In this chapter I have drawn on diverse theories to argue that thought expresses itself in and through the body, the sensory body, in embodied action, and further that our very sense of identity is not based on disembodied thought, but rather the feeling we have of our body and the way it connects us to the social world and to our relationships with others in this world. Thus the concept of embodiment is understood in terms of emplacement, since the different spaces in which people live are essentially social spaces, where communication can be achieved through performance or utterance.

This point was highlighted by the Anlo-Ewe example, which also demonstrated the way in which the symbolic is connected to the material in society and how it is not possible to separate or to fuse these spheres. In the museum the New Woodlands case study leant on the Anlo-Ewe experience of being embodied as mediated through cultural representations, focusing on the stool. The New Woodlands work pointed to the importance of the expanded museum/school space, not only to benefit cross-cultural understanding and knowledge construction, but also to empower the economically disadvantaged boys with EBD through a new sense of being embodied.

Next in my concluding chapter I shall offer some concise reflection on what has been achieved in *Learning at the Museum Frontiers*. I shall highlight the key relationships between the three sections and suggest areas for future research in my concluding remarks.

Conclusion:
Pedagogy in Museums

Voicing Human Rights and Making Meaning through Storytelling

Let me open this concluding section with a story that draws together some critical threads of *Learning at the Museum Frontiers*. I outline one story, taken from a museum programme that was designed to hold appeal for an adult audience by successfully drawing together a range of ideas and collections, which later served as inspiration for creative writing exercises with a range of new audiences.

> Imagine! Sister Goose swimming at dead of night in a huge pond shimmering under the moonlight, observed by Bra (Brer/Brother) Fox from the waters edge. As Sister Goose swims closer Brother Fox can no longer contain his appetite for her and communicates his intention to 'eat you up bones an' all for me dinner.' Sister Goose protests her freedom and contests his right to eat her. She invokes the law that she understands is a means of protecting her right to swim in her own environment, free from fear of being eaten by anyone passing by, and asserts her right to take her case against him to the Court.

> Admirably reasonable, Bra Fox agrees to follow her project in the Court, after which he intends to accomplish his own project of eating her up. Sister Goose is permitted entry to the court by the officials, who are all foxes. Ushers, court scribes, jury, lawyers and judge, indeed the entire apparatus of the system is composed of foxes. The court verdict is given in favour of Bra Fox, who after waiting for Sister Goose to see the legal process in action, promptly eats her up for his dinner! (Adapted from Anim-Addo 2007: 88)

This tale clearly highlights human rights and the nature of trust, which is vital to collaborative praxis. At Horniman I have seen it provoke much dialogue on justice within an adult 'Tales from Around the World' programme. Indeed storytelling has been found to be a key interpretive strategy for adults visiting museums and generally a way of making meaning or sense of lives, all over the globe (Roberts 1997; Falk and Dierking 2000). As Lois Silverman states:

> Visitors "make meaning" through a *constant process of remembering and connecting*. ... visitors' needs affect the memories and connections that become salient during a visit. Humans share a *basic need to express* the meanings we

make by telling them, often *in the form of stories*, to ourselves and to others. The museum setting lends itself well to this storytelling, not only by curators and educators, but by visitors as well. (Silverman 1995: 162) [my emphasis]

Here Silverman contends that storytelling provides a means of making and sharing meanings in the museum, which satisfies a basic human 'need', to communicate or 'express' personal meaning making. In this book I have I examined the ways in which museums, notably Horniman in UK, the Museum of World Culture in Sweden and District Six Museum in South Africa, have given support to this meaning making process through facilitating the representation of personal and community stories, herstories for CWWA. I aimed to show that working in partnership through such storytelling projects provides a powerful way of museums to engage in a dynamic dialogue with new audiences, which can enable collections and the ideas we attach to them to gain in relevance for diverse local and global audiences beyond the story-givers. This is a strong claim, which detailed examples attempted to justify throughout. At this point I should like to examine some questions that have emerged.

It is becoming a commonplace statement in the museum profession that 'objects can tell many stories' and that these stories are only limited by our imaginations. Yet perhaps an important question that arises here concerns truth and interpretation. Are all objects open to interpretation by any visitor at any time? Are all 'stories' equally valid? Should some visitors be permitted to tell stories with mildly sexist or racist undertones, perhaps inherent in traditional tales? Does the museum have the authority or responsibility to expunge such undesirable elements from their interpretation? Should certain voices, such as those of CWWA considered in Section 1 or voices from originating communities take precedence, due to their silencing in a colonial past for example? How do these questions of contested histories impact on the national story and the need to build socially cohesive local communities in the twenty-first century where we see division at local and global levels?

These are large questions. In short I have argued throughout this book for museums to promote democracy and citizenship through the critical pedagogy, informed by feminist-hermeneutics, which I have outlined with reference to museum examples. Such pedagogy is based on collaboration and the telling of more diverse stories, which does not imply passivity on the part of either partner, but rather an active dialogical exchange imbued with mutual respect, which can ultimately lead to 'intercultural' understanding and more cohesive communities through highlighting a common sense of belonging. In this respect the book reinforces the Council of Europe's 2008 White Paper, which states:

Museums and heritage sites have the potential to challenge, in the name of common humanity, selective narratives reflecting the historical dominance of members of one or other ethnic or national community, and to offer scope for mutual recognition by individuals from diverse backgrounds. (Council of Europe, White Paper 2008: 33 <http://www.coe.int/t/dg4/intercultural/Source/White%20Paper_final_revised_EN.pdf> accessed on 07.02.2009)

The concept of the frontiers and the privileging of the arts as a route to embodied knowledge(s) that thread through this book also resonate in the 2008 Paper. The Paper specifically highlights the 'arts' as a powerful means of 'allowing for individual expression, critical self-reflection and mediation', since they 'naturally cross borders and connect and speak directly to people's emotions' (ibid.). I have outlined a number of museums that have engaged in successful artist and community collaborations to further intercultural understanding in *Learning at the Museum Frontiers*, such as Horniman with CWWA and the Museum of World Culture (MWC) with Fred Wilson. Yet collaboration may provoke dissent along the way as we saw for example at MWC. However as Lagerkvist and Luke observe, museum controversy is not to be feared but welcomed as prompting a meeting ground between belief systems (Lagerkvist 2006; Luke 2006).

Gadamer also notes the value of misunderstanding that is helpful here in taking a first step towards the horizon of the other. He states:

> It is generally true that even when one misunderstands something, if one has been listening carefully, more has probably been understood than if the most exact knowledge had been applied without listening to the poem as a whole. (Gadamer 1997: 186)

Stories and creative writing are helpful to museum collaboration since they challenge the notion of one true view. Gadamer further notes on this: 'I am convinced that it is a serious mistake for one to think it is an advantage to have in mind what is 'correct' (Gadamer 1997: 133). For Gadamer in interpretation 'correct' is always relative, since in terms of poetry, 'the poet himself reads it differently each time' (ibid. 183). *Learning at the Museum Frontiers* has attempted to show that opening up the museum to a range of diverse voices can enliven the museum and promote social inclusion in the wider world.

On the other hand this inclusive praxis does not argue for an anything goes approach and Gadamer is not a relativist. He declares that human beings share common bonds, such as language, which presents us with the possibility of understanding. While aligning myself with certain elements of 'postmodernism' such as the raising of new voices, I have defended the right to say certain discourses, for instance racism, sexism and homophobia, is always and everywhere wrong. In this sense I hold fast to specific tenets of modernism and highlighted The International Convention on the Rights of the Child (CRC) as particularly important.

I write here on the 60th anniversary of The Universal Declaration of Human Rights (UDHR) in 2008. The UDHR condemns all discrimination and it is to the importance of this document for the museum context that I shall turn to next.

Values: National and Universal Declarations

British museums in the twenty-first century are working within a national framework that is increasingly insular, fearful of 'otherness' and protective of 'us' standing firm for civilised values against 'them' and it is to these ideas that I now turn. The Prime Minister, Gordon Brown, defines British values as 'liberty, responsibility and fairness', while his predecessor Tony Blair highlighted British values as a 'belief in democracy, the rule of law, tolerance, equal treatment for all' (Brown 2006; Blair 2006).

One may wonder, in the wider world of European museums and in post-Apartheid South Africa for example that I have considered, whether these are peculiarly British values, or whether they are more aligned with the international principles of human rights and the expressed values of modern democracy in Nation States the world over. The Universal Declaration of Human Rights (UDHR) adopted by the United Nations General Assembly in 1948, is a foundational document posing the notion of all human beings as members of a human 'family', with consequent entitlement to equality in dignity and rights, from which global justice and peace ensues. At the outset The Declaration asserts the need for:

> [R]ecognition of the inherent dignity and of the equal and inalienable rights of
> all members of the human family is the foundation of freedom, justice and peace
> in the world. (United Nations Organization, 1948 Preface; UNESCO, 2002)

Widening this notion of the 'family' is important in the context of feminist-hermeneutics museum work since it highlights the African 'ethics of care' within the social group, respect for the rights of others and reciprocity (Hill-Collins 1991). As Doctor Martin Luther King, wrote from his prison cell in Birmingham Alabama, 'an inescapable network of mutuality' binds our futures 'in a single garment of destiny, since 'whatever affects one directly, affects all indirectly' (King 1962: 77 in Banks et al. 2005: 7).

At Horniman we long considered how we might work with an understanding of the universality of human rights, a moral and legal framework, to include as human beings all those in need even if they do not hold national citizenship. In this we observed the UDHR, requirement of member nations to 'disseminate the text and expound the principles' widely throughout 'educational institutions', which tacitly includes the museum (<http://www.un.org/en/documents/udhr/> accessed on 29.04.2008). We saw the UDHR as a vital document that offered an ethical framework to promote dialogical exchange and the recognition of every voice at the museum frontiers. Specifically: Article 2 declaring no-one shall be subject to unfair discrimination; Article 5 that prohibits treating anyone in a degrading manner; Article 10 stating a fair hearing should be vouchsafed to all; Articles 12 and 18 highlighting respect for privacy and diverse religious beliefs; Article 19 demanding people listen to alternative views even those with which they disagree and Article 20 valuing peaceful association and the right to protest.

It is worth emphasising that Horniman is not alone in anti-discriminatory activity and observance of the UDHR. To briefly highlight UK museums that are countering the British National Party's (BNP)[1] false representation of Black and Minority Ethnic (BME) peoples through exhibition, 'Sanctuary' (2003) at the Gallery of Modern Art in Glasgow (GoMA) and 'Belonging' (2006) at the Museum of London (MoL) are notable in the work with refugee communities. Museum learning here has been seen to work with visitors' curiosity and human empathy, whether they are members of the dominant majority or of a minority group, to welcome diversity and reinforce human rights as normative values within the local nation state and in the wider world.

Within this brief discussion of Universal Human Rights I would like to advocate a notion of 'nation' that is fluid and has been characterised as comprising 'imagined communities' (Anderson, 1991). In *Learning at the Museum Frontiers* I have suggested that the museum of the twenty-first century has a vital role in developing the imagined community of the nation-state, which I recommend might profitably be viewed as a global 'community of communities', through creative exhibitions and programming (Parekh 2000). Now let us turn to examine this notion of communities, which has wider implications for other parts of the globe.

Nation as a Community of Communities

The *Future of Multiethnic Britain* or *The Parekh Report* is an important document offering guidelines for public institutions, including the museum (Parekh 2000). Parekh's remit was to 'analyse the current state of multiethnic Britain' and 'propose ways of countering racial discrimination and disadvantage' to 'make Britain a confident and vibrant multicultural society at ease with its rich diversity. The preface to the Report is especially valuable, providing six 'fundamental beliefs' or values around which British people may unite and develop a sense of community cohesion. Parekh's first principle recognises the difficult notion of promoting 'equal worth' within economic or social inequalities. Secondly Parekh envisions Britain as a 'community of communities' who may need to reconcile, if not resolve, conflict. For the purpose of the museum Parekh's third, fourth and fifth principles may be summed up as encompassing the need to nurture a mutual respect for differences within a cohesive sense of belonging and shared identity that affirms the values of tolerance and dialogue; while the final principle is to tackle the 'subtle and complex phenomenon' of 'racism' (ibid. iix). These points have resonance for museums located in the port cites of the newly democratic South Africa and Sweden, as I have attempted to demonstrate in Section 2.

---

1   The BNP is a far right political group in the UK who gained some power in recent local government elections.

Parekh notes that museums located in Britain's ports are sites where the self/ other dichotomy and issues of racism may be productively explored. For example he writes of the 1999 NMM (National Maritime Museum) exhibition that showed a 'Jane Austin-like figure sipping tea with a sugar bowl on the table beside her', while from under the 'floor beneath her feet a manacled black arm reached out as if from the hold of a slave ship' (Parekh 2000: 159). This exhibition is notable for drawing attention to the historical roots of the wealth gained during the Transatlantic Slave Trade that lies at the hearts of many British Museums but it can be criticised in postcolonial theory. Specifically in presenting the 'silent native' as a poor object, reduced to an identity as 'oppressed victim', and so reinforcing the dominant European self as subject at the centre of representation (Chow 1996: 123-5, 132). It has also been argued that in terms of the visitor's meaning making perhaps an excessively challenging display may merely serve to position the shocked visitor at a greater distance' from the displayed 'other', to reject or contest complicity in histories of atrocity as oppressor and prevent an appeal to the notion of shared humanity as Riegel notes (Riegel 1996: 88).

Diverse Stories of Nation to Challenge Racism

The NMM exhibition certainly made uncomfortable viewing for many visitors, demonstrating in stark visual terms the white female 'self' sitting in such 'civilised' surroundings at the expense of the Black 'other' who is regarded literally as beneath the human and may therefore be subjected to appalling cruelty. In the British media reports criticised the exhibit for 'depriving the British people of any aspect of their history in which they can take justifiable pride' to which the director replied that museums are 'not just there to perpetuate the old view. We want galleries to be challenging' (Parekh 2000: 159). Yet while Parekh emphasises the need to address the causes of 'racist violence' and how perpetrators attempt to justify it, in reality the NMM, like all museums with a national and international responsibility, treads a fine line between alienating its traditional customer base – the white middle-classes – and may shy away from involvement in the more challenging aspects of antiracism. For example, as Ratan Vaswani of the UK Museums Association points out, the NMM 'ignored the racist murder of the teenager Stephen Lawrence in Eltham, a few miles from the NMM, despite the families high profile campaign that led to the Macpherson Report' (Vaswani MJ 5, 2000: 19).

I have referred to Macpherson in *Learning at the Museum Frontier*, but here I want to note the importance of museums addressing 'othering' in their displays and programmes. I emphasise that new approaches do not aim to erase dominant histories of the powerful historical oppressor – an impossible task – but simply to tell different stories and provide fuller, deeper histories, which might facilitate points of contact between viewers. My case study museum examples have attempted to show this is beneficial for the whole 'community of communities' not just for the Black communities whose histories have been suppressed within the museum walls. Parekh quotes the novelist Ben Okri on this point. Okri states

> Nations and peoples are largely the stories they feed themselves. If they tell themselves stories that are lies, they will suffer the consequences. If they tell themselves stories that face their own truths, they will allow us all to free histories for future flowerings. (Okri quoted in Parekh 2000: 103)

What The Parekh Report highlights for the museum here and elsewhere is the possibility to involve the many different contributions of diverse communities to the national story, which is essentially an intertwined history between Black and white citizens. A major value for the museum context, is the opportunities presented by museums for exhibitions to show historical events 'through more than one pair of eyes, and narrated within more than one story, which calls for a 'democratising approach' (Parakh 2000: 163). In this regard Parekh highlights the 'Liverpool Museum on the Slave Trade' as a courageous exception to the selective amnesia about Britain's former empire. In 2007 the International Slavery Museum (ISM) opened on the third floor of the Maritime Museum in Liverpool and replaced the older gallery. ISM dedicated a gallery to the memory of a local student Anthony Walker who was murdered by racists in the summer of 2005. In this way Liverpool helps to give what Vaswani at the UK Museum Association, called for, 'a responsible history of slavery', which 'cannot help but raise the issue of how to treat the wounds of racism' (Vaswani MJ 5, 2000: 17).

Racism does not disappear if museums ignore it and perpetuate old colonial stories. As I noted earlier more diverse stories need not be told in a simple hectoring manner in the museum, which would be counterproductive, nevertheless institutions such as ours should be 'reflexive, serious and sustained' in our thought on 'change as a consequence of cultural diversity' (Hall 1980, 2000: 51). I find the notion of playful approaches to objects helpful in this task.

Play, Story and the Impact of the Museum Experience

In this book I have emphasised the value of material culture and the biographies that surround it. I have also made a case for extending the right to creatively tell different stories of material culture, with due regard for raising diverse voices on what has been unthinkingly taken as the one 'truth', eternally and universally. In Section 1 Anim-Addo highlighted the importance of playing with language and telling personal her/stories for members of CWWA with African objects, noting Gadamer's influence in this regard (Gadamer 1981). Section 2 also emphasised the values of such storytelling for previously oppressed and marginalised communities at the Museum of World Culture (MWC) in Sweden, which at the District Six Museum (D6M) in South Africa seemed to provide some healing of the painful memories that were evoked (Morrison 1988, 1991; 1994b). Then in Section 3 the idea of playful storytelling was examined with respect to young peoples' learning, where storytelling and creative writing based on African objects offered a pathway towards literacy, through the enunciation of new identities.

A recent study of the way young children interpret various types of exhibition environment including a: traditional art gallery, interactive science centre, natural history museum and a social history museum, supports the idea of play and story being important elements of the exhibition experience for the child. It seems to be through the familiar socio-cultural context and the familiar learning modes of play and story that childrens' learning is best facilitated, since the child is able to link the new exhibits and knowledge to the prior understandings embedded in their everyday world (Anderson et al. 2002: 213).

The evidence for Anderson et al.'s assertion rests on the significant impact of play and story on the children's memory of their visits. For example, the experience of climbing on large-scale outdoor sculptures at the art gallery proved to be particularly memorable and the study concluded that since playing on climbing apparatus outdoors was a highly familiar context in which the children had previously explored and learnt in their everyday lives, this accounted for the children being able to easily recall the new experience in detail (Anderson et al. 2002: 222). Similarly, the children in the study clearly remembered the stories they had been asked to develop while sitting and looking closely at particular artworks in the gallery. This storytelling experience with the art helped to provide conducive learning environments by building upon the frequent occurrences of story in the children's lives and the familiar context in which children learn (ibid. 223). In contrast the interactive science centre where the exhibits were not related to everyday experiences, was less well-remembered and mentioned at interview.

Clifford casts light on the idea of play for adults. He speaks of 'intimate encounters' with artifacts in anthropology collections, which gives us permission to become 'adult-children', exploring 'territories of danger and desire' (Clifford 1994: 216). At Horniman collaborative research teams have found that these territories are 'tabooed' zones because they reveal the complexity of individual identities *and* a common humanity; our differences *and* our similarities; our past *and* our present. Similarly in Sweden and South Africa I observed objects providing points of human contact across time and space and illuminating a brighter future for all. Roger Simon illuminates this point. The museums I have considered offer spaces for a public narrative, a 'story space', where we may come to recognise ethical relationships between self and others 'lives lived in times and places other than our own' (Simon 2006: 190). Simon defines this as an interhuman, 'holding the present', to open up broader future possibilities (Simon 2006: 203).

In *Learning at the Museum Frontiers* the notions of diaspora identities and hybridity were considered vital to museum education projects, which presented audiences with the more optimistic futures Simon highlights. It may be helpful to briefly recap the key points here.

Diaspora Hybrid Identities and Points of Suture

Stuart Hall defines the Black experience as a '*Diaspora* experience', which carries with it a 'process of unsettling, recombination, hybridization and "cut and mix"' (Hall 1994: 258). Hall further elucidates this experience as 'profoundly fed and nourished by ... rich cultural roots', which encompass 'the African experience; the reconnection with Afro-Caribbean experience' (ibid.). He also emphasises the complexity of the Diaspora experience, which demands 'creative enunciation' through 'the categories of the present' (Hall 1994: 258).

'Diaspora identities' are seen in terms of a vital mixture and movement of historical and contemporary elements, across temporal and spatial borderlands from Africa, the Caribbean and the west. Hall's thesis on identity opposes the either-or of dualist thought and he rejects any simple reversing of binary oppositions. For example he denies a 'new essentially good black subject' as well as the old stereotype of the lazy degenerate. His primary concern is with political transformation and he aims to build 'forms of solidarity and identification which make common struggle possible but without suppressing real heterogeneity of interests and identities' (Hall 1994: 254-5).

This profoundly anti-essentialist and anti-dualist thought stands in contrast to racism and sexism, which fixes people into rigid categories. Paul Gilroy cites the 'ubiquitous theme' of racism as an 'absolutist view of black and white cultures, as fixed, mutually impermeable expressions of racial and national identity' (Gilroy 1996: 263). This view fears 'contamination' and harbours a fantasy of Imagined Communities, of 'return' to 'pure origins' (Anderson 1983).

The collaborative praxis at the museum frontiers I have expounded in this book highlights the dynamic nature of identity construction today. Movement and change is recognised as positive forces for creating new forms of art, writing, and ways of being in the world. Identity is not seen as predetermined or fixed by racial characteristics, nor as one continuous entity, but as a process of active hybrid construction from disparate fragments of similarity and difference. I have argued that the museum proves an ideal site for such construction and re-construction. It provides a discursive space of 'suture' or connection between the local and the global; past and present; individual and group (Hall 1997: 5-6). In this book feminist-hermeneutics has been shown to affect various points of temporary suture, or joining of subjects in different structures of meaning. Suture roots identity in complex political structures: of temporary affiliation, attachment, and ways of belonging. It also involves a perpetual re-conceptualisation of 'subjectivity' to permit a variety of fruitful new positionings.

Writing Subjects Remapping Identities in the Museum

At Horniman I have found that Hall and Gilroy's re-writing of dominant or 'colonial' discourse(s) and their Diaspora scholarship can help to bring vibrant new voices from out of the 'shadow' to illuminate traditional debates, in ways that are useful to museum praxis, as I showed with reference to CWWA in Section 1 (Spivak 1984: 83). Diaspora theory marks a fragile space of alternative voice and visibility, which permits the objects of colonial discourse to reconstruct themselves as subjects. Trinh T. Minh-ha emphasises this point. She says.

> Writing the body' is that abstract-concrete, personal-political realm of excess not fully contained by writing's unifying structural forces. ... It is a way of making theory in gender, of making theory a politics of everyday life, thereby re-writing the ethnic female subject as a site of differences. (Trinh 1989: 44, 59)

Throughout this book I have highlighted the importance of agency, of all 'subjects' actively claiming identity, and for the museum to engage in the ongoing process of hermeneutic 'listening' to the identities claimed in the 'uprising' textualities of diverse communities. In Section 2 the book attempted to show how a radical consciousness of the possibilities for creative 're-mapping' of identities might be developed at the museum frontiers, at (D6M) in South Africa , Edo-Tokyo Museum in Japan, in Oxford during outreach, as well as in the MWC in Sweden and at Horniman London. Furthermore feminist-hermeneutics was presented as a useful method to facilitate such re-mapping (Boyce-Davis 1994: 108-9).

Remapping has been seen here to address the issues of misrecognition that Taylor warns is harmful to identities. He states:

> ... our identity is partly shaped by recognition or its absence, often by the misrecognition of others, and so a person or group of people can suffer real damage, real distortion, if the people or society around them mirror back to them a confining or demeaning or contemptible picture of themselves. Nonrecognition or misrecognition can inflict harm, can be a form of oppression, imprisoning someone in a false, distorted, and reduced mode of being. (Taylor 1994: 26)

Taylor also emphasises commonalities alongside differences, helpfully highlighting for the museum context the way individual identities and community identities overlap. Human identity, he notes is negotiated and constructed in dialogical exchange *with* significant others who include family, friends, teachers as well as the institutions such as the museum they operate within, and since this negotiation continues throughout life museums offer opportunities to progress lifelong and life wide learning. As I have been considering African collection in this book it is worth highlighting the African concept of 'umbuntu', which roughly translates as 'I am because you are', which similarly emphasises an African ethics of care for the wider community group that individuals can progress through dialogue in the museum (Hill-Collins 1991).

Similarly Amy Gutman notes the human capacity of individuals to 'integrate, reflect upon, and modify their own cultural heritage and that of other people with whom they come into contact', which the museums I have discussed are ideally placed to facilitate in the museum as forum space (Gutman 1994: 7). She agrees Taylor's view that human identity is constructed dialogically in human relationships and asserts the need for a politics that enables public recognition of and debate on 'those aspects of our identities that we share, or potentially share, with other citizens' (ibid.).

Music, like language and art, is a widespread characteristic of human society. Music and musical instruments have featured and proved highly motivating in the museums and programmes I have considered in this book and it is to this aspect that I shall turn next.

Motivation, Music and the Senses

Briefly, musical instruments act as vital 'hooks' to capture young peoples attention, which if museums are able to connect with the long-term interest in music that is such a widespread phenomena amongst young people around the world, can promote 'flow' learning (Csikszentmihalyi and Hermanson 1995). In Section 3 I suggested pupils were engaged in flow learning, intrinsically motivated in the object-based activities for their own sake, and not the extrinsic reward of an exam for example. With respect to musical engagement the state of flow was seen to be deeply pleasurable, inspiring the desire to repeat the musical experience and revisit the museum.

At Horniman, in the pupil's musical engagement we observed all four dimensions of the 'aesthetic' experience: perceptual, emotional, intellectual and communicative, which Csikszentmihalyi and Robinson highlight with reference to elite employees in Western museums of the visual and decorative arts. Csikszentmihalyi and Robinson note perceptual qualities extending beyond the visual to embrace other senses, notably touch, which reveals the balance, weight, temperature and mechanisms – the precise way a clasp fastens a gold necklace for example (Csikszentmihalyi and Robinson 1990: 32). In Section 3 I considered how through touch pupils were able to have an impact on the world and affect change. For example, pupils found musical instruments could be made to issue sounds and the sense of power this imparted was enhanced by wearing textiles that transformed the bodies they adorned, which served to lift and lighten mood (Tuan 2005: 75-78).

We observed music, like Csikszentmihalyi and Robinson's visual aesthetic experience, to be a 'thrilling' sensual, emotional and intellectual communicative media (Csikszentmihalyi and Robinson 1990: 36). Pupils found the sensual bodily contact with the objects enriching emotionally and intellectually and this holistic experience was enhanced when the object provided communication routes with the past era when the objects were made. In this sense the pupils were moved or 'touched' figuratively by the culture of others. Being touched figuratively speaking also means to be concerned. Since touch can arouse sympathy and empathetic feelings for the distant world of others, the sensual embodied experience of pleasure in touch is said to be 'self-affirming and self-transcending' (Classen 1993: 69, 76).

Communication here is seen as a multidimensional experience of bridging a time space gap by integrating perceptual, emotional and intellectual aspects. The metaphor of 'transport' can describe something of this communicative quality for individuals – a unifying of the senses and a releasing of the self in communication with the other – to more fully recognise the self (Csikszentmihalyi and Robinson 1990: 68). Transport requires active and creative work of decoding over time. To be transported in this way implies a positive way to focus on the wider world, to share the dreams, emotions and ideas of others from different times and places that are encoded in the work. In the words of Homi Bhabha:

> What is crucial to such a vision is that we must not merely change the narratives
> of our histories, but transform our sense of what it means to live, to be, in other
> times and different spaces, both human and historical. (Bhabha. 1995: 256)

In 2008, when the African American Barack Obama has been elected President of the USA, museums and their visitors may feel justly optimistic that Bhabha's words may come to fruition, despite Trevor Philip's contention that this could not happen in the UK (Philips 2008). I conclude this book in a spirit of hope and look forward to 'listening' museums working collaboratively for the sake of the future millennium, by embracing their role in progressing democracy and citizenship (Parekh 2000: 151; Osler and Starkey 2005).

Bibliography

Allen, J. and Littlefield, J. 2000, *Without Sanctuary* <http://www.withoutsanctuary.org/> [accessed 01.09.2008].

Ames, M. 1995, *Cannibal Tours and Glass Boxes*, U.B.C. Press, Canada.

Anderson, B. 1983, *Imagined Communities: Reflections on the Origins and Spread of Nationalism*, Verso, London.

Anderson, D. et al. 2002, 'Children's museum experiences: Identifying powerful mediators of learning', *Curator* 45(3), July, 213-231.

Anderson, D. 1999, *A Commonwealth: Museums and Learning in the United Kingdom: Report to the Department of National Heritage*, London.

Anim-Addo, J. 1998a, 'Another Doorway? Black Women Writing the Museum Experience', *Journal of Museum Ethnography* 10: 93-104.

Anim-Addo, J. (ed.) 1998b, *Another Doorway. Visible in the Museum*, Mango Publishing, London.

Anim-Addo, J. 1999, 'Introduction', in Ross, J, and Anim-Addo, J. (eds) 1999, *Voice, Memory, Ashes*, Mango Publishing, London: 9-10.

Anim-Addo, J. 2007a, *Touching the Body: History Language and African-Caribbean Women's Writing*, Mango Publishing, London.

Anim-Addo, J. 2007b, 'Inventing the Self: An Introduction to the Black Woman Subject/Object in Britain from 1507' in Anim-Addo, J. and Scafe, S. (eds) 2007, *I am Black / White / Yellow: An Introduction to the Black Body in Europe*, Mango Publishing, London: 17-36.

Anim-Addo, J. 2008, *Imoinda or She Who Will Lose Her Name*, Mango Publishing, London.

Anzaldua, G. 1987, *Borderlands/La Frontera, The New Mestiza*, Spinsters/Aunt Lute, California.

Appiah, K. 1995, 'Why Africa? Why Art?' in Phillips, T. (ed.) 1995, *Africa: Art of a Continent*, Royal Academy Publication, Prestel, Munich and New York: 21-26.

Appiah, K. 1991, 'Is the Post-in Postmodernism the Post-in Postcolonialism' in Mongia, P. (ed.) 1996, *Contemporary Postcolonial Theory, A Reader*, Arnold Hodder Headline Group, London: 55-109.

Appleton, J. 2001, 'Museums for "The People"?' in Watson, S. (ed.) 2007, *Museums and their Communities*, Routledge, London: 114-126.

Araeen, R. 1993, 'From Primitivism to Ethnic Arts' in Hiller, S. (ed.) 1993, *The Myth of Primitivism*, Routledge, London: 158-182.

Arinze, E. 2000, 'Keynote Address', *Journal of Museum Ethnography* 12: 1-5.

Aristotle, *Poetics*, Telford, K. (trans) 1961, Gateway Editions Ltd., Indiana.

Ashton, C. 2002, 'Speech' Mayor of London, 2002, 'Towards a Vision of Excellence London Schools and the Black Child Conference Report' <http://www.london. gov.uk/mayor/education/lsbc/black_child.pdf> [accessed 26.08.2007].

Back, L. and Solomos, J. (eds) 2000, *Theories of Race and Racism a Reader*, Routledge, London.

Banks, J. et al. 2005, *Democracy and Diversity Principles and Concepts for Educating Citizens in a Global Age* <http://depts.washington.edu/centerme/ home.htm>.

Bann, S. 1984, 'Poetics of the Museum: Lenoir and Du Sommarard' in Preziosi, D. and Farago, C. (eds) 2004, *Grasping the World. The Idea of the Museum*, Ashgate, Aldershot: 65-84.

Barnes, C., Mercer, G. and Shakespeare, T. 2002, *Exploring Disability A Sociological Introduction*, Polity Press, Cambridge.

Bell, D., Caplan, P. and Karim, W. (eds) 1993, *Gendered Fields, Women, Men and Ethnography*, Routledge, London.

Benedict, R. 1943, 'Race: What it is Not' in Back, L. and Solomos, J. (eds) 2000, *Theories of Race and Racism A Reader*, Routledge, London: 113-118.

Bennett, T. 1996, *The Birth of the Museum*, Routledge, London.

Bennett, T. 1988, 'The Exhibitionary Complex' in Preziosi, D. and Farago, C. (eds) 2004, *Grasping the World. The Idea of the Museum*, Ashgate, Aldershot: 413-441.

Bernal, M. 1987, *Black Athena: The Afroasiatic Roots of Classical Civilization*, Rutgers University Press, New Jersey.

Bettleheim, B. 1991, *The Uses of Enchantment*, Penguin, London.

Bhabha, H. 1995, *The Location of Culture*, Routledge, London.

Biebuyck, D. and Herreman, F. 1995, 'Central Africa' in Phillips, T. (ed.) 1995, *Africa: Art of a Continent*, Royal Academy Publication, Prestel, Munich and New York: 231-326.

Birkett, D. 2006, 'Child Benefit', *Museums Journal* (2006) August, 30-33.

Blair, T. 2006, 'Our Nations Future: Multiculturalism and Integration', Speech given at 10 Downing Street 8 December <http://www.number10.gov.uk/ output/Page10563.asp> [accessed 08.03.2006].

Boyce Davis, C. 1994, *Black Women, Writing and Identity, Migrations of the Subject*, Routledge, London.

Braidotti, R. 1994a, *Nomadic Subjects, Embodiment and Sexual Difference in Contemporary Feminist Theory*, Colombia University Press, New York.

Braidotti, R. 1994b, 'Body Images and the Pornography of Representation' in Lennon, K. and Whitford M. (eds) 1994, *Knowing the Difference*, Routledge, London: 17-31.

Brown, G. 2006, 'Who do we want to be? The future of Britishness', Speech given to the Fabian Society, 16 January <http://fabians.org.uk/events/new-year-conference-06/brown-britishness/speech> [accessed 12.03.2006].

Bryson, N. 1992, 'The Politics of Arbitrariness' in Bryson, N. et al. (eds) 1992, *Visual Theory, Painting and Interpretation*, Polity Press in association with Blackwell, Oxford: 95-100.

Bulmer, M. and Solomos, J. (eds) 1999, *Racism*, Oxford University Press, Oxford.

Burnside, I. 1995, 'Themes and Props: Adjuncts for Reminiscence Therapy Groups' in Haight, B. and Webster, J. (eds) 1995, *The Art and Science of Reminiscing, Theory, Research, Methods and Applications*, Talyor Francis, London: 153-163.

Cantle, T. (Chair) 2002, Home Office Report, *Community Cohesion. Report of the Independent Review Team* <http://www.oldham.gov.uk/cantle-review-final-report.pdf> [accessed 12.12.2008].

Chapman, W.R. 1985, 'Arranging Ethnology: A.H.L. F Pitt Rivers and the Typological Tradition' in Stocking, G.W. (ed.) 1985, *Objects and Others. Essays on Material Culture*, University of Wisconsin Press, Wisconsin: 15-48.

Chow, R. 1994, 'Where Have all the Natives Gone?' in Mongia, P. (ed.) 1996, *Contemporary Postcolonial Theory, A Reader*, Arnold Hodder Headline Group, London: 122-147.

Cixous, H. and Clement, C. 1987, *Newly Born Woman*, Manchester University Press, Manchester.

Classen, C. 1993, *Worlds of Sense: Exploring the Senses in History and Across Cultures*, Routledge, London.

Classen, C. 2005, 'McLuhan in the Rainforest: The Sensory Worlds of Oral Cultures' in Howes, D. 2005, *The Empire of the Senses*, Berg, Oxford: 179-191.

Classen, C. (ed.) 2005, *The Book of Touch*, Berg, Oxford.

Classen, C. and Howes, D. 2006, 'The Museum as Sensescape: Western Sensibilities and Indigenous Artifacts' in Edwards, E., Gosden, C. and Philips, R. (eds) 2006, *Sensible Objects*, Berg, Oxford: 199-222.

Clifford, J. 1994, *The Predicament of Culture, Twentieth-Century Ethnography, Literature and Art*, Harvard University Press, Cambridge, MA.

Clifford, J. 1994b, 'Diasporas', *Cultural Anthropology* 9: 302-38.

Clifford, J. 1997, 'Museums as Contact Zone' in Boswell, D. and Evans, J. (eds) 1999, *Representing the Nation: A Reader Histories, Heritage and Museums*, Routledge, London: 435-459.

Clifford, J. 1997, *Routes, Travels and Translation in the Late Twentieth Century*, Harvard University Press, Cambridge, MA.

Clifford, J. and Marcus, G.E. (eds) 1989, *Writing Culture. The Poetics and Politics of Ethnography*, University of California Press, California.

Cole, T. 1989, *Apart or A Part? Integration and the Growth of British Special Education*, Open University Press, Milton Keynes.

Cole, T., Visser, J. and Upton, G. 1998, *Effective Schooling for Pupils with Emotional and Behavioural Difficulties*, David Fulton Publishers, London.

Coombes, A.E. 1994, *Re-inventing Africa. Museums, Material Culture and Popular Imagination*, Yale University Press, New Haven and London.

Coombes, A.E. 2003, *History after Apartheid. Visual Culture and Public Memory in a Democratic South Africa*, Duke University Press, Durham and London.

Cope, P. 1999, *Voudou*, exhibition text, Horniman Museum.

Corrin, L. 2004, 'Mining the Museum: Artists Look at Museums, Museums Look at Themselves' in Carbonbell, B. (ed.) 2004, *Museum Studies. An Anthology of Contexts*, Blackwell Publishing Ltd., Oxford: 381-402.

Corsane, G. (ed.) 2005, *Heritage, Museums and Galleries: An Introductory Reader*, Routledge, London.

Court, E. 1999, 'Africa on Display: Exhibiting Art by Africans' in Barker, E. (ed.) 1999, *Contemporary Cultures of Display*, Yale University Press, New Haven, CT: 147-173.

Crary, J. 1995, *Techniques of the Observer, On Vision and Modernity in the Nineteenth Century*, MIT Press, USA.

Crimp, D. 1985, 'On the Museum's Ruins' in Foster, H. (ed.) 1985, *Postmodern Culture*, Pluto Press, London: 43-56.

Csikszentmihalyi, M. 1975, *Beyond Boredom and Anxiety. The Experience of Play in Work and Games*, Jossey-Bass Publishers, California, USA.

Csikszentmihalyi, M. 1995, 'Intrinsic Motivation in Museums: Why Does One Want to Learn?' in Falk, J. and Dierking, L. (ed.) 1995, *Public Institutions for Personal Learning: Establishing a Research Agenda*, American Association of Museums, Washington: 67-77.

Csikszentmihalyi, M. and Robinson, R.E. 1990, *The Art of Seeing, An Interpretation of the Aesthetic Encounter*, The J. Paul Getty Trust Office of Publications, California.

Davidson, P. 1995, 'Central Africa' in Phillips, T. (ed.) 1995, *Africa: Art of a Continent*, Royal Academy Publication, Prestel, Munich and New York: 179-230.

Davies, P. 1999, *Ecomusuems: A Sense of Place*, Leicester University Press, Leicester.

Delport, P. 2001, 'Digging Deeper in District Six: Features and Interfaces in a Curatorial Landscape' in Rassool C. and Prosalendis, S. (eds) 2001, *Creating and Curating the District Six Museum. Recalling Community in Cape Town*, 154-164.

Delport, P. 2001, 'Museum or Place for Working with Memory?' in Rassool C. and Prosalendis, S. (eds) 2001, *Creating and Curating the District Six Museum. Recalling Community in Cape Town*, 11-12.

Denham, J. (Chair) 2002, Home Office Independent Review Team, *Building Community Cohesion: A Report of the Ministerial Group on Public Order and Community Cohesion*.

Denniston, H. 2003, *Holding up the Mirror. Addressing Cultural Diversity in London's Museums.* London Museums Agency, London <http://londonmuseums.org> [accessed 24.11.2008].

Department for Education and Skills (DfES), 2001, Special Educational Needs Code of Practice (DfES 0581/2001), London.

Desai, P. and Thomas, A. 1999, *Cultural Diversity: Attitudes of Ethnic Minority Populations Towards Museums and Galleries*, Museum and Galleries Commission (MGC) Report, London: BMRB International Ltd. (commissioned by the Museums and Galleries Commission), January 1998 <http://www.gem.org.uk/culture.html> [accessed 17.04.2008].

Dewey, J. 1968, *Experience and Education*, Collier-Macmillan Press, London.

Dodd, J. and Sandell, R. (eds) 2001, 'Including Museums. Perspectives on Museums, Galleries and Social Inclusion' <www.le.ac.uk/ms/research/rcmgpublicationsandprojects.html> [accessed 09.05.2009].

Donald, J. and Rattansi, A. (eds) 1994, *Race, Culture and Difference*, Sage Publications in association with the Open University, London.

Dubin, S. 1999, *Displays of Power: Memory and Amnesia in the American Museum*, New York University Press, NY and London.

Du Bois, W.E.B. 1903, in Bulmer, M. and Solomos, J. (eds) 1999, *Racism A Reader*, Oxford University Press, Oxford: 125-129.

Duncan, C. 1995, *Civilising Rituals Inside Public Art Museums*, Routledge, London.

Duncan, M. 1972, *A Historical Survey of the Ethnographical Collections in the Horniman Museum London*, Unpublished Museums Association Diploma Thesis.

Ebrahim, N. 2001, 'Guided moments in the District Six Musuem' in Rassool C. and Prosalendis, S. (eds) 2001, *Creating and Curating the District Six Museum. Recalling Community in Cape Town*, 55-59.

Ebrahim, N. 2005, 'Noor's Story', *My Life in District Six, District Six*, D6Museum Press Memorial Text, Digging Deeper D6M, 2006.

Edwards, E., Gosden, C. and Philips, R. (eds) 2006, *Sensible Objects. Colonialism, Museums and Material Culture*, Berg, Oxford, New York.

Eichstedt, J. and Small, S. 2002, *Representations of Slavery. Race and Ideology in Southern Plantation Museums*, Smithsonian Institution Press, Washington and London.

Evans, G. 1995, 'Learning and the Physical Environment', in Falk, J.H. and Dierking, L. (ed.) 1995, *Public Institutions for Personal Learning. Establishing a Research Agenda*, American Association of Museums, Washington: 119-126.

Falk, J.H. and Dierking, L. 2000, *Learning from Museums*, Whaleback Books, Washington, USA.

Falzon, C. 1998, *Foucault and Dialogue, Beyond Fragmentation*, Routledge, London.

Fanon, F. 1970, *Towards the African Revolution*, Pelican, Harmondsworth.

Fanon, F. 1990, *The Wretched of the Earth*, Penguin, London.

Fanon, F. 1993, *Black Skin, White Masks*, Pluto Press, London.

Feld, S. 1996, 'Places Sensed, Senses Placed' in Howes, D. 2005, *The Empire of the Senses*, Berg, Oxford: 179-191.

Fleming, D. 1999, 'Power to the People', *Museum Practice* 11(1999) 16.

Foller, M. and Thorn, H. (eds) 2005, *No Name Fever Aids in the Age of Globalisation*, Lund, Göteborg University, Studentlitteratur.

Fortune, L. 2001, 'A Record of History: Extracts from the District Six Museum Diary' in Rassool, C. and Prosalendis, S. (eds) 2001, *Creating and Curating the District Six Museum. Recalling Community in Cape Town*, 47-54.

Foster, H. (ed.) 1985 *Postmodern Culture*, Pluto Press, London.

Foucault, M. 1980, *Power/Knowledge, Selected Interviews and Other Writings 1972-1977*, The Harvester Press, Hertfordshire.

Foucault, M. 1995, *Madness andCivilisation. A History of Insanity in the Age of Reason*, Routledge, London.

Freire, P. 1972, *Cultural Action for Freedom*, Penguin, Harmondsworth.

Freire, P. 1985, *The Politics of Education*, Bergin and Garvey Publishers Inc., New York.

Freire, P. 1996, *Pedagogy of the Oppressed*, Penguin, London.

Freire, P. 1998, *Pedagogy of Freedom Ethics Democracy and Civic Courage*, Rowman and Littlefield Publishers Inc., New York.

Freire, P. and Shor, I. 1987, *A Pedagogy for Liberation*, Macmillan, Basingstoke.

Gable, E. 1996, 'Maintaining Boundaries, or 'Mainstreaming' Black History in a White Museum' in Macdonald, S. and Fyfe, G. (eds) 1996, *Theorising Museums Representing Identity and Diversity in a Changing World*, Blackwell Publishing, Oxford: 177-202.

Gadamer, H.G. 1973, *Gadamer on Celan. 'Who am I and who are you?' and Other Essays*, Heinemann, R. and Krajewski, B. (trans. and eds) 1997, Suny University of New York Press, New York.

Gadamer, H.G. 1980, *Dialogue and Dialectic. Eight Hermeneutical Studies on Plato*, Yale University Press, New Haven.

Gadamer, H.G. 1981, *Truth and Method*, Sheed and Ward, London.

Gadamer, H.G. 1986, *The Idea of the Good in Platonic-Aristotelian Philosophy*, Yale University Press, New Haven.

Gardner, H. 1993, 'Multiple Intelligences' in Durbin, G. (ed.) 1996, *Developing Exhibitions for Lifelong Learning*, Stationary Office, London: 35-37.

Gardner, H. 2000, *Intelligence Reframed: Multiple Intelligences for the 21st Century*, Basic Books, New York.

Gascoigne, L. 2005, *Musuem Practice* Issue 31, Autumn: 57-59.

Gell, A. 1996, 'Vogel's Net: Traps as Artworks and Artworks as Traps' in Morphy, H. and Perkins, M. (eds) 2006, *The Anthropology of Art*, Blackwell, Oxford: 219-236.

Genoways, H.H. (ed.) 2006, *Museum Philosophy for the Twenty-first Century*, Alta Mira Press, USA.

Gibson, F. 1994, *Reminiscence and Recall, A Guide to Good Practice*, Age Concern, London.

Gieryn, T. 1998, 'Balancing Acts: Science, Enola Gay and History Wars at the Smithsonian' in Macdonald, S. (ed.) 1998, *The Politics of Display. Museums, Science*, Culture, Routledge, London: 197-228.

Gillborn, D. 1995, *Racism and Antiracism in Real Schools: Theory, Policy, Practice*, Open University Press, Buckingham.

Gillborn, D. and Gipps, C. 1996a, *Recent Research on the Achievements of Ethnic Minority Pupils*, OFSTED, HMSO publication.

Gillborn, D. and Gipps, C. 1996b, *TES*, 6.9.96.

Gilborn, D. and Mirza, H. 2000, *Educational Inequality, Mapping Race, Class and Gender A Synthesis of Research Evidence* <http://www.ofsted.gov.uk>.

Gilman, S. 1987, 'Black Bodies, White Bodies. Towards an Iconography of Female Sexuality in Late Nineteenth-Century Art, Medicine and Literature' in Donald, J. and Rattansi, A. (eds) 1994, *Race, Culture and Difference*, Sage Publications in association with the Open University, London: 171-197.

Gilman, S. 1991, 'Are Jews White?' in Back, L. and Solomos, J. (eds) 2000, *Theories of Race and Racism: A Reader*, Routledge, London: 229-237.

Gilroy, B. 1994, *Black Teacher*, Bogle-L'Overture Press, London.

Gilroy, B. 1998, *Leaves in the Wind: Collected Writings*, Mango Publishing, London.

Gilroy, P. 1990, 'The End of Antiracism' in Donald, J. and Rattansi, A. (eds) 1994, *Race, Culture and Difference*, Sage, London: 49-61.

Gilroy, P. 1991, 'The Whisper Wakes, the Shudder Plays: Race, Nation and Ethnic Absolutism' in Mongia, P. (ed.) 1996, *Contemporary Postcolonial Theory, A Reader*, Arnold Press, London: 248-274.

Gilroy, P. 1994, *Small Acts: Thoughts on the Politics of Black Cultures*, Serpents Tail, London.

Gilroy, P. 1997, 'Diaspora and the Detours of Identity' in Woodward, K. (ed.) 1997, *Identity and Difference*, Sage Publications, London: 299-346.

Giroux, H. 1993, *Border-crossings. Cultural Workers and the Politics of Education*, Routledge, London.

Giroux, H. and McLaren, P. 1994, *Between Borders. Pedadgogy and the Politics of Cultural Studies*, Routledge, London.

Golding, V. 1997, 'Meaning and Truth in Multicultural Museum Education' in Hooper-Greenhill, E. (ed.) 1997, *Cultural Diversity. Developing Museum Audiences in Britain*, Leicester University Press, Leicester: 203-225.

Golding, V. 2000, *New Voices and Visibilities at the Museum Frontiers*, unpublished PhD thesis, University of Leicester, Leicester.

Golding, V. 2005, 'The Museum Clearing: A Metaphor for New Museum Practice' in Atkinson, D. and Dash, P. (eds) 1995, *Social and Critical Practice in Art Education*, Trentham Books, Staffordshire: 51-66.

Golding, V. 2006, 'Carnival Connections: Challenging Racism as the Unsaid at the Museum/School Frontiers with Feminist-hermeneutics' in Inglilleri, M. (ed.) 2006, *Swinging her Breasts at History*, Mango Publishing, London: 290-309.

Golding, V. 2007a, 'Challenging Racism and Sexism at the Museum Forum' in Anim-Addo, J. and Scafe, S. (eds) 2007, *I am Black, White and Yellow An Introduction to the Black Body in Europe*, Mango Publishing, London: 148-166.

Golding, V. 2007b, 'Learning at the Museum Frontiers: Democracy, Identity and Difference' in Knell, S., MacLeod, S. and Watson, S. (eds) 2007, *Museum Revolutions*, Routledge, London: 315-329.

Golding, V. 2007c, 'Using Tangible and Intangible Heritage to Promote Social Inclusion for Students with Disabilities: 'Inspiration Africa!' in Watson, S. (ed.) 2007, *Museums and their Communities*, Routledge, London: 358-378.

Gombrich, E. 1968, *Art and Illusion*, Phaidon, London.

Goodnow, K. 2006, *Challenge and Transformation: Museums in Cape Town and Sidney*, UNESCO Publishing, Paris.

Greenblatt, S. 1991, 'Resonance and Wonder' in Karp, I. and Lavine S. (eds) 1991, *Exhibiting Cultures, the Poetics and Politics of Museum Display*, Smithsonian Institution Press, Washington DC: 42-56.

Grinter, R. 1985, 'Bridging the Gulf: The Need for Anti-Racist Multicultural Education', *Multicultural Teaching* 3(2) 7-10.

Guarracino, S. 2007, 'Imoinda's Performing Bodies: An Interview with Joan Anim-Addo' in Anim-Addo, J. and Scafe, S. (eds) 2007, *I am Black / White / Yellow: An Introduction to the Black Body in Europe*, Mango Publishing, London: 212-223.

Guerts, K.L. 2005, 'Consciousness as 'Feeling in the Body': A West African Theory of Embodiment, Emotion and the Making of Mind' in Howes, D. (ed.) 2005, *The Empire of the Senses. The Sensual Culture Reader*, Berg, Oxford: 164-178.

Gundara, J. 2000, *Interculturalism, Education and Inclusion*, Sage, London.

Gupta, A. and Ferguson, J. 2002, 'Beyond "Culture": Space, Identity and the Politics of Difference' in Xavier, J. and Renato, R. (eds) 2002, *The Anthropology of Globalization*, Blackwell, Oxford: l65-80.

Gutman, A. 1994, 'Introduction' in Taylor, C. and Gutman, A. (eds) 1994, *Multiculturalism*, Princeton University Press, New Jersey.

Gutman, A. 2003, *Identity in Democracy*, Princeton University Press, Princeton and Oxford.

Hall, S. 1980, 'Teaching Race', *Multiracial Education* 9(1) 3-13.

Hall, S. 1990, 'Cultural Identity and Diaspora' in Mongia, P. (ed.) 1996, *Contemporary Postcolonial Theory, A Reader*, Arnold Press, London: 110-121.

Hall, S. 1994, 'New Ethnicities' in Donald, J. and Rattansi, A. (eds) 1994, *Race, Culture and Difference*, Sage, London: 252-259.

Hall, S. 1997, 'Who Needs Identity' in Hall S. and du Gay, P. (eds) 1997, *Questions of Cultural Identity*, Sage, London: 1-17.

Hallam, E. and Street, B. (eds) 2000, *Cultural Encounters Representing Otherness*, Routledge, London and New York.

Haraway, D.J. 1991a, 'A Cyborg Manifesto: Science, Technology and Socialist Feminism in the Late Twentieth Century' in Haraway, D.J. 1991, *Simians, Cyborgs and Women: The Reinvention of Nature*, Free Association Books, London: 149-181.

Haraway, D.J. 1991b, 'Situated Knowledges: The Science Question in Feminism the Privilege of Partial Perspectives' in Haraway, D.J. 1991, *Simians, Cybourgs and Women: The Reinvention of Nature*, London Free Association Books, London: 183-201.

Hein, G.E. 1998, *Learning in the Museum*, Routledge, London.

Heumann Gurian, E. 1991, 'Noodling Around with Exhibition Opportunities' in Karp, I. and Lavine, S. (eds) 1991, *Exhibiting Cultures: The Poetics and Politics of Museum Display*, Smithsonian Institution Press, Washington and London: 176-190.

Hill-Collins, P. 1991, *Black Feminist Thought Knowledge, Consciousness and the Politics of Empowerment*, Routledge, London.

Hiller, S. 1993, *The Myth of Primitivism*, Routledge, London.

Hirschi, K.D. and Screven, C.G. 1988, 'Effects of Questions on Visitor Reading Behaviour' in Durbin, G. 1998, *Developing Exhibitions for Lifelong Learning*, Stationary Office, London: 189-192.

Holiday, A. 1998, 'Forgiveness and Forgetting: The Truth and Reconciliation Commission' in Coetzee, C. and Nutrall, S. 1998, *Negotiating the Past: The Making of Memory in South Africa*, Oxford University Press, Oxford: 43-56.

Home Office, 2001, *Building Cohesive Communities.*

Home Office, 2004, *Strength in Diversity: Towards a Community Cohesion and Race Equality Strategy.*

Home Office, 2005, *Improving Opportunity, Strengthening Society: The Government's Strategy to Increase Race Equality and Community Cohesion.*

hooks, b. 1989, *Talking Back, Thinking Feminist, Thinking Black*, South End Press, Boston, MA.

hooks, b. 1991, 'Postmodern Blackness' in Williams, P. and Chrisman, L. (eds) 1994, *Colonial Discourse and Postcolonial Theory. A Reader*, Harvester Wheatsheaf, Hertfordshire: 421-427.

hooks, b. 1992, *Black Looks, Race and Representation*, South End Press, Boston, MA.

hooks, b. 1994, *Teaching to Transgress, Education as the Practice of Freedom*, Routledge, London.

hooks, b. 1995, *Art on My Mind, Visual Politics*, The New Press, New York.

Hooper-Greenhill, E. 1989, 'The Museum in the Disciplinary Society' in Pearce S. (ed.) 1989, *Museum Studies in Material Culture*, Leicester University Press, Leicester: 61-72.

Hooper-Greenhill, E. 1990, 'The Space of the Museum' in *Continuum* 3(1) 56-69.

Hooper-Greenhill, E. 1992, *Museums and the Shaping of Knowledge*, Routledge, London.

Hooper-Greenhill, E. 1999, *The Educational Role of the Museum*, Routledge, London.

Hooper-Greenhill, E. 2006, 'The Power of Museum Pedagogy' in Genoways, H.H. (ed.) 2006, *Museum Philosophy for the Twenty-first Century*, Alta Mira Press, USA: 235-246.

Howell, S. 1993, 'Art and Meaning' in Hiller, S. 1993, *The Myth of Primitivism*, Routledge, London: 215-237.

Howes, D. (ed.) 2005, *The Empire of the Senses*, Berg, Oxford.

Insoll, T.A. et al. 1995, 'Northern Africa' in Phillips, T. (ed.) 1995, *Africa: Art of a Continent*, Royal Academy Publication, Prestel, Munich and New York: 535-596.

Irigaray, L. 1977, 'The Sex Which Is Not One' in Marks, I. and de Courtivron, E. (eds) 1981, *New French Feminisms*, Harvester Wheatsheaf, Hemel Hempstead: 99-110.

Jary, D. and Jary, J. 2000, *Collins Dictionary of Sociology*, HarperCollins Publishers, Glasgow.

Jordanova, L. 1993, 'Objects of Knowledge: A Historical Perspective on Museums' in Vergo, P. (ed.) 1993, *The New Museology*, Reaktion Books, London: 22-40.

Karp, I. 1991, 'Other Cultures in Museum Perspective' in Karp, I. and Lavine, S. 1991, *Exhibiting Cultures. The Poetics and Politics of Museum Display*, Smithsonian Institution Press, Washington and London: 373-386.

Karp, I. and Lavine, S. 1991, *Exhibiting Cultures. The Poetics and Politics of Museum Display*, Smithsonian Institution Press, Washington and London.

Karp, I. and Wilson, F. 1996, 'Constructing the Spectacle of Culture in Museums' in Greenberg, Ferguson and Nairne, *Thinking about Exhibitions*, Routledge, London: 251-74.

Kathrada, A. Postcard [Prison no. 468/64].

Kauffman, J. 2001, *Characteristics of Emotional and Behavioural Disorders of Children and Youth*, 7th edn, Merrill Prentice Hall, New Jersey.

Kavanagh, G. 2000, *Dream Spaces, Memory and the Museum*, Leicester University Press, London.

King, M. in Banks, J. et al. 2005, *Democracy and Diversity Principles and Concepts for Educating Citizens in a Global Age* <http://depts.washington.edu/centerme/home.htm> 7 [accessed 15.07.2006].

Kitwood, T. 1990, *Concern for Others: A Psychology of Conscience and Morality*, Routledge, London.

Kreps, C. 2003, *Liberating Culture. Cross-cultural Perspectives on Museums, Curation and Heritage Preservation*, Routledge, London.

Lagerkvist, C. 2002, Horizonter Brief 2001.

Lagerkvist, C. et al. 2004, *Voices from a Global Africa*, Elanders Print, Sweden.

Lagerkvist, C. 2006, 'Empowerment and Anger: Learning How to Share Ownership of the Museum' in *Museum and Society*, July 2006, 4(2) 52-68 <http://le.ac.uk/museumstudies> [accessed 23.08.2007].

Lagerkvist, C. 2007, 'The Museum of World Culture: A 'Glocal' Museum of a New Kind', *Museums and Diversity*, UNESCO, Editions.

Lavine, S. and Karp, I. 1991, 'Introduction: Museums and Multiculturalism' in Karp, I. and Lavine, S. 1991, *Exhibiting Cultures. The Poetics and Politics of Museum Display*, Smithsonian Institution Press, Washington and London: 1-9.

Leicester, M. 1986, 'Multicultural Curriculum or Anti Racist Education: Denying the Gulf', *Multicultural Teaching* 4(2) 4-7.

Lennon, K. and Witford, M. (eds) 1994, *Knowing the Difference*, Routledge, London.

Lidchi, H. 2003, 'The Poetics and the Politics of Exhibiting Other Cultures' in Hall, S. (ed.) 2003, *Representation: Cultural Representations and Signifying Practices*, 151-222.

Loomba, A. 2002, *Colonialism/Postcolonialism*, Routledge, London.

Lorde, A. 1996a, 'The Cancer Journals' in *The Audrey Lorde Compendium. Essays, Speeches and Journals. The Cancer Journals. Sister Outsider. A Burst of Light*, Pandora, London: 3-62.

Lorde, A. 1996b, 'The Masters Tools Will Never Dismantle The Masters House' in *The Audrey Lorde Compendium. Essays, Speeches and Journals. The Cancer Journals. Sister Outsider. A Burst of Light*, Pandora, London: 158-161.

Lorde, A. 1996c, 'Age, Race, Class and Sex: Women Redefining Difference' in *The Audrey Lorde Compendium. Essays, Speeches and Journals. The Cancer Journals. Sister Outsider. A Burst of Light*, Pandora, London: 162-171.

Lorde, A. 1996d, 'Eye to Eye' in *The Audrey Lorde Compendium. Essays, Speeches and Journals. The Cancer Journals. Sister Outsider. A Burst of* Light, Pandora, London: 191-219.

Lowenthal, D. 1993, 'Remembering to Forget' *Museums Journal* 93(6) 20-22.

Lownsbrough, H. and Beundernam, J. 2007, 'Equally Spaced? Public Space and Interaction Between Diverse Communities', A Report for the Commission for Racial Equality, Demos publication, <http://www.demos.co.uk/publications/equallyspaced> [accessed 28.05.2009].

Luke, T. 2006, 'The Museum: Where Civilizations Clash or Clash Civilizes?' in Genoways, H. (ed.) 2006, *Museum Philosophy for the Twenty-first Century*, Alta Mira Press, USA: 19-26.

Lyotard, J. 1984, *The Postmodern Condition*, Manchester University Press, Manchester.

MacDonald, S. (ed.) 2006, *A Companion to Museum Studies*, Blackwell Publishing, Oxford.

MacDonald, S. and Basu, P. (eds) 2007, *Exhibition Experiments*, Blackwell Publishing, Oxford.

Mack, J. 1995, 'Eastern Africa' in Phillips, T. (ed.) 1995, *Africa: Art of a Continent*, Royal Academy Publication, Prestel, Munich and New York: 117-178.

Mandela, N. Postcard Museum Prison no. 466/64.

Mandela, N. 1996, 'Truth and Reconciliation' <http://www.anc.org.za/ancdocs/history/mandela/1996/sp0213.html> [accessed 28.06.2007].

Mandela, N. 1997, Heritage Day Address <http://www.anc.org.za/ancdocs/history/mandela/1997/sp0924a.html> [accessed 28.06.2007].

Mandela, N. 2000, *Long Walk to Freedom*, Abacus, London.

Martin, D. 1996, 'Outreach', *Museum Practice* 1, 36-79.

Martin, D. 1999, 'Update on Outreach', *Museum Practice* 11, 68-97.

Marwick, S. 1995, 'Learning from Each Other: Museums and Older Members of the Community – The People's Story' in Hooper-Greenhill, E. (ed.) 1995, *Museums Media, Message*, Routledge, London: 140-150.

Mastusov, E. and Rogoff, B. 1995, 'Evidence of Development from People's Participation in Communities of Learners' in Falk, J.H. and Dierking, L. (ed.) 1995, *Public Institutions for Personal Learning. Establishing a Research Agenda*, American Association of Museums, Washington DC: 97-104.

Mathers, K. 1993, 'Why do South Africans Choose Not to Visit Museum? An Analysis of a National Survey of the Museum Visiting Habits of South African Adults', paper presented at the conference *South African Museum and its Public: Negotiating Partnerships*, SAM, Cape Town, 1993.

Mayor of London, 2002, *Towards a Vision of Excellence London Schools and the Black Child*, Conference Report <http://www.london.gov.uk/mayor/education/lsbc/black_child.pdf> [accessed 26.08.2007].

Macpherson, W. 1999, *The Stephen Lawrence Inquiry*, Government Report, cm 4262-1.

McCabe, C. 1988, 'Foreward', in Spivak, G. 1987, *In Other Worlds, Essays in Cultural Politics*, Routledge, London: ix-xix.

McGivney, V. 2000, *Recovering Outreach: Concepts, Issues and Practices*, Leicester: NIACE.

McLeod, M. 1999, 'Museums Without Collections: Museum Philosophy in West Africa' in Carbonbell, B. (eds) 2004, *Museum Studies. An Anthology of Contexts*, Blackwell Publishing Ltd., Oxford: 455-460.

McLeod, J. 2000, *Beginning Postcolonialism*, Manchester University Press, Manchester.

McManus, P. 1989, 'Label Reading Behaviour' in Durbin, G. (ed.) 1996, *Developing Exhibitions for Lifelong Learning*, Stationary Office, London: 183-188.

McMoreland, A. 1997, 'I Hear it in My Heart: Music and Reminiscence' in *Widening Horizons in Dementia Care, A Conference of the European Reminiscence Network: Conference Papers*, Age Exchange London: 110-113.

Meek, M. 1991, *On Being Literate*, Bodley Head, London.

Meltzer, L. 2001, 'Past Streets' in Rassool, C. and Prosalendis, S. (eds) 2001, *Creating and Curating the District Six Museum. Recalling Community in Cape Town*, 21-22.

Mill, J.S. 1859, *Essays on Equality, Law, and Education*, Robson, J.M. 1984 (ed.) Routledge, London, cited in Young, R. 2001, *Postcolonialism. An Historical Introduction*, Blackwell Publishing, Oxford: 86-87.

Miller, D. 1993, 'Primitive Art and the Necessity of Primitivism to Art' in Hiller (ed.) 1993, *The Myth of Primitivism*, Routledge, London: 50-71.

Milner, D. 1983, *Children and Race*, Penguin, Harmondsworth.

Misztel, B. 2003, 'Memory Experience' in Watson, S. (ed.) 2007, *Museums and their Communities*, Routledge, London: 379-396.

Morrison, T. 1984, 'Rootedness: The Ancestor as Foundation' in Evans, M. (ed.) 1984, *Black Women Writers (1950-1980): A Critical Evaluation*, Doubleday, Garden City New York: 339-45.

Morrison, T. 1988, *Beloved*, Picador, London.

Morrison, T. 1990, *The Bluest Eye*, Picador, London.

Morrison, T. 1991, *Sula*, Picador imprint Macmillan Publishers Ltd., London.

Morrison, T. 1993, *Playing in the Dark. Whiteness and the Literary Imagination*, Picador, London.

Morrison, T. 1994a, 'Living Memory: A Meeting with Toni Morrison' in Gilroy, P. 1994, *Small Acts: Thoughts on the Politics of Black Cultures*, Serpents Tail, London: 173-182.

Morrison, T. 1994b, 'In the Realm of Responsibility: A Conversation with Marsha Darling' in *Conversations with Toni Morrison* (edited by Danielle Taylor Guthrie), University Press of Mississippi Jackson, USA: 246-254.

OFSTED, 1999, Available at <http://www.ofsted.gov.uk> [accessed 25.09.2006].

Oliver, M. 1996, *Understanding Disability: From Theory to Practice*, Macmillan, Basingstoke.

Osler, A. (ed.) 2000, *Citizenship and Democracy in Schools: Diversity, Identity, Equality*, Stoke-on-Trent, Trentham.

Osler, A. and Starkey, H. 2005, *Changing Citizenship: Democracy and Inclusion in Education*, Maidenhead: Open University Press.

Osler, A. and Starkey, H. 2005, 'Education for Democratic Citizenship: A Review of Research, Policy and Practice 1995-2005', BERA Review <http://www.bera.ac.uk/files/2008/09/oslerstarkeyberareview2005.pdf> [accessed 20.05.2009].

Parekh, B. 2000, *The Future of Multi-Ethnic Britain. The Parekh Report*, Profile Books, London.

Passerini, L. quoted in Sangster, J. 2003, 'Telling Our Stories: Feminist Debates and the Use of Oral History' in Perks, R. and Thomson, A. (eds) 2003, *The Oral History Reader*, Routledge, London: 87-100.

Pearce, J. 1998, *Centres for Curiosity and Imagination*, Calouste Gulbenkian Foundation.

Pearce, S.M. (ed.) 1992, *Museums, Objects and Collections*, Routledge, London.

Pearce, S.M. (ed.) 1994, *Interpreting Objects and Collections*, Routledge, London.

Pearce, S.M. 2003, *On Collecting*, Routledge, London.

Philip, M.N. 1992, *Frontiers. Essays and Writings on Racism and Culture*, The Mercury Press, Ontario, Canada.

Philip, M.N. 1993, *She Tries Her Tongue, Her Silence Softly Breaks*, Women's Press, London.

Philips, R. 2003, 'Community Collaboration in Exhibitions Towards a Dialogic Paradigm' in Peers, L. and Brown, A. 2003, *Museums and Source Communities: A Routledge Reader*, Routledge, London: 155-170.

Philips, R. 2007, 'Exhibiting Africa: After Modernism: Globalization, Pluralism and the Persistent Paradigms of Art and Artifact' in Pollack, G. and Zemans, J.

(eds) 2007, *Museums after Modernism Strategies of Engagement*, Blackwell Publishing, Oxford: 81-103.

Picton, J. 1992, 'Desperately Seeking Africa, New York, 1991', *The Oxford Art Journal* 15(2) 104-112.

Picton, J. 1995, 'West Africa and the Gunea Coast' in Phillips, T. (ed.) 1995, *Africa: Art of a Continent*, Royal Academy Publication, Prestel, Munich and New York: 327-478.

Picton, J. 1998, 'Observers are Worried: The "Tribal Image" is No More', *Internationales Afrikaforum* 13(34) 281-289.

Porter, G. 1996, 'Seeing through Solidity: A Feminist Perspective on Museums', in Macdonald, S. and Fyfe, G. (eds) 1996, *Theorising Museum Representing Identity and Diversity in a Changing World*, Blackwell Publishing, Oxford: 105-126.

Pratt, M.L. 1992, *Imperial Eyes: Travel Writing and Transculturation*, Routledge, London.

Predazzi, M., Vercauteren, R. and Loriaux, M. 2000, 'The Culture of the Meeting of Generations to Overcome Social and Ethnic Discrimination' in *Towards a Society for all Ages: The Time of all Possibilities*, Vol. II, European Union.

Prins, D. 2005, 'The Art of Memory-Making' in Atkinson, D. and Dash, P. (eds) 2005, *Social and Critical Practice in Art Education*, Trentham Books, Staffordshire, UK: 67-79.

Prosalendis, S., Marot, J., Soudien, C. and Nagia, A. 2001, 'Punctuations: Periodic Impressions of a Museum' in Rassool, C. and Prosalendis, S. (eds) 2001, *Creating and Curating the District Six Museum. Recalling Community in Cape Town*, 74-94.

Quick, R. 1896, Horniman Museum, London, Correspondence Scrapbook, Mrs Keddie from Gaya Bengal.

Quick, R. 1897, *Annual Report of the Horniman Free Museum*, London.

Quick, R. 1897, Illustrated London News, 10 April, 493.

Quick, R. 1899, *Annual Report of the Horniman Free Museum*, London.

Quick, R. 1899, 'Notes on Benin Carvings', *Reliquary* v: 248-255.

Raasool, C. 2006, 'Community Museums, Memory, Politics and Social Transformation in South Africa: Histories, Possibilities and Limits' in Karp, I., Krantz, C., Szwaja, L. and Ybarra-Frausto, T. et al. (eds) 2006, *Museum Frictions. Public Cultures/Global Transformations*, Duke University Press, Durham and London: 286-321.

Rassool, C. and Prosalendis, S. (eds) 2001, *Creating and Curating the District Six Museum. Recalling Community in Cape Town*.

Reigel, H. 1996, 'Into the Heart of Irony: Ethnographic Exhibitions and the Politics of Difference' in Macdonald, S. and Fyfe, G. (eds) 1996, *Theorizing Museums. Representing Identity and Diversity in a Changing World*, Blackwell Publishing, Oxford: 83-104.

Rice, D. 2001 'The Museum Ambassadors Programme: A Youth Development Initiative in District Six' in Rassool, C. and Prosalendis, S. (eds) 2001, *Creating and Curating the District Six Museum. Recalling Community in Cape Town*, 60-65.

Ricouer, P. 1982, *Hermeneutics and the Human Sciences* (edited and translated by Thompson, J.), Cambridge University Press, Cambridge.

Rincon, L. 2005, 'My Voice in a Glass Box', ICME Papers, 2005 <http://icme. icom.museum> 1-7 [accessed 26.10.2008].

Roberts, H. (ed.) 1981, *Doing Feminist Research*, Routledge, London.

Roberts, L.C. 1997, *From Knowledge to Narrative, Educators and the Changing Museum*, Smithsonian Institution Press, Washington.

Rosaldo, M. 2005, 'The Shame of Headhunters and the Autonomy of Self' in Wulff, H. (ed.) 2005, *The Emotions*. A Cultural Reader, 205-217.

Rosaldo R. 1984, Grief and a Headhunter's Rage. On the Cultural Force of Emotions' in Bruner, E. (ed.) 1984, *Text, Play and Story*, American Ethnological Society, Washington: 178-195.

Rosen, H. in Rosen, B. 1988, *And None of it was Nonsense: The Power of Storytelling in School*, Mary Glasgow Publications, London.

Russmann, E.R. 1995, 'Ancient Egypt and Nubia' in Philips, T. (ed.) 1995, *Africa: Art of a Continent*, Royal Academy Publication: 41-167.

Said, A. 2004, in Lagerkvist, C. et al. (eds) 2004, *Voices from a Global Africa*, Elanders Print, Sweden: 49.

Said, E. 1985, *Orientalism*, London.

Said, E. 1993, *Culture and Imperialism*, Chatto and Windus, London.

Said, E. 1994, *Representations of the Intellectual*, the 1993 Reith Lectures, Random House Publishing, London.

Sandahl, J. 2002, 'Site Unseen: Dwelling of the Demons' <http://www.worldculture. se/smvk/jsp/polopoly.jsp?d=877&a=4543&l=en_US> [accessed 14.01.2008].

Sandahl, J. 2002, 'HIV/AIDS *No Name Fever*' <http://www.worldculture.se/ smvk/jsp/polopoly.jsp?d=877&a=4547&p=0> [accessed 14.01.2008].

Sandahl, J. 2002, 'Fluid Boundaries and False Dichotomies – Scholarship, Partnership and Representation in Museums?' <http://www.intercom.museum/ conferences/2002/sandahl.html> [accessed 01.02.2008].

Sandell, R. 1998, 'Museums as Agents of Social Inclusion' in *Museum Management and Curatorship*, 17(4) 401-418.

Sandell, R. 2002, 'Museums and the Combatting of Social Inequality: Roles, Responsibilities, Resistance' in Sandell, R. (ed.) 2002, *Museums Society and Inequality*, Routledge, London.

Sandell, R. 2003, 'Social Inclusion, the Museum and the Dynamics of Sectoral Change', *Museum and Society* 1(1) 45-62.

Sandell, R. 2007, *Museums, Prejudice and the Reframing of Difference*, Routledge, London.

Sargent, L. 2002, *Words and Wings* <http://www.mlasoutheast.org.uk/assets/ documents/1000033Cwordswings_last.pdf>; <http://lindasargent.co.uk/html/ resources.html> [accessed 17.03.2008].

Schildkrout, E. 1991, 'Ambiguous Messages and Ironic Twists: Into the Heart of Africa and the Other Museum' in Messias Carbonell, B. (ed.) 2004, *Museum Studies. An Anthology of Contexts*, Blackwell, Oxford: 181-192.

Schweitzer, P. 1993, *Age Exchanges, Reminiscence Projects for Children and Older People*, Age Exchange, London.

Scott, M. 2007, *Rethinking Evolution in the Museum Envisioning African Origins*, Routledge, London.

Shelton, A. 1992, 'The Recontextualisation of Culture in UK Museums', *Anthropology Today* 8(5).

Shelton, A. 2000, 'Curating African Worlds' in *Journal of Museum Ethnography* 12: 5-20.

Silverman, L. 1995, 'Visitor Meaning–Making in Museums for a New Age', *Curator, The Museum Journal* 38(3) 161-170.

Simon, R. 2006, 'The Terrible Gift: Museums and the Possibility of Hope Without Consolation', *Journal of Museum Management and Curatorship* 21(3) September, 187-204.

Simpson, M. 1996, *Making Representations. Museums in the Post-Colonial Era*, Routledge, London.

Siraj-Blatchford, I. 1994, *The Early Years. Laying the Foundations for Racial Equality*, Trentham, Essex.

Small, S. 1997, 'Contextualising the Black Presence in British Museums: Representation, Resources and Response' in Hooper-Greenhill, E. (ed.) 1997, *Cultural Diversity. Developing Museum Audiences in Britain*, Leicester University Press, Leicester: 50-66.

Solomos, J. and Back, L. 1996, *Racism and Society*, Macmillan Press Ltd., Basingstoke.

Soudien, C. and Meltzer, L. 2001, 'District Six: Representation and Struggle' in Rassool, C. and Prosalendis, S. (eds) 2001, *Creating and Curating the District Six Museum. Recalling Community in Cape Town*, 66-73.

Spalding, J. 2002, *The Poetic Museum. Reviving Historic Collections*, Prestel, Munich, London and New York.

Spivak, G. 1987, *In Other Worlds, Essays in Cultural Politics*, Routledge, London.

Stoller, P. 1989, *The Taste of Ethnographic Things*, University of Pennsylvannia Press, USA.

Stone, M. 1985, *The Education of the Black Child*, Fontana Press, London.

Swann, Lord 1985, Committee of Inquiry into the Education of Children from Ethnic Minority Groups (Chairman: Lord Swann), *Final Report: Education For All*, London: HMSO (Cmnd. 9453).

Taylor, C. 1994, 'The Politics of Recognition' in Taylor, C. and Gutman, A. (eds) 1994, *Multiculturalism*, Princeton University Press, New Jersey: 25-73.

Taylor, C. and Gutman, A. (eds) 1994, *Multiculturalism*, Princeton University Press, New Jersey.

Taylor, E. 1997, 'Working with Groups at the Age Exchange Reminiscence Centre' in *Widening Horizons in Dementia Care, A Conference of European Reminiscence Network*, Conference papers, London, Age Exchange: 140-1.

Trevelyan, V. (ed.) 1991, 'Dingy Places with Different Kinds of Bits', An attitudes Survey of London Museums amongst non-visitors, London Museums Service, London.

Trinh, T.M. 1989, *Woman, Native, Other: Writing Postcoloniality and Feminism*, Indiana University Press, Bloomington and Indianapolis.

Tuan, Y.-F. 1993, 'The Pleasures of Touch' in Classen, C. (ed.) 2005, *The Book of Touch*, Berg, Oxford: 74-79.

United Nations Convention on the Rights of the Child <http://www.unicef.org/crc/> [accessed 30.02.2007].

UNESCO, 1995, Universal Declaration on Cultural Diversity <http://www.unesco.org/culture/pluralism/> [accessed 04.11.2007].

Usher, R. and Bryant, I. 1994, *Postmodernism and Education*, Routledge, London.

Valuing People: A New Strategy for Learning Disability for the 21st Century, A White Paper, Department of Health, 2001 <http://valuingpeople.gov.uk/>.

Valuing People, 2004 <http://whssb.n-jnhs-uk/partner/cd_strategy_2006>.

Vaswani, R. MJ 5 (2000) 16-18.

Vergo, P. 1993, *The New Museology*, Reaktion Books, London.

Visser, J. 2003, *A Study of Children and Young People who Present Challenging Behaviour*, University of Birmingham (3849 EBD).

Vogel, S. et al. (ed.) 1988, *ART/Artifact*, The Centre for African Art, New York and Prestel Verlag.

Vogel, S. 1991, 'Always True to the Object, in Our Fashion' in Karp, I. and Lavine, S. (ed.) 1991, *Exhibiting Cultures: The Poetics and Politics of Museum Display*, Smithsonian Institution Press, Washington and London: 191-204.

Vygotsky, L. 1996, *Thought and Language*, The MIT Press, Cambridge, MA.

Warnock, M. 1987, *Memory*, Faber and Faber, London.

West, C. 1995, 'Preface' in Philips, T. 1995, *Africa: Art of a Continent*, Royal Academy Publication: 9-11.

White, N.R. 1994, 'Making Absences: Holocaust Testimony and History' in Perks, R. and Thomson, A. 2003, *The Oral History Reader*, Routledge, London: 172-182.

White, M. and Epston, D. 1990, *Narrative Means to Therapeutic Ends*, W.W. Norton Press, New York.

White, M. and Epston, D. <http://white&epston/narrative_therapy> [accessed 12.06.2007].

White Paper on Arts, Culture and Heritage (4 June 1996) South Africa.

White Paper on Intercultural Dialogue, 'Living Together as Equals in Dignity', Council of Europe, F-67075 Strasbourg Cedex, June 2008, <http://www.coe.int/t/dg4/intercultural/Source/White%20Paper_final_revised_EN.pdf> [accessed 30.05.2009].

220 *Learning at the Museum Frontiers*

Whitford, M. 1991, *Luce Irigaray. Philosophy in the Feminine*, Routledge, London.
Wittgenstein, L. 1974, *Philosophical Investigations*, Blackwell, Oxford.
Wulff, H. 2007, *The Emotions*, Berg, Oxford.
Young, R. 2001, *Postcolonialism. An Historical Introduction*, Blackwell Publishing, Oxford.

Websites

Age Exchange <http//:www.age-exchange.org,uk> [accessed 16.8. 2004].
Black Body in Europe <http://www.goldsmiths.ac.uk/blackbodyineurope/about.php> [accessed 12.7.2007].
Cloth of Gold <http//:www.clothofgold.org.uk.html> [accessed 15.9. 2007].
Critical Pedagogy, Peter McLaren <http://www.gseis.ucla.edu/faculty/pages/mclaren/> [accessed 30.05.2009].
Diversify, Museums Association <http://www.museumsassociation.org/diversify> [accessed 13.12.2008].
East Midlands Oral History Archive (EMOHA) <http//:www.emoha.org.html> [accessed 17.08.2004].
Edo-Tokyo Museum <http://www.edo-tokyo-museum.or.jp/english/index.html> [accessed 17.06.2004].
Inspiring Learning for All <http://www.inspiringlearningforall.gov.uk> [accessed 05.09.2008].
International Coalition of Historic Site Museums of Conscience <http://www.sitesofconscience.org/en/> [accessed 13.12.2008].
Museums Association <http://www.museumsassociation.org> [accessed 13.12.2008].
Museum Loan Boxes <http://www.museumse.org.uk/making_the_most_of_museums/benefits_of_using_museums/Loan_Boxes.html>; <http://www.museumsloansnetwork.org.uk/learning.htm>; <http://www.ucl.ac.uk/museums/loanboxes.html>; <http://www.leics.gov.uk/moving_objects>; <http://www.objectdialoguebox.com/>; <http://www.gem.org.uk/grassroots/GR%20Resources/makeloansbox.html>; <www.mlasouthwest.org.uk/docs/Resource-Box-Report.pdf> [accessed 20.11.2008].
Museum of Anthropology, British Columbia, Canada, Spirit of Islam Resource <http://www.moa.ubc.ca/spiritofislam/resources/educationoverview.html> [accessed 23.09.2008].
Museum of World Culture, Göteborg, Sweden, Reports <http://www.actupny.org/reports/WorldCultureMuseum.html> [accessed 28.01.2008].
National Curriculum England, Quality and Curriculum Authority <http://www.qca.org.uk/7907.html> [accessed 28.08.2007].
Research Centre for Museums and Galleries (RCMG) Reports <www.le.ac.uk/ms/research/rcmgpublicationsandprojects.html> [accessed 09.05.2009].

South Africa, Demographic Statistics <http://www.ststssa.gov.za/keyindicators/mye.asp> [accessed 23.09.2008].

South Africa, Department of Arts, Culture, Heritage and Sport. White Paper on Arts and Culture, 1996 <http://www.dac.gov.za/legislation_policies/white_papers/white_paper_on_arts_culture_heritage.htm> [accessed 21.02.2008].

South Africa, District Six Museum <http://www.d6.co.za/>.

South Africa, District Six Museum, A Site Museum of Conscience <http://www.sitesofconscience.org/eng/d6_how.htm> [accessed 23.09.2008].

South Africa, Education <http://www.africawithin.com/mandela/bantu_education_0657.htm> [accessed 23.09.2008].

South Africa, Freedom Charter <http://www.anc.org.za/ancdocs/history/charter.html> [accessed 23.09.2008].

South Africa Department of Arts, Culture, Heritage and Sport, White Paper on Arts and Culture, 1996 <http://www.dac.gov.za/legislation_policies/white_papers/white_paper_on_arts_culture_heritage.htm> [accessed 21.02.2008].

United Nations, Convention on the Rights of the Child <http://www.unicef.org/crc/> [accessed 04.05.2008].

United Nations, Office of the High Commission for Human Rights, Declaration of the Rights of the Child <http://www.unhchr.ch/html/menu3/b/25.htm> [accessed 04.05.2008].

United Nations Organization <http://www.un.org> [accessed 04.05.2008].

United Nations, Universal Declaration of Human Rights <http://un.org./en/documents/udhr/> [accessed 04.05.2008].

US Constitution <http://www.usconstitution.net/declar.html> [accessed 21.02.2008].

Victoria and Albert Museum <http://vam.ac.uk> [accessed 20.03.2009].

Index